TURMOIL
&
TRUTH

Philip Trower

*The Historical Roots of the Modern Crisis
in the Catholic Church*

Family Publications · Oxford
Ignatius Press · San Francisco

© Family Publications, Oxford, 2003
All rights reserved

published by
Family Publications
King Street, Oxford OX2 6DF
ISBN 1-871217-40-7
and
Ignatius Press
San Francisco, U.S.A.
ISBN 0-89870-980-6
Library of Congress Control Number 2003105702

Cover art:
Rembrandt van Rijn
Storm on the Sea of Galilee
© Burstein Collection/CORBIS
Cover design by Riz Boncan Marsella

Printed in England

by the same author
A Danger to the State (Ignatius Press, 1998)

Contents

PREFACE

My original intention in writing this book was to cover the whole story of reform and rebellion in the Catholic Church in modern times from its beginnings in the nineteenth century down to the present, with the Second Vatican Council as the centre-piece. But the more I went into the subject, the clearer it became that the beginnings of the story were the most important part and needed a book to themselves. As is always the case with great historical events, whatever took place at the Council or has happened since had been in preparation for a long time. So the greater part of the book is about events before the Council. It is from the study of these, I believe, that most is to be learned.

Since I have tried to make the book as intelligible as possible to readers of every kind, I ask well-informed Catholic readers to bear with me if I sometimes explain in detail things which they take for granted.

Most of what I have to say is about conditions and events in what we call "the West", by which I mean Western Europe, North America, Australia and New Zealand – the countries of European culture, inundated with wealth since World War II. This should not be taken to mean that the Church elsewhere is regarded as of small account. But it is in "the West", as just defined, that we find the roots of most of the initiatives and aberrations we shall be considering.

Finally a few words about that difficult subject, heresy. I say "difficult" because, although a technical term, it now has, owing to past religious and ideological conflicts, an almost exclusively abusive sound. Yet it describes a fact which has to be kept in mind when considering any upheaval in the Catholic Church like the one taking place today. By refraining from using the word or using softer-sounding alternatives, as I have mostly done, we do not alter the fact.

In principle, everyone who believes in a divine revelation accepts the fact or possibility of heresy – whatever claims to be part of revelation or true belief, but in some way contradicts, distorts or is an unauthorised addition to it. For other Christians, many Catholic beliefs are, in the technical sense, heresies. The word has no meaning except in reference to a divine revelation, real or supposed. Its use to describe deviations from the opinions of purely human teachers like Marx, Darwin and Freud is a misuse of language, and the equivalent of treating them as gods. All knowledge coming solely from men can only claim to be such on the basis of evidence or logic.

Much the same can be said about "dogma". If there has been a revelation, dogma – a succinct and unchangeable formulation of some aspect of what has been revealed – is something altogether reasonable, and indeed necessary; just as the attempt to give human opinions the status of dogmas is unreasonable or downright silly.

A further point: although other Christians believe certain things which, in the view of the Catholic Church, are objectively heresies, the Church recognises that it is possible for them to do so in good faith since they do not believe in a Church which teaches with authority. For Catholics it is otherwise. Having once known and accepted the Church's claims and teachings in their totality, it is impossible for them to reject one or more of them without fault. A Catholic, if truly such, cannot fall into heresy blamelessly.

Finally, a word about Catholics who adopt or promote heresies, and about why fully-believing Catholics are bound, not only to continue loving them, but also, out of love, to oppose them. Not to oppose them would be equivalent to saying that the revelation of God is a matter of opinion, is not to be found fully in the teaching of the Catholic Church, or that in handing it on the Church has got parts of it wrong.

These may be acceptable opinions for anyone else, but neither can be a tenable position for a Catholic, since the converse – God has made a revelation that can be certainly known and the Church is its guardian and interpreter – is the very heart of our religion. Loving, as even the most closely knit families know, has never excluded resisting or speaking out about what one believes to be seriously wrong. What counts is the spirit in which it is done.

In a sense, the sole subject of this book is the revelation of God: the efforts of its guardians to make it bear fruit in the present, and its vicissitudes at the hands of men who believe that, in order for it to survive, it must be altered.

PART I

A BIRD'S-EYE VIEW

Chapter One

REFORM

When people ask, as I imagine they sometimes still do, "What on earth is going on in the Catholic Church?" the best answer, I believe, is "Two contradictory things at once". One can then go on to show, according to the time at one's disposal, how they are related, which is one of the purposes of this book.

In the 1960s, one will explain, a lawful General Council, a gathering of the world's Catholic bishops with and under the Pope to discuss the affairs of the Church (the twenty-first such Council in her history and the second to be held at the Vatican in just under a hundred years) launched the Church on a major programme of reforms. Summoned by Pope John XXIII (1958–1963), the assembly met for two months in four successive autumns, 1962, 1963, 1964, 1965. Between these general assemblies the work was carried on by committees and commissions. Pope Paul VI, who succeeded Pope John in 1963, presided over the second, third and fourth sessions.

However, the Council was hardly over before a great rebellion against the Church's teaching and authority broke out, carried on for the most part in the name of the Council.

In this opening chapter I will look at the first of these contradictory currents – the movement for reform.

As with all true calls for reform, at the heart of the Council's teaching is a call for Catholics to return to greater personal holiness. This is religious reform in the most fundamental sense. If Catholics were holier, such seems to have been Pope John's initial idea, the separated Christians would be drawn back into the Church by her sheer attractive power, and all could then go out and convert the modern world.

But it was not necessary to gather more than 2000 bishops in Rome for four consecutive autumns in order to make such an elementary demand. Those who took the lead at the Council had more specialised concerns.

Most Catholics before the Council lived in countries that had long been publicly Christian, their attitudes and outlook being formed accordingly. In such countries a certain religious easy-goingness prevails. It is like family life. There is no one to impress. No one is shocked by what has come to be called "the gap between faith and life", i.e. the way people lived too often barely or not sufficiently corresponding with what they professed to believe. Believe they did. Practice fell too much behind.

Another characteristic of Christian countries of long standing was the assumption that there was no-one, or hardly anyone immediately at hand to convert. In theory at least, everyone was already a Christian, so the missionary spirit tended to atrophy. Converting other people, it was felt, could safely be left to those with a special call to spread the Gospel to the heathen.

But the number of countries which could still in any true sense be called Christian was rapidly diminishing. Christians were everywhere becoming a minority, a situation where their faults, as far as the mission of the Church is concerned, become of much greater consequence. A minority, just because it is a minority, will always be looked at to some degree critically, and if it is a religious minority its behaviour will be taken as the measure of the truth of its beliefs.

If, therefore, the Church was to continue to fulfil its mission, and even in certain countries to survive, the faithful must at all cost be moved out of living mentally and spiritually in a Christendom that no longer existed. They must be brought to realise that they are called to preach Christ by example as well as by word, and must learn to see themselves as missionaries, like the early Christians.

However, such a change of outlook cannot be worked by a simple word of command and without some hard thinking. It presupposed on the part of the Church something similar to the fresh look a man takes at himself, his life and beliefs when he goes on retreat. In the Second Vatican Council the Church in a sense "went into retreat" (even if, as we shall shortly see, a troubled one), and the outcome was a reflection on its own nature, as well as on its mission and relation to the world, leading to a reform of theology or its manner of presenting its beliefs. For those concerned with these questions, a reform of Catholic theology was a prerequisite for a reform of Catholic life. If the beliefs of the faithful did not make the impact on them they should, that was because those beliefs were inadequately presented. They did not sufficiently understand all their implications. There were "black holes" in their understanding. The "black holes" were responsible for the gap between faith and life.

A reform of theology does not mean new beliefs. But the conciliar decrees do contain important shifts of emphasis and perspective (they are usually referred to as the "new orientations"), and the beginnings of some theological developments (the drawing out of the implications of aspects of the faith not explicitly expressed in the original "deposit") whose purpose is not only to make Catholics more fervent and apostolic, but to make the faith more easily understood by our contemporaries by removing unnecessary causes of misunderstanding and giving what is intended to be a fuller, better-balanced, and if possible more attractive presentation of the faith.

For the Church, the purpose of the shifts of emphasis was not to exclude what had previously received most attention, but to give greater prominence to what it was felt had hitherto not received enough in order to correct an imbalance.

The mysteries revealed by God, like the facts of nature are a harmony of parts many of which appear to us as complementary opposites. Just as in nature there is light and dark, joy and sorrow, change and stability, so in the Christian mysteries God is One and Three, Christ is divine and human, king and servant, the Mass is the sacrifice of Calvary made present without blood-shed, and a sacred meal. The human mind cannot keep the whole faith in view at any one time in all its details. But it should have a vision of the whole based on a properly balanced presentation of fundamentals. This overall vision is what the world-wide teaching of the faith, Sunday by Sunday, through the liturgy, from the pulpit, and via other forms of instruction, is meant to produce. But its faithfulness depends on the proper distribution of the weight of emphasis. Not only must all the salient features be present; they must be shown in the right relationship both to each other and the whole. If the balance is not right, understanding of the sense and import of the whole will be to some extent affected. Plenty of examples will be mentioned along the way.

The fuller, better-balanced presentation of the faith which the conciliar teachings are intended to provide has been the theoretical basis for the practical changes: altered liturgy, revised canon law, ecumenical initiatives, simplified rules for religious orders, new administrative and consultative bodies like the triennial episcopal synods in Rome, national episcopal conferences, diocesan commissions, priests' senates, parish councils, and so on. The conciliar decrees, however, only gave guidelines about the shape the reforms ought to have. The practical changes have been the work of the Pope and bishops together, or the reigning Pope alone, since the Council. In many cases they go considerably beyond what the decrees suggest or positively require.[1]

Making Catholics more fervent and apostolic, and the faith better understood by outsiders, would also, it was believed, be advanced by the process Pope John called *aggiornamento*, translated into English as "updating" or "renewal".

Aggiornamento was the Council's second major undertaking. People frequently talk about *aggiornamento* or updating as though it were identical with reform. However there is a difference. *Aggiornamento* is not in the strict sense reform at all.

Reform in the strict sense means bringing back to its original shape something that has been partially knocked out of shape or deformed. In religion it may be morals, spirituality, modes of worship, ecclesiastical institutions, styles of government, or, as we have just seen, prevailing ways of presenting the faith. This will often involve restoring good things which in the course of history have been cast aside or neglected, or removing accidental accretions that prevent the original beauty or effectiveness of what is being reformed from being seen.

Aggiornamento or updating, on the other hand, is the weighing up by the Church of new ideas and practices in a surrounding culture, the sifting of the wheat from the chaff, and then the "baptising" or taking into her thinking and practice of whatever it is judged lawfully can be "baptised" so that she will not impede her mission by opposing what is naturally good, and will make her teaching as understandable as possible to whatever people she has to preach to. At the level of ideas it means showing the relationship between natural and revealed knowledge.

A monastery is *reformed* for example if the monks have given up communal prayer and a strong-minded abbot gets them out of bed and back into Church again in the morning. It is *updated* if, for good reasons, he decides to install a telephone, or includes some talks on modern psychology in the moral theology courses for his novices.

The process now called "inculturation" (what the missionary does when, with ecclesiastical permission, he uses certain local artistic styles in church architecture and decoration, certain local customs in the liturgy, or certain local modes of expression and behaviour in teaching or living the faith) is just *aggiornamento* or updating applied to new places instead of new times.

Since the history of Christianity has been a continual meeting with new cultures, both things, *aggiornamento* and inculturation have always gone on in the Church.

The Church was engaged in aggiornamento and inculturation when she first took the measure of Graeco-Roman civilisation and then adjusted herself to its collapse: when she started to extract and appropriate the gold in Greek philosophy and imperial law; when she mitigated the severity of her penances to make it easier for the lapsed to return after periods of persecution; when, listening to the voice of contemporary science, she accepted for practical purposes, not as part of her faith, the reigning Ptolemaic cosmology;

when in the west she switched from Greek to Latin in her liturgy after the majority of the faithful ceased to be Greek-speaking; when with the decline of the empire she moved increasingly out of the towns to convert the country people; when she took to anointing kings, fostered the spirit of chivalry, instituted the truce of God, excluded the turbulent Roman nobility and populace from the election of popes and confined it to the college of cardinals, made the copying of manuscripts one of the chief works of her monks, gave birth to the universities, put Aristotelian and Arabian philosophy under the microscope, embraced what was worthwhile in renaissance humanism (and temporarily some things that were not), introduced seminary training for her priests so that they could talk on an equality with educated laymen, and in the 17th century started to come to terms with the new scientific learning.

Unfortunately, in carrying out this very necessary work, the Church will frequently be hampered by the fact that a number of her children will be carrying on an impassioned love affair with "the times" – the feudal and renaissance periods provide some notable examples whose consequences will later take holy churchmen much time and effort to undo. Those of the 21st century are plainly going to have a big job of this sort. Often too she has to tolerate things she disapproves of but cannot for the time remedy. The best she may be able to do is mitigate the more serious evils.

These meetings with new times and places, however, no more cause the Church to change her beliefs than theological reform does, though the need to answer objections may lead her to clarify certain aspects, define them more precisely, organise them systematically or explain their consequences. In other words they can be the catalyst for theological or doctrinal development.

So much for *aggiornamento* in the past. That there should have been a special need for it in recent times is easily understood when one considers the tremendous changes over the last 150 years in the way people live and the cataract of new ideas and ideologies they have been exposed to.

For the Church they present a mixture of opportunities and obstacles to her mission which, even in the most favourable circumstances, would make some kind of stock-taking appropriate.

In spite of this, making the faithful holier and more apostolic remains the first consideration. The purpose of everything else – reform, *aggiornamento*, inculturation – is to reshape the faithful's inner dispositions, and revive or release their spiritual energies, hitherto partially blocked or thought to have been, by bad habits, the spirit of routine, an inadequate grasp of the implications of their beliefs, inefficient or no longer effective ways of conducting

Church affairs, or failure to take advantage of new opportunities.

But why this sudden interest in change on the part of ecclesiastical authority around 1960?

In fact it was not sudden. There had long been a movement in the Church for both the kinds of "reform" I have mentioned (its origins go back to the early 19th century), and a great deal had already been achieved in the ninety-odd years between the First and Second Vatican Councils.

However, during the 1930s, 1940s and 1950s there began to take shape a party of mainly French, and German, theologians and scholars wanting more radical shifts of emphasis, bolder adaptations and the "baptism" of a greater number of contemporary ideas. The resulting presentation of the faith, which they offered the Church for its approval, has come to be called "the new theology" *(la nouvelle théologie)*.

During the pontificate of Pius XII (1939–1958), Pope John's immediate predecessor, the new theologians had been out of favour, the Pope and his advisers considering a number of their ideas too extreme. The encyclical *Humani Generis* (1950) singled out what the Pope took exception to. Some of them were forbidden to teach or write for a time. However Pope John decided they should be allowed to have their say. Most of the leading representatives attended the Council. Some were invited to work on the commissions which drafted the documents for discussion. Others were present as theological advisers to individual bishops.

The term "new theology", originally with a pejorative meaning, is said to have been coined by the French theologian Fr. Garrigou-Lagrange O.P., a leader of the rival, quasi-official neo-scholastic theology.[2]

The confrontation between the neo-scholastics and the new theologians underlay many of the conflicts at the Council. It was not unlike the dispute between the theological schools of Antioch and Alexandria beginning around A.D. 400 about the relationship between Our Lord's divine and human natures, which was fought out over three hundred years and half a dozen general councils. The difference today is that the new theology is a new-comer, while the schools of Antioch and Alexandria were rivals of almost equal age.

In France, the leading "new theologians" were: Fr. Henri de Lubac, based at the Jesuit house at Fourvière in Lyons, and his fellow Jesuit Fr. Jean Daniélou, and the Dominicans Fr. Yves Congar and his teacher and friend Fr. Marie-Dominique Chenu, both teachers for the greater part of their lives at the Dominican house of higher studies at Le Saulchoir in Belgium, later moved to the outskirts of Paris. Fr. Teilhard de Chardin, the Jesuit palaeontologist, a key figure as an influence in the background, had died in 1955, seven years before the Council opened.

The Jesuit Fr. Karl Rahner was the chief representative of the new tendencies in Germany, and the Dominican Fr. Edward Schillebeeckx in the Low Countries. The Swiss theologian, Fr. Hans von Balthasar did not attend the Council. He had left the Jesuits some years before to found a small community of his own, but was a close friend of Fr. de Lubac, whose pupil he had been, and was in sympathy with most of his views. Jacques Maritain, a layman and leading neo-scholastic, did not belong to the circle of new theologians. But they mostly approved his social and political ideas, which, along with those of his disciple Emmanuel Mounier, had a profound influence on the Council's social teaching.

The new theologians, backed by a minority of influential bishops, were the driving force behind the "reform party" at the Council.

By "reform party" I mean the much wider body of men who supported most of the new theologians' initiatives without necessarily subscribing to all their ideas, or always grasping all their implications.

In addition there were, throughout the Church, numbers of clergy and laity anxious for changes of one kind or another without having a comprehensive programme. The philosopher Dietrich von Hildebrand, who later protested vehemently against liturgical and other abuses, wanted the teaching of philosophy broadened to include the German phenomenological method, and, in its immediate aftermath, spoke of the "greatness of the Second Vatican Council", while the teaching of the founder of Opus Dei, the Spanish St. Josemaría Escrivá de Balaguer, is recognised as having anticipated the Council's teaching on the laity, in particular its teaching on the universal call to holiness and the place of human work in God's creative plan.[3]

To conclude this chapter, three other points about the Council should be mentioned.

Pope John, who called the Council, said it was to be "pastoral", that is to say chiefly concerned with getting the Church's teachings to "tell" more in the faithful's minds and lives. There were to be no solemn definitions, or *anathemas* (condemnations). From this, not a few Catholics have concluded that its doctrinal teachings are of little consequence, that they can ignore what is seemingly novel, or, according to taste, not novel enough. But this is a misunderstanding. Popes, like other men, may propose, but in the end God disposes. No solemn definitions or anathemas there may have been, but the two primary documents (on the Church and on the sources of revelation) are entitled "dogmatic constitutions", and throughout the decrees as a whole there is a wealth of doctrinal material of the greatest value, for which it would be unfair not to give the new theologians and the reform party most of the credit.

The second point concerns the famous passage in Pope John's opening speech at the Council. The Church's "unchangeable doctrine", he said "has to be presented in a way that is demanded by our times. One thing is the deposit of faith, which consists of the truths contained in sacred doctrine; another is the manner of presentation, however always with the same signification and meaning" .[4]

How the passage was to be understood and applied became one of the key issues at the Council and has been the cause of many of the problems since. Was the fresh presentation to involve a change of words and style only, or also of concepts? And can you change concepts without changing the meaning?

A glance at the nursery rhyme about Jack and Jill will highlight the difficulties of the undertaking. "Jack and Jill went up the hill to fetch a pail of water". Now substitute the word "liquid" for "water". You haven't explicitly altered the meaning. But it is less precise. It is now possible to suggest that what they were carrying was a pail of white wine or arsenic.

It is largely by taking advantage of the Council's often looser terminology that, since the Council, theologians in rebellion against the Church have been able to introduce changes of meaning under cover of the Council's authority.

The third point is that the influence of the Conciliar teaching and reforms has not been confined to the Catholic Church. Most other Christian bodies have had their practices and certainties to some degree stirred or disturbed by it.

Was Pope John's decision to call a Council an inspiration from God, as he believed, or not? In other words, was it a work of God's active or permissive will? No one can know[5]. But even if only the latter, that does not rule out God's having used the Council to put across some important messages.

Notes to Chapter One

[1] Altars facing the people, not mentioned in the decree on the liturgy, are an example of an initiative going beyond what the Council asked for. On the other hand, the widespread abandonment of Thomist philosophy and theology is a departure from the conciliar teaching.

[2] The term "new theology" was initially used for the ideas emanating from French theological circles. Subsequently the term was extended to include like-minded thinkers across the Rhine and in the Low Countries. While neo-scholastic theology tended to

present the Church's teachings in a timeless form, the new theology accented the element of historical development. In philosophy it favoured a subjective starting point and an evolutionary view of reality, where becoming is considered more important than being.

[3]   "Your ideal is truly great. From its very beginnings it anticipated the theology of the laity that was later to characterise the Church after the Council." John Paul II, homily to members of Opus Dei, 19th Aug. 1997. For the reasons why St. Josemaría Escrivá declined two invitations to participate directly in the Council as head of a religious institute or *peritus*, see Alvaro Portillo, *Immersed in God*, Scepter, Princeton, 1992, pp. 9–14.

[4]   The first English translation of the Council documents (Abbott-Gallagher) omits the crucial phrase, "always with the same sense and meaning", and it was later claimed that Pope John never used it; it is said to have been smuggled into the official printed text by unprincipled Vatican officials after the speech was given. The claim was effectively refuted by Professor John Finnis of Oxford in the correspondence columns of *The Tablet* (Jan.–Feb. 1992). The main point is, why would Catholics be anxious for the Pope not to have said "always with the same sense and meaning" unless they did want a change of meaning?

[5]   Pope John was beatified by John Paul II on 3 September 2000, becoming Bl. John XXIII. I leave the reader to draw his own conclusions.

Chapter Two

REBELLION

We now come to the second of the two currents I mentioned at the beginning of the last chapter – the rejection of the Church's teaching and authority, along with the attempt to substitute new beliefs.

There have been mass rejections of Catholic belief before, but never I think on the same scale. There is almost no point of Catholic teaching that has not been called into question or repudiated, from the divinity of Christ to belief in eternal life. Many have left the Church openly. But still more have remained on, in appearance at least "inside" the Church, where for over thirty-five years they have been spreading their new beliefs among the rest of the now thoroughly confused faithful.

Warnings from the highest authorities have been continuous. Pope Paul's are epitomised in his well-known cry in 1972 that "the smoke of Satan" had entered into the Church. He also spoke of "the ravages being inflicted on the Christian people by . . . venturesome hypotheses" (Paul VI, Apostolic Exhortation, fifth anniversary of Council's closure, 1970).

Here are three more examples from the highest authorities.

> "We must admit realistically . . . that the majority of Christians today feel bewildered, confused, perplexed, and even deceived: ideas contradicting revealed truth as taught from the beginning are liberally spread abroad; in the dogmatic and moral fields real heresies have been propagated, creating doubts, confusions, rebellions; even the liturgy has been manipulated" (John Paul II, address to priests, 6th February 1981).

> "Not a few of today's attacks are going for the jugular, the very fundamentals of our faith: the divinity of Christ, the resurrection from the dead of his true Body, our own immortality and so forth" (Cardinal Oddi, former head of the Congregation for the Clergy in Rome, symposium on catechetics, 15th May 1981).

> "No one can deny that the last ten years have been harmful to the Church. Instead of the promised renewal, they have given us a process of decadence which to a large extent began in the name of the Council and has done nothing but discredit the

Council itself. We can therefore affirm that there will be no renewal in the Church until there is a change of course and an abandonment of the errors adopted after the council." (Cardinal Ratzinger, when Archbishop of Munich).

There has also been the evidence of statistics, newspaper reports, and direct experience. It has been a record of mass departures from the priesthood and religious life; a devastating drop in priestly and religious vocations; an equally devastating drop in attendance at Mass (the heart of Catholic Christianity), infant baptisms and conversions; the almost complete abandonment over wide areas of the sacrament of confession; in many places a stripping of churches and sale of their furnishings and sacred vessels reminiscent of the Protestant reformation; the closing down of countless schools, seminaries, religious houses, hospitals, and orphanages; a rocketing number of divorces and annulments; whole generations growing up in ignorance of the faith; and now in Latin American countries a mass exodus of Catholics into the fundamentalist sects because the latter continue to preach about the seriousness of sin, the reality of hell and salvation in another life. These things are now so well known that there is no need to labour them.[1]

Looking at the situation as a whole, one could describe it as a rebellion of intellectuals who have won the support of large numbers of the Western laity through an unspoken compact.

For reasons that will appear later, a proportion of the Catholic intelligentsia, having lost or partially lost their faith, wanted to alter Catholic doctrine. With the laity morals were usually the problem, especially the Church's teaching about marriage and procreation. So in return for being allowed to have contraception and divorce the majority of the Western laity have let the theological rebels put much of the rest of Catholic teaching through the pulping machine. This is a simplification of events, but not one, I think, which distorts them.

In this great doctrinal-moral rebellion the trouble started well before the Council with theologians, thinkers and scholars who had been converted, or partially converted, to that latest in the long line of attempts to alter the religion of Christ to suit the opinions or convenience of men, called *modernism*.

Modernism can be considered a by-product of that more than a century-old movement for cultural and intellectual *aggiornamento* mentioned in the last chapter.

In the whole business of sifting and "baptising" secular ideas and practices, the significant word is *lawfully*. It marks the boundary between true and false *aggiornamento*. Genuine practitioners of *aggiornamento* are those who stay on the right side of the boundary. But from the start of the movement around 1815, a trickle of thinkers, swept off their feet by the theories they were studying, began to lose their faith, cross the boundary line, and agitate for the baptism of ideas and practices the Church cannot lawfully baptise.

To begin with, those who crossed the boundary eventually broke with the Church. But as the 20th century succeeded the 19th and the subjects under study multiplied and grew more complicated, increasing numbers with doubts about this or that article of belief, stayed on inside the Church. The trickle eventually became a stream, and by the 1950s a small lake. Or, changing the metaphor, an heretical movement devoted to altering the meaning of the Church's beliefs developed like a cancer in the entrails of the movement for reform and *aggiornamento*.

In origin at least, modernism can be regarded as a failed attempt at *aggiornamento*, its shadow side or occupational disease, *aggiornamento* itself being a thoroughly legitimate activity.

Most of the damage can be attributed to the kind of radical biblical scholarship, dating from the late 18th century, which cast varying degrees of doubt on the authenticity and truthfulness of the Bible. The doubts included the Resurrection. But if the Resurrection was not an historical fact, on what was Christianity based? This led to a new theory about the way God reveals himself.

For modernists there has been no revelation with an unchanging content given by God through specially appointed spokesmen and ending with the death of the last apostle St. John. In so far as God speaks to men he does so mainly or solely through personal religious experience, and what he says continually changes or is modified as the world and men's situations change. Today this idea is called "on-going revelation", and its interpretation by theologians "process theology".

From this it would follow that Christian doctrine only has a symbolic significance and must continually be reinterpreted. In its present form it represents the efforts of earlier less enlightened Christians to interpret what God was saying to them through their particular experiences. Similarly with the Bible. The Bible is basically a record of what the Jews and early Christians felt or thought about their inner experiences, not about what was actually said or happened to them. In modernism everything takes place in the mind, rather than externally.[2]

These two views of the way God reveals himself, the Catholic and the modernist, are often described, and contrasted, as the "deductive" and "inductive" approaches.

Deduction is the mental process by which we move from established facts or knowledge to their implications or consequences. This is what theologians do when they try to explain the more mysterious aspects of divine revelation. Since Christianity gets the greater part of what it knows directly from God, they are thinking deductively.

We think inductively when, starting from what we can touch and see (sense experience), we climb to a knowledge of the causes, laws and first principles underlying them. Natural religions, like Confucianism and Buddhism are based on inductive thinking. They are dependent solely on what the human mind can tease out of things. In giving primacy to the "inductive" approach modernism is pushing Christianity back to the status of a natural religion.

These theories made their first appearance in the Catholic Church between 1880 and 1907 when the movement was arrested, or was thought to have been, by St. Pius X's encyclical *Pascendi*. But they reappeared at the time of the Council apparently as strong as ever. Meanwhile, under the influence of contemporary secular ideas, they had received some important additions, justifying the title neo-modernism.

By the 1950s Christianity had ceased to be the majority religion in most Western countries. In so far as most Westerners could be said to have had a religion, it was some kind of belief in perpetual progress and an earthly paradise, in liberty, equality and fraternity as the indispensable ingredients of human happiness, and in democracy as the only means of achieving them. Neo-modernism is the incorporation of these ideas into the early modernist theory of revelation through personal experience.

If revelation is through personal experience, the Christian people are the final arbiters of what is to be believed and done. The government of the Church should therefore be remodelled more along the lines of a modern popular democracy. After an exchange of experiences the people reach a consensus, which, when sufficiently widely accepted, the bishops ratify, the consensus becoming the Church's official teaching for the time being. The bishops are merely the people's delegates. However a closer look at the theory reveals that it is theologians, not the people, who hold the determining position. On their own, the people are unable to articulate their experiences properly. Only with the help of theologians can they discover what God is saying to them. Theologians are the midwives of popular experience.[3]

It also seems that, in revealing himself through the people's experiences, God is subject to the laws of Hegelian logic (truth can only be arrived at through argument – thesis, antithesis, synthesis).

At any given moment in the Church's history, the new ideas of theologians represent the experiences and insights of the believing community's most alert members, and therefore the Deity's most recent thoughts and instructions. These, however, will automatically be resisted by bishops. Bishops, being naturally conservative, will want to hang on to current teaching, although it in large part reflects past life situations and dead experiences. There follows a "creative clash", with theologians dissenting and bishops threatening anathemas. Eventually the bishops surrender and give the new ideas their approval. But once again they mistakenly imagine that what they have endorsed will remain official teaching forever. So when the faithful's life situations and experiences change once more, a further creative clash becomes necessary. And so on. This is how modernism understands the development of doctrine. Although the theory has a supposedly democratic basis, it in fact turns theologians into bishops and bishops into errand boys.

Neo-modernism also changes the concept of salvation. Salvation means being delivered from physical and spiritual misery in this world, not deliverance from sin in this world and its consequences in the next. "Transforming the world" materially and politically therefore replaces spreading the Gospel and sanctifying men as the heart of the Church's mission. Salvation in the next world is more or less a certainty.

Needless to say, only a minority of Catholics, if we can call them that, adhere consciously to these hard-core modernist principles. Nevertheless their influence is widespread right down to the parish level. The chief effect has been to suggest that, in the words of a well-known member of a religious order, "everything is up for grabs". The most thorough-going attempts to put hard-core modernism into practice so far have been in Holland and in the South American "base communities" inspired by liberation theology.[4]

The attempt to impose on Catholics or other Christians such a total reversal of what they have always believed can only be described as a revolution, which is in fact how its advocates and sympathisers admit to seeing it.

It is of course a revolution mainly of ideas and therefore without unpleasant or frightening physical consequences. There are no bombs or firing squads. The wheels of diocesan and parish life continue to turn, while the revolutionaries themselves, and their now numerous sympathisers well entrenched in most Western ecclesiastical bureaucracies, are respectable professional men and women with, for the most part, friendly smiles, agreeable manners and what they regard as the highest intentions, who talk the language of religion and use catch-phrases and theories rather than dynamite. Now therefore that the first shocks and excitements are over, many Catholics find it fairly easy to persuade themselves that nothing all that important has happened, or if it has, whatever it was is over. But a revolution, or attempted revolution it still is even if the transformations are now mostly worked out of sight in the minds and hearts of the faithful without their being aware of it.[5]

From theologians, the great revolt I have been describing spread to priests (not a few being drawn in by the expectation that the Church was going to be forced to change her laws about clerical celibacy), and from priests to lay people for the reasons noted earlier. On a large scale it was only later and more slowly joined by bishops. But, tragically, this also eventually happened.

When we find numbers of bishops permitting or even actively encouraging teaching at variance with that given by the Pope, and that given constantly by the Church through the centuries, one can only presume they have come to believe at least some of the doctrinal novelties. Inevitably many of the faithful have concluded either that heresy does not matter all that much, or that the Pope and a local hierarchy have equal authority and one can follow which teaching one pleases.

This episcopal revolt or collapse has been the second main cause of chaos and loss of faith.[6]

Why does Rome allow it? Why did Paul VI initiate a policy of teaching and giving warnings, while refraining (except in one instance) from disciplining or punishing? This is a question which it will be easier for future historians than for us to answer. But we can perhaps see the beginnings of an explanation in the Council's teachings on *collegiality* and *ecumenism*.

The doctrine of collegiality is about bishops taking a greater share in the government of the whole Church. To implement it the Holy See, immediately after the Council, embarked on a policy of decentralisation. With regard to dissenting theologians, Rome let it be known that it wanted local bishops to do the disciplining.

Ecumenism also made the use of strong measures difficult. How were good relations with separated Christians to be maintained if the Church started punishing or excommunicating theologians or bishops for holding views similar to those of the separated brethren themselves?[7]

Another conciliar initiative was bringing about a rapprochement between the Church and "the modern world" (Western secular culture). This seems to have generated the desire to have the Church appear as much as possible the friend of freedom of opinion.

However the requirements of these three goals have not always been easy to harmonise. In 1968, for instance, Cardinal O'Boyle of Washington disciplined nineteen of his priests who had challenged the teaching of Paul

VI's recently issued encyclical *Humanae Vitae* upholding the Church's position on the unlawfulness of contraception. The priests appealed to Rome and, three years later, under pressure from the head of the Congregation for the Clergy, Cardinal O'Boyle reinstated those of the original nineteen who had not by this time left the priesthood. None of them was required to make a public retraction.

Similarly, in 1978, the Bishop of Baton Rouge, Louisiana was summoned to Rome and rebuked by the Congregation for Bishops, though this time it seems without the knowledge of the Holy Father, because he had forbidden the dissenting moral theologian Fr. Charles Curran from preaching in his diocese.

In both these cases, respect for liberal susceptibilities seems to have taken precedence over the principle of collegiality.

Whatever the pros and cons of the new policy – and it may well be that by this time strong measures would push large numbers of Western Catholics into more openly expressed schism – it has, nevertheless, been one of the most difficult things for the faithful loyal to the Holy See to understand. They had been taught to think of heresy as on a level with murder, theft and adultery. Yet here it was being tolerated apparently as if it were of little consequence. But just because they are loyal they remain so in spite of the strategy of headquarters being often beyond their understanding.[8]

In practice, by the end of Pope Paul's reign the revolutionary theologians had established a *de facto* right to teach their errors in the Church on a par with the teaching of the faith. They could thus be said to have won the first round in their campaign to take over the Church and change its constitution and teaching.

Notes to Chapter Two

[1] Divorce followed by remarriage is not allowed in the Catholic Church. But in many areas, divorced remarried couples are quietly allowed to receive Holy Communion, which amounts to its being locally sanctioned in practice, while annulments (declarations that there was not a valid marriage in the first place), are often given for insufficient reasons, leaving the impression that they are just a Catholic form of divorce.

[2] Parents will recognise here the origins of "experiential" catechesis – religion classes in which, rather than being taught the truths of the faith, the children are encouraged to write or discuss what they think or feel about God, his world and the way to please Him. As a result over the last thirty years the majority of young Catholics in the West have grown up largely ignorant of their faith. The experience of living our beliefs can deepen our understanding of them but does not alter or add to them. Similarly, mysti-

cal theology makes use of the experiences of the saints in their prayer life, but without regarding those experiences as a rival revelation.

[3] See, for example Bernard Lonergan S.J., *Method in Theology*, especially chapter 5, where it is suggested that the starting point for theology should not be divine revelation but "Christian living", and doctrines are apparently judged worthwhile according to whether they promote or impede Christian living of the "best kind".

[4] "These denials, which I have described with all the severity of their consequences, are seldom spoken of so openly. The movements, however, are clear and they do not confine themselves to the realm of theology alone." (Cardinal Ratzinger addressing the presidents of European doctrinal commission in the winter of 1992–3) Indeed, the cardinal continued, they are "even more pronounced" in preaching and catechesis "than in strictly theological literature".

[5] In the winter of 1982-83, the London Catholic weekly *The Tablet*, ran a series of articles on the meaning of the Second Vatican Council called *The Vatican II Revolution*. When the present writer suggested to the editor that a revolution means replacing what exists by something altogether different and that this was not the Council's object, he continued to insist that the word "revolution" accurately described the Council's work. Oxford English Dictionary definition of revolution: "complete change, turning upside down, great reversal of conditions, fundamental reconstruction, esp. forcible substitution by subjects of a new ruler or policy for the old".

[6] It should be said in fairness that in the period following the Council, many bishops, and many priests later to become bishops, were put through updating courses by experts, often either heterodox or confused themselves.

[7] There seems to be reason to think that at the time of the Council the highest authorities were persuaded that had Luther not been excommunicated, the reformation would never have happened. A little more dialogue and Luther and his followers would have returned to the fold. This would explain the handling of Fr. Hans Küng. Ironically, Fr. Küng has shown every sign of wanting to be a new Luther. He has done everything in his power to get himself excommunicated. However the Holy See seems equally determined not to oblige him. He must be a deeply disappointed man.

[8] Explaining the new policy over a decade and a half ago, the then secretary of a Roman congregation (now the cardinal prefect of a different one), told the author that, rather than condemning errors, the Holy See today preferred to "swamp errors with truth", or in the words of John Paul II to André Frossard, allow "error to destroy itself" (*Catholic World Report*, Nov. 1995). This is simply an extension of Pope John's principle "it is better to use the means of mercy than of condemnation". Most Catholics thought Pope John was talking about its use at the Council. They did not realise the principle would continue to be applied more or less indefinitely. However, Cardinal Ratzinger has thrown the clearest light on the origins of the new policy in his *Principles of Catholic Theology* (Ignatius Press, 1987, p. 229: German original, 1982). After speaking of the "great tension and turmoil" in the Church, of the demand by many of the faithful for "a clear drawing of lines", and the inability of "the Pope and bishops as yet to decide in favour of such an action", he attributes it to "the resentment that has grown up in the last half century because of innumerable faulty decisions, and above all because of the

too narrow handling of Church discipline (in the past)", a resentment he describes as "like an inward-growing boil on the ecclesial conscience" that "has created an allergy to condemnation, from which we can more readily expect an increase of the ill than its cure". As to whether truth will succeed in swamping error in the long run, the cardinal confines himself to the cautious statement "we shall have to see whether . . . this approach to discipline in matters of doctrine can serve as a model for the future."

Chapter Three

THE REFORM PARTY – TWO IN ONE FLESH

If things are really as I have described them, then it is going to be impossible to understand what has happened unless one keeps both aspects of the situation – the movement for reform and the attempted revolution – squarely before the mind and in balance. However, large numbers of Catholics plainly find this difficult.

They tend to concentrate on one aspect more or less to the exclusion of the other. Either they see any and every change as a more or less legitimate expression of reform, or they detect signs of revolutionary intent where in fact there are none – that is, if they do not view the Council as an unqualified disaster which it would have been better never to have embarked on.

The reason is simple enough. Reform and rebellion have been closely intertwined, both having sprung from the same source. By the same source I mean the body of theologians, mentioned in Chapter One, who led the reform party and were responsible for what is new or seemingly new in the Council documents. Although they did not see eye to eye on every point, their aims were sufficiently alike for them to work together during the Council more or less as one, and they rapidly became its chief interpreters.

Books explaining what they had in mind or what they thought needed to be done had been pouring from Catholic publishing houses from the moment Pope John announced the Council, and during the Council itself or between meetings of the general assembly they gave lectures, some official, some not, to groups of bishops and their assistants in order to familiarise them with the new thinking. Thus they were able to win over numbers of bishops to their view of what the Council was about, while much of its work was still to be done.

They had other advantages. Since 1963 they had had their own news agency, IDOC, started by the Dutch hierarchy, and from 1965 their own theological quarterly *Concilium* to explain to theologians and the higher clergy what the Council was doing. They also had the backing of the world press. They were the party of change and change suggested that the Church might be about to abandon some of her more "unpalatable" doctrines.

In these circumstances, it is not surprising that the new theology, of which they were among the chief representatives, rapidly came to be identified with the voice of the Church.

But were they identical? As the Council proceeded, more and more people began to realise that the errors beginning to circulate in the Church at large were not coming from men on the fringes of the theological world but from within the reform party itself; that not only were some of the reformers trying to influence the decrees in a way unacceptable to the magisterium, but that the new theology carried within it − in addition to ideas the Church could make use of − the seeds of a revived modernism.[1]

If this estimate of events is incorrect, if there was not something amiss with the new theology, or elements in it, the revival of modernism becomes impossible to explain. It could not conceivably have been the work of outsiders alone. By the end of the Council the prestige of the new theologians was unparalleled. They would only have had to band together and shout "Hold your tongues. That isn't what we were saying", and any outsiders would have been silenced.

The crucial conflicts at the Council were about these attempts to give a heterodox or partly heterodox meaning to the new orientations. The most dramatic concerned the passage in the decree on the Church (*Lumen Gentium*, the Council's key document) about collegiality. Does the fact that the bishops together with the Pope rule the Church as a "college" mean that the Pope is merely the college's spokesman? Pope Paul had to intervene at the last minute to make clear that it did not. He also had to issue two encyclicals during the Council, one on the Church (*Ecclesiam Suam*), the other on the Eucharist (*Mysterium Fidei*), to explain how the Council's teaching on these subjects was and was not to be understood.

For a time, the authorities were able to keep the more disagreeable of these facts partially out of sight. Concealment was made easier by the post-conciliar euphoria. The euphoria was natural enough. There is always something appealing in new beginnings, and any of the faithful who thought about it knew there was plenty in Catholic life that could be improved. But with the publication of Pope Paul's encyclical *Humanae Vitae* against contraception in 1968, disguise was no longer possible. Headed by Fr. Karl Rahner and Fr. Edward Schillebeeckx, with the help of Fr. Hans Küng (not an original thinker but a propagandist of the first rank), the rebellion became public. For the next 10–15 years, Rahner and his allies were to be the interpreters of the Council for the media and the majority of Western Catholics.[2] Not only *Humanae Vitae*, but a whole spectrum of Catholic beliefs was openly challenged.

It was as though Luther's rebellion had been delayed fifty years, breaking out immediately after the last sessions of the Council of Trent, with Luther,

Melancthon and Zwingli having first taken part in it as theological experts.

Pope Paul had prepared for the explosion by declaring the 12 months from June 1967 to June 1968 a "Year of Faith", and closing it with the publication of his *Creed of the People of God*, which, taking the articles of the creed one by one, reaffirmed the Church's beliefs on each contested point.

None of this means that the Council was not a work of God as well as man, but it was clearly a much more mysterious work of God than many people seem to have been willing to recognise.

The doctrinal and moral teaching of a general council ratified by the reigning Pope, will always be capable of a Catholic interpretation. But they are not directly inspired as Christians believe the text of the Bible to be. Nor does the fact that the participants receive the assistance of the Holy Spirit mean that those taking part will fully correspond with his inspirations. They will not necessarily do their work perfectly or in every detail as God wanted. The teaching of the Council of Ephesus (431) about the relationship of Christ's two natures had to be tightened up and clarified by the Council of Chalcedon twenty years later. The presence of proto-monophysites at the second Council of Constantinople about a hundred years later (553) led to some of its condemnations being phrased in a way that provoked misunderstanding and revolt in the western empire, and a schism in northern Italy lasting about half a century. Of the Fifth Lateran Council (1517), the historian Philip Hughes remarked that one can scarcely read many of its decrees without impatience, so ineffective were they, given the need for reform.

Nor is it without precedent for the Church to take some of a famous theologian's ideas and reject others, or for such a theologian afterwards to go off the rails. When it comes to truth, the Church is not choosy about the source. She holds in high regard the writings of the Church Fathers Tertullian, Origen, and Theodoret, although Tertullian left the Church to join the Montanists, a sect believing in the imminent arrival of the New Jerusalem, and Origen and Theodoret, while remaining in the Church, had some of their ideas condemned after their deaths by general councils. Novatian, before he went into schism in the middle of the third century, gave the western Church its first full treatise on the Trinity, from which Pope John Paul II quoted a passage to illustrate his encyclical *Veritatis Splendor*. Nearer our times, Fr. Rosmini, who gave two new religious orders to the Church, had a large number of philosophical propositions censured[3], and the Fr. Passaglia who worked on the bull *Ineffabilis Deus* (1854) defining the Immaculate Conception, afterwards ranged himself against the papacy in its struggle with the government of Turin.

The mixed nature of the reform party and the new theology is the first and chief reason why reform and rebellion have been so bewilderingly tangled up and why the rebellion began to manifest itself not only simultaneously with the Council but in a certain sense through it.

There is an additional problem. If we could make a clear division between the two wings of the reform party, attributing all the good it achieved to the orthodox members and the deficiencies to the heterodox, things would be reasonably simple. But the heterodox made positive contributions to the conciliar teachings. Not all their ideas were harmful, even if, carried too far, they could become so. Rahner, for instance, helped to promote the idea of the Church as the "universal sacrament of salvation", a concept taken from 19th-century German theologians. On the other hand, not everything proposed by the orthodox has proved innocuous. The Church is far from having endorsed all their views. In spite of this they have often continued to press them on her regardless.[4]

If the reformers had a common weakness, it would seem to have been an inability to accept the fact that the Council was God's, not theirs; that he had other instruments in his tool chest besides themselves; that although they were his principal agents for formulating the new orientations, many of their ideas only became acceptable after they had been pruned, tailored or knocked into shape by bishops and theologians of a quite different stamp, even (horror of horrors) "conservative" ones.

On the contrary, not a few of them appear to have regarded the new theology with its mixture of acceptable and unacceptable or less acceptable ideas as the true expression of God's mind, while regarding the limitations put on their ideas as purely human obstacles, permitted no doubt by God, but contrary to his will, which the next general council, or a pope more to their way of thinking, would one day remove.

Perhaps the best way of picturing the situation is to see the Council as a sieve, which God held out for the Church's leading thinkers to pour their ideas into. Then the sieve was shaken (by the conciliar debates and voting) and into the documents fell more or less what God wanted. I say "more or less", because for the analogy to be exact we would have to imagine some of the new theologians punching the odd hole here and there in the mesh so that more of certain substances and not enough of others came through, and the resulting mixture was thus not in all cases perfectly balanced. What did not come through should then have been thrown onto the rubbish tip. But theologians, like parents, tend to love all their children, even the ugly ones. So they went to the rubbish tip, rescued their discarded offerings, mixed them up again with what the Church had accepted and, through their books and lecture tours, served this up to the faithful as the conciliar teaching.

What most of the faithful throughout the West have been receiving over the last twenty years as the conciliar teaching, when not overt modernism, is only too often, I believe, nothing but the new theology before it was purified by the conciliar process.

Why were the more orthodox reformers so slow to react once they saw their one-time associates going off the rails?

Partly, I think, for the same reason that the magisterium was slow to react – the difficulty of providing an explanation that would not totally discredit the Council in the eyes of the faithful. How could one admit that some of the men who had influenced the drafting of the conciliar documents were now attacking fundamental doctrines without the documents themselves being compromised?[5]

On top of this there was the bond of shared aims and interests, transcending disagreements about particular doctrines. In spite of the disagreements, the thinking of orthodox and heterodox still had the same starting point: adjustments of some kind in the Church's practice and ways of presenting her teaching were necessary; and the same final goal – an apostolate specially aimed at modern man, however defined. There was also a large measure of agreement about which aspects of modern life and thought could and should be "baptised". The questions that divided them were what precisely these borrowings from secular culture were to mean when incorporated into the Church's theology.

Where these sympathies and affinities were strongly felt, one has the impression that reform and updating had come to be seen as almost more precious and in need of protection than the faith and Church they are meant to serve. Anyone claiming to be on the side of reform and *aggiornamento* was automatically regarded as an ally, even if the person in question showed signs of doubting truths revealed by God, while anyone expressing reservations, even legitimate ones, about the possible wisdom of certain conciliar initiatives, was classified as an opponent, even though he believed everything the Church teaches.

This state of mind partly, I think, explains Pope Paul's more unfortunate episcopal appointments; also why he gave some of the more loyal members of his flock the unsettling impression that he found them an embarrassment while hankering after the approval of the sheep who were defying him and fleeing into heresy. His unusual psychology – more like that of a hypersensitive 19th-century poet than of the average pope – increased their bewilderment.

It was as though Leopardi had been called to do battle with Danton and Robespierre, or Gerard Manley Hopkins with Lenin.

In the end, however, the rapid unfolding of events forced the orthodox reformers to bite the bullet.

The theological quarterly *Concilium* had originally been regarded as an organ of the reform party; up to the early 1970s, all the leading reformers had written for it. But the main intentions of the founders – a Dutch businessman, Mr Anton van den Boogard, a Dutch publisher, Mr Paul Brand, and Fr. Edward Schillebeeckx – had in fact been to provide a platform for Fr. Karl Rahner, and Rahner and his allies had all along been the preponderant influence.

By 1972 the magazine's policies had become so manifestly subversive and so much of its contents questionable that Frs. von Balthasar, Ratzinger and de Lubac detached themselves and founded the rival international theological quarterly *Communio*, to which other members of the reform party still loyal to the Holy See, like Frs. Louis Bouyer and René Laurentin, soon adhered. Fr. Congar, perhaps the most solid of the new theologians, adopted, one deeply regrets having to say, a fence sitting position. From time to time he would express regrets or doubts about this or that *Concilium* initiative, but remained on the editorial board well into the 1980s.[6]

Concilium's editorial offices in the Dutch university town of Nijmegen (Fr. Schillebeeckx's university) can be considered modernism's international nerve centre. It gives modernism whatever unity it has, and from it most of the agitation against Rome is orchestrated.[7]

The founding of *Communio* was the first public sign of serious disagreement within the reform movement, and as such, I believe will be seen as a crucial date or turning point in the history of the Church since the Council. In Fr. von Balthasar, Rahner was confronted with a rival of equal theological "weight" and erudition, who rapidly moved into position as chief interpreter of the Council for the followers of the orthodox wing of the reform party. By 1980 he had become a kind of Karl Rahner for the orthodox in general.

Concilium and *Communio* have since become the two poles towards which theologians tend to gravitate according to the Catholicity or uncatholicity of their ideas, conducting a theological star wars over the heads of the faithful, though not without the faithful being hit by a lot of *Concilium*'s flak and other fallout.

If the mixed nature of the reform party and the new theology has been the main cause of confusion among the faithful, a supplementary cause, I think, has been the new terminology which came in at the time of the Council, with its borrowings from German idealist philosophy, neo-Protestant theology, and French personalist humanism.

The faithful no longer or only rarely heard about sin, grace, sanctification and salvation. Sermons overflowed with words like commitment, encounter, community, pluralism, dialogue, reconciliation and faith experiences. In place of the soul, they were told to think about the "whole man". Instead of divine revelation, they heard about "God's saving deeds". The Faith was no longer taught or preached, only proclaimed. Christ's life death and resurrection were referred to as "the Christ event".

Although the new terminology can have a perfectly Catholic meaning – the reasons for its introduction will appear later – it is hardly surprising that, hearing the conciliar teaching and heresy simultaneously preached in this unfamiliar tongue, many of the faithful, either with dismay or rejoicing, concluded that the Council really was changing the meaning of the Church's teaching.

A third and final cause of confusion has been the special nature of the Council's work. It introduced, as we have said, important shifts of emphasis and the beginnings of new doctrinal developments. But these things are much more difficult to control than defining doctrines and pinpointing errors (which almost all previous Councils had done).

Let me explain.

When a teacher moves the weight of emphasis from one part of his subject to another what he is really moving is his audience's focus of attention. Ultimately, he wants it to be centrally focused. But we are assuming it has hitherto been turned too much to one side. So to begin with he must start moving it towards the opposite side. However, once you set people's minds moving, it is difficult to bring the movement to a halt precisely where you want.

It is this tendency of the mind to be carried along by ideas as though they had a momentum of their own like physical bodies which has worked so momentously to the advantage of the theological innovators.

If, for instance, you talk all the time about God's love and rarely if ever about his holiness and justice, your listeners are eventually going to conclude they are all but sinless and that their salvation is a certainty. Tell them often enough that they are as important as the clergy and eventually a proportion is going to imagine they can say Mass and forgive sins. Dwell exclusively on the goodness of this world and the importance of making the best of it, and many will forget about heaven, or at least ignore the obstacles to getting there. Speak solely of what Catholics, Christians and other religions have in common, and they will decide that what is peculiar to each of them is of no consequence. In other words, speak only or mainly about the points the Council wanted given greater but not exclusive attention to and, under the appearance of fidelity to the Council, you will have produced a different religion.

It has been the same with the new developments. In an effort to resolve certain pressing theological problems (like the salvation of non-believers or the role of civilisation and progress in the plans of God), the Council allowed the introduction of a number of solutions without defining their precise limits. With regard to these, and borrowing the words of another writer about a very different gathering, the Council could be said to have "opened doors" more than "resolved issues". All this was in keeping with Pope John XXIII's decision that the Council should be "pastoral". But open doors make it easier for unwelcome as well as welcome guests to pass through. In this way a greater and more dangerous imbalance than existed before the Council has temporarily been created.

The difficulty of controlling both processes once under way can perhaps best be illustrated by a scene from an imaginary movie.

Six men are pushing a heavily loaded car which has run out of fuel. Three of them, who have been riding in the car, want to push it twenty yards to get it into a lay-by. The other three, who have offered to help, mean to push the car fifty yards and shove it over a cliff followed by the car owner and his two friends. Once the pushing begins and the car starts moving it is probable the car is going to come to rest more than twenty yards from the starting point, even if it does not end up at the cliff's foot.

Now let us imagine what a group of people watching from a nearby hilltop will make of the incident. They will start by assuming that all six men have the same intentions. The car is moving steadily forward. Then they see three of the men detach themselves from the back of the car, run round to the front and try to stop it. Which are the trouble-makers? Those surely who are now opposing the process that has been started.

So it has been with the conciliar teaching and reforms. Whenever the Holy See or an energetic bishop has endeavoured to correct or contain the abuses, the innovators, with every appearance of plausibility, have been able to accuse them of trying to reverse the Council's work. They have only had to cry "Touch us and you touch the Council and reform too" for large numbers of the faithful to believe them.

Notes to Chapter Three

[1] Fr. Chenu, with characteristic candour, has given a number of examples of the way he and his colleagues were able to influence the texts, sometimes to their advantage, sometimes not. In one case he describes how, when the main text had been voted on and therefore could not be changed, they were able to get an additional paragraph introduced contradicting the previous one. See *Un théologien en liberté, Jacques Duquesne intérroge le Père Chenu* (T.L.), Le Centurion, Paris, 1975, pp. 17, 18, 63, 81, 106, 177–9, 184. For Fr. Congar, Vatican II "wasn't perfect, but due to its broad outlook . . . it was able to promote movements which went beyond the Council itself" (*Forty Years of Catholic Theology*, S.C.M. Press, 1987, pp. 56 & 68).

[2] Is the Council responsible for the present crisis? "The answer to this question, put in such general terms, must be a resolute No . . . However we don't deny that the Council has played a part in what has grown into the crisis." Fr. Congar, *Challenge to the Church*, (Collins 1976, pp. 50-51). Fr. Chenu goes further. The cause of the crisis "is in the Council itself . . . in the logic of its proceedings and dynamism." (T.L. 195).

[3] John Paul II, more sympathetic than his predecessors to Rosmini's philosophical ideas, and, perhaps because of this, understanding better what he was trying to achieve, had the censures lifted.

[4] A small example, to avoid more complicated and controversial topics at this point: Fr. Chenu was fond of saying that obedience is a "mediocre" virtue. It was silly and wrong-headed, even if he was thinking of cases where what appears to be obedience is in fact being used as an excuse for cowardice or shirking one's responsibilities. But it became positively pernicious with the greater part of the Church's intelligentsia in a state of open revolt. He continued to state it nevertheless. (T.L. 22)

[5] In fact, doubts about the activities of some of the *periti* were already fairly widespread before the Council ended. Cardinal Heenan of Westminster's comments at the time are well known.

[6] See *The Tablet*, 8 June 1991. At a theological forum in Cambridge organised by *Concilium* in 1981, which the author reported, Mr van den Boogard, "a formidable fundraiser," gave the impression that he saw Vatican II as completing or continuing the work of the Protestant reformation. The U.S. *National Catholic Reporter* and, in England, *The Tablet* are the main channels through which *Concilium* theology and viewpoints reach the English-speaking laity. Fr. Congar's friends claim that he remained on *Concilium's* editorial board to act as a restraining influence. If true, it was like von Papen imagining he could restrain Hitler.

[7] For example, the series of signed protests in the early 90s, by theologians of one country after another against the policies and teachings of John Paul II. The "We Are Church" movement in Austria, Germany and elsewhere can be seen as a lay by-product. "We Are Church" is a movement for bringing pressure on the hierarchy to modify Church teachings which conflict with the European middle-classes' new lifestyle.

Chapter Four

NAMES AND LABELS

Before we move on, a word needs to be said about the terms "liberal" and "conservative", "progressive" and "traditionalist". Their use and abuse have contributed to the confusion too. Taken from politics, they have to do with change. Should there be much, or little, or none at all?

If "conservatism" only meant conserving what is good, and "liberalism" only changing what is bad or welcoming the good in what is new, every man and woman should and probably would be both conservative and liberal. But which of the many things that history has handed down or new times have presented are good and which bad? This is where the disagreements begin.

In the early days of the Council, the application of the two terms to describe the differing approaches of the participants still bore some relationship to what was happening. Things instituted or permitted by the Church under its authority to "bind and loose" – prayers, practices, methods of government or ways of presenting its teaching – can change, and there can be legitimate differences of opinion about what will be beneficial.

On the other hand, the idea that there can be "progressive" and "conservative" opinions about what God has revealed is on a level with thinking there can be "progressive" and "conservative" views about lying, the circulation of the blood, or the date of Napoleon's death.

When, therefore, it became apparent that there were two subjects of debate, not one, the first about reform, the second about belief, and that a proportion of the reformers were not reformers but religious revolutionaries, terms like "liberal" and "conservative", "progressive" and "traditionalist" became not only inadequate but positively misleading. In fact, the debates were often three-, four-, or five-way ones.

Take, for example, the simplification of the prayers of the Mass and the introduction of the vernacular. Bishop A, we will say, favoured change because he genuinely believed it would help the faithful understand and take part in the Mass more fruitfully, Bishop B because it would make the Mass sound more like a simple memorial meal of bread and wine, which is what he had now come to believe the Mass is, while Bishop C, though not in principle opposed to the vernacular and a degree of simplification, opposed the initiatives of Bishop B and his followers because he rightly suspected them of trying to introduce a Protestant conception of the Mass, and Bishop D was against change because he believed the liturgy of the Mass to be satisfactory as it was.

This partly explains the uneven tenor of many passages in the conciliar decrees. It is normal for there to be different schools of thought and conflicts at a general council. It is different when the integrity of the faith becomes an issue.

Among those calling themselves Catholics today there are in fact not two but three recognizable bodies of belief or opinion. First, there are Catholics in the hitherto universally recognised sense; they accept all the Church's teachings. Then come the modernists or semi-modernists dedicated to altering some aspect of faith or morals. We can also call them innovators or dissenters. It seems the politest name consistent with accuracy. Finally, there are the followers of the French Archbishop, Marcel Lefebvre.

Circulating around, between or within these more consolidated groups are vast numbers of clergy and laity, Catholic in intention no doubt, but whose uncertain beliefs and wavering loyalties make them, in regard to belief at least, difficult to classify. After nearly 35 years of pick-and-choose religious instruction, many have been turned into either neo-Episcopalians (a liking for dignified worship is retained but each believes as much or as little as he chooses); praying Bible-reading Protestants; secularised "democratised" activists; adherents of a trivialised psychologised religion of togetherness with only two doctrines – "God loves you" and "everybody is basically nice"; or a mixture of two or more of these different "faiths".[1]

Catholics in the recognised sense can be known by their willingness to follow the teaching of the successor of St. Peter. Why did Christ give St. Peter and his successors their special position if not for just such a situation? But though one in belief and obedience, they are often divided about how the reforms should be applied in practice when this has not been clearly laid down by Rome; or about the kind of accommodations with the times that are wise or possible. They may also feel different degrees of enthusiasm for the reforms. Disagreements of this sort can be partly a matter of temperament.[2]

In this area, talk about "progressives" and "conservatives" still makes some kind of sense.

However, while some of those described by the media as "conservative" may be motivated largely by dislike of change, the majority are chiefly concerned with preventing change being used to alter belief.

At the same time, priests anxious to implement the Council's teaching as fully as they can are sometimes called "progressive" with the possible implication that they are unorthodox, when they are not.

The difficulty here is that neighbouring parish priests making the same changes, and therefore all called "progressive", may have different motives. The first may have removed the altar rails because he wants to make the distinction between clergy and laity less sharp, the second because he no longer believes there *is* any distinction. The activities of a third may be a mixture of authentic implementations of the reforms, and initiatives unconsciously inspired by heterodox influences. So even in connection with believing Catholics, the words "progressive" and "conservative" tend to be ambiguous.

In the modernist or innovating camp – the second body of belief or opinion – there is no absolute unity of belief. The only unifying factors are opposition to Rome, and the conviction that many of the Church's teachings can no longer mean what they appear to mean and must be altered accordingly.

The crucial conflict is between these first two groups, the Catholics and the theological innovators, about the very substance of Catholic belief, not about legitimately different ways of interpreting and implementing the Council. It is a struggle which varies in intensity from region to region. Where orthodox bishops and clergy have the upper hand it may be barely noticeable. But wherever it goes on, however confusedly and obscurely, it takes place at every level – parish, school, university, diocese, religious order, even within the Roman curia.

Our third body of belief or opinion, the followers of the late French Archbishop Lefebvre, represents, by comparison, a kind of skirmishing on the perimeter. Beginning as a justifiable attempt to resist modernism, Lefebvrism went off the rails largely, I would say, because so many authorised guardians of the faith did little or nothing to protect it.

Scandalised by their negligence, the Lefebvrist reaction could be summed up as: "since change and heresy came in together, change nothing. Stick to tradition." However, they include under "tradition", not only what has always been believed or was instituted by Christ (Tradition in the strict sense, or with a big "T", which is indeed unchangeable), but a great deal of what, however good in itself, the Church does have power to modify or adapt (tradition in the looser sense – tradition with a small "t"). Fidelity to the old liturgy became the focus of their opposition to change, because the new liturgy was instantly seized upon by the innovators as their principal instrument for altering belief at the parish level.

The fact that Pope Paul singled out Archbishop Lefebvre for disciplinary action while leaving uncensured cardinals and bishops tolerating rampant heresies, inevitably increased traditionalist suspicions, hardened their opposition, and drove them increasingly to question the Council as such.[3]

However, the idea that, as a schismatic "rebellion of the right", Lefebvrism is a danger to the Church comparable in size and importance to the modernist "rebellion of the left" does not remotely correspond with the facts.

Confusion is compounded by the use of the term "traditionalist". The Lefebvrists regard themselves as or call themselves "traditionalists". But so often do Catholics who remain obedient to the Pope but attached to the old liturgy and doubtful about the wisdom or necessity of most of the reforms.

Under these circumstances, talk about "liberals" and "conservatives", "progressives" and "traditionalists", though difficult to avoid altogether, has worked almost exclusively to the advantage of the innovators.

Giving the impression, as it does, that there is only one subject under debate (reform), with only two parties to it, the innovators are able to pass themselves off as merely an "extreme left" of the reform party whose attempts to alter the meaning of belief are a legitimate contribution to *aggiornamento*, while branding as a "conservative" anyone who opposes those attempts, the Pope included. What else can the Pope be but a "conservative" if they are merely "liberals"? What the Church has taught for twenty centuries on the one hand, and what modernism now says those teachings mean on the other, are made to appear as equally valid versions of the Catholic faith, to either of which Catholics may assent. Defending the traditional meaning of the Church's teachings is merely the peculiarity of one brand of Catholics, the "conservative" brand, while altering their meaning is a legitimate "liberal" or "progressive" alternative.

I shall, therefore, make as little use of these terms as possible. The word "liberal" when it does appear will have its long-established sense. It will refer to Catholics who since the beginning of the 19th century have been anxious to have the Church approve as much as she can in contemporary life, and allow the greatest degree of freedom compatible with the maintenance of belief. For those who want to alter belief, I will mainly use the term "dissenters".

Returning for a moment to the fully believing Catholics, the weakness of their opposition to false teaching has certainly been another reason for the rebellion's successes. With many, this may be due to lack of interest. But it is also, I think, to be explained by habit, training and belief.

They know that obedience to lawful authority is a virtue. Their religion also tells them to be charitable and not to judge. All this makes them fearful of sinning against these virtues. The "other side" plays on these susceptibilities to undermine their resistance. They want, too, as the saying goes to "think with the mind of the Church". They recognise in a general way the possibilities for good in the reforms. But in the prevailing confusion it is often all but impossible for them to discover precisely what the mind of the Church is; to distinguish between genuine and spurious interpretations of the decrees; or when faced with some change, to determine whether it really has the backing of Rome or not. The Catholic press will not enlighten them. The greater part has accepted the dissenters' interpretation of the Council, or performs a balancing act, trying to please all comers.

Such are the circumstances in which the Church has for 35 years been trying to implement the Second Vatican Council's decrees.

By now, whatever it is considered can be done by external means has been done. The practical adaptations have been made. And among orthodox Catholics scattered about the world — though they are not usually those who speak loudest about reform or renewal — there are signs that the Council's true work is beginning to bear fruit. A genuine spiritual revival seems to be underway. The signs are chiefly noticeable in the new lay, or lay and priestly religious communities founded in the 20th century, some before the Council, but also growing numbers since. There are also many conversions in Africa and countries like Korea.

But in most of the West these new beginnings are like the first shoots of plant life in early spring held back by the persisting frosts and the debris littering the ground after a succession of hurricanes. The number of outsiders that the reforms have succeeded in attracting to the Church is still small compared with the numbers of the faithful whom revolution and dissent have been sweeping away from Catholic belief.

For any Pope, the situation would plainly require the most delicate handling. John Paul II's estimate of it, like Pius XII's over Hitler and the Jews, would seem to be that strong measures — however much apparently the right thing — would at this point only make matters worse. For nearly thirty-five years the Church has been living with the beginnings of a second reformation. Can he defuse the bomb without detonating it? Can he detach errant bishops from the rebel theologians, with whom so many of them seem to be in love? Can the rebel theologians be drawn back before irrevocable breaks with Rome?

How many, too, of the straying laity can he recover? How many can he persuade to listen to him rather than to the rebels? The principal purpose of his many journeys abroad would seem to be get at the people where necessary over the heads of the local theological establishment.

At the same time he is clearly determined to let it be seen that combating the abuses and false teaching does not mean putting the Council into the lumber room. This is not just a matter of tactics. He is in every sense a "man of the Council", by which I mean an unquestionable believer in its value and importance, as anyone realises who knows the part he played at the Council or has read his *Sources of Renewal*, written for the guidance of his priests when he was Archbishop of Krakow. One knows of no other bishop who made such conscientious efforts to understand what God wanted from the Council and to apply it.

His numerous sermons and addresses can be seen as a catechism course for the whole Church, anchoring the new orientations and initiatives in the bed rock of traditional Catholic belief so that they no longer float about in an ocean of modernist and semi-modernist ambiguities.[4]

The *Catechism of Catholic Church* (CCC) has the same purpose. Requested by Cardinal Law at the end of the 1985 Synod to commemorate the 20th anniversary of the closing of Vatican II, it first appeared in French in 1992, to be followed by an official Latin version in 1997.[5] Ever since the Council, modernists had opposed the composition of such a catechism. A catechism, of its very nature, limits private interpretation.

Although the conflict is far from over, with the publication of the *Catechism* the Church could be said to have won the second round in its struggle with modernism.

The question that now faces us is why large numbers of the faithful surrendered so rapidly to the siren songs of the innovators.

Notes to Chapter Four

[1] According to a German poll in the mid-1980s, 23% of German Catholics regard papal decisions as binding, and 64% are said to regard them as binding when they agree with them! (Allensbach Institute Poll, cited by *The Tablet*, 7th Dec. 1985).

[2] Practices which are changeable in principle may nevertheless be important safeguards of belief. The abandonment throughout most of the West, for instance, of Corpus Christi and May processions – often rather snobbishly referred to as "popular devotions" – have contributed to the weakening of belief in the Real Presence and the intercessory power of Our Lady.

[3] In 1976 Pope Paul suspended the Archbishop *a divinis*, that is from the exercise of his priestly and episcopal powers, for ordaining more priests after he had been ordered to close his seminary. He was already well known for his opposition to the liturgical reforms and questioning of the conciliar decree on religious liberty. His excommunication

in the summer of 1988 was the result of his illegal consecration of four bishops to carry on his work after his death. Under canon law, any bishop who consecrates another bishop against the command of the reigning pope is automatically excommunicated. Modernist animosity towards the archbishop is due to his having been responsible during the Council for checking a number of their more questionable initiatives. He also represented a French right-wing socio-political tradition opposed to the "left-inclining" socio-political views of the French reformers.

[4]   In January 1985 he began his extended series of addresses on the Creed, now published in book form (six volumes) by Pauline Press, Boston, Mass.

[5]   Cardinal Law would appear to have been responding to the wishes of the Pope. According to the Jesuit editor of a U.S. periodical, there had been requests for a new catechism incorporating the teachings of Vatican II at every episcopal synod in Rome from 1974. But not until 1985 did Rome feel it had enough episcopal support to take action. The editor in question had reported every Synod since 1974.

PART II

A BACKWARD GLANCE

Chapter Five

THE SHEPHERDS

Looked at from outside, Catholic life in the decade and a half between 1945 and 1960 seemed in the main healthy and strong, and the Church's prospects rather splendid.

The United States, the most powerful country in the world, had a growing population of apparently fervent and faithful Catholics. Indeed it looked as if the Catholics would soon turn the United States into a Catholic country simply by having more babies and outvoting their fellow citizens at the polls. The Americans, Germans, Irish, Dutch gave money liberally and along with the Italians sent abroad large numbers of missionaries. France, Germany and Italy, for generations ruled by politicians hostile to the Church, had suddenly produced a clutch of exceptionally able statesmen or parliamentarians and Catholic parties with majorities or near majorities. Spain and Portugal were in the control of capable Catholic autocrats. Sunday Mass was still mainly well attended. In spite of losses, Rome seemed to be holding on to her members better than the mainline Protestant churches.

The Church had also experienced a remarkable if limited recovery of intellectual prestige, and for several generations had been attracting a stream of notable converts; writers, thinkers, men of science. These converts contributed to the recovery, as well as being the fruit of it. Nobody of course believed that everything was perfect. There are no perfect periods in the Church's history. But there seemed reason for looking to the future with confidence, and for most people the Council did not immediately shake these rosy expectations.

Then in July 1968, Pope Paul VI issued *Humanae Vitae*, and deeper and quite different realities were laid bare.

Contradicting what they had solemnly taught only four years before in the Council's document on the Church, *Lumen Gentium* – namely that "religious submission of mind and will must be shown in a special way to the authentic teaching and authority of the Roman pontiff even when he is not speaking *ex cathedra*", and what they had equally explicitly said about contraception in the document *Gaudium et Spes* – most Western hierarchies and a few elsewhere now repudiated the Pope's encyclical in a series of joint statements, some rejecting the teaching openly, others with circumlocutions.[1]

Meanwhile rebellious priests and lay people were crowding into the radio and television studios, assuring their listeners how compassionate and well-informed they were, and urging their fellow Catholics not to listen to the Pope. There was now a higher authority in the Church: "the mature Catholic conscience".

The violence of the explosion is usually blamed on the length of time Pope Paul took to make up his mind, and that would certainly seem to have been a factor. The delay gave the impression that the teaching was certain to be changed. Many Catholic couples had therefore started practising contraception, and bishops tacitly allowed it. Now the bishops were faced with having to tell their flocks that they had led them astray, and that they must give up what had become a habit.

On the other hand, if Pope Paul had not had the subject thoroughly studied, he would have been blamed for acting impetuously.

But *Humanae Vitae* was not the only problem. It quickly became clear there was much else in Catholic teaching that many of the clergy and laity could no longer stomach.

What had gone wrong? I do not want to give support to the many caricatures of Catholic life before the Council that have been spread abroad in recent years. But, behind the grand-looking façade of religious practice, there must have been something amiss, something in need of reform. Catholics do not suddenly abandon large numbers of their beliefs and moral principles if they have been serving God as they ought.

I will begin with the shepherds. For a Catholic, the bishop is "Christ in the diocese". He is the chief sanctifier of his flock. But he is also human like the rest of us. If he is not in every respect the shepherd he should be, he is not going to stand firm when the wolf looks out of the wood.

One of the things the world took for granted before the Council was that Catholic bishops always gave the same teaching as the Pope. Since many of them were suddenly defying the Pope, did this mean that all the orthodoxy and fidelity to the Holy See which had been so conspicuous in the reign of Pius XII was a sham? No. But much of it may have sprung from natural as much as from supernatural motives. Bishops at that time had strong natural reasons for remaining faithful. In the world's eyes, a bishop is a success, and since all favours flowed from Rome, continued success depended on doing what Rome wanted. It was not just a matter of cold calculation. Most of us are kept on the straight and narrow by social pressure as much as by virtue. If natural motives for loyalty are removed, only grace and the supernatural virtues will keep a bishop in union with and obedient to the successor of St.

Peter. It is then that bishops are most exposed to the temptation which is, as it were, built into the episcopal office; the temptation to resent the Pope's higher office and authority, and his unique gift which they do not share. The Council's teaching about episcopal collegiality has greatly enhanced the possibilities of temptation in this area.

Another danger for bishops is to take as their model the contemporary man of influence and power.

There have been armoured bishops wielding maces, princely renaissance bishops with splendid households and great art collections; history has also known leisurely land-owning bishops devoted mostly to hunting and shooting. Now the man of power is the company president or grand administrator. So the temptation today is very great for a bishop with a large diocese, and a great deal of temporal and purely administrative work, to slide into being an efficient businessman more than a bishop. The apostle vanishes inside the executive, and the transformation is unnoticed, above all by the subject of it.

Now an administrator exists to keep the company running. It does not much matter to him what the company is producing or selling, providing it continues in existence and works smoothly. That is the characteristic administrator's point of view.

Under Pius XII, the bishop administrator or businessman at least knew what the boss in Rome wanted. The corporation was producing orthodoxy in faith and morals and no public scandals or dissensions. Very well, if that was what the boss wanted, he should have it. No doubt the businessman-bishop of those days wanted them too. His faith had not yet been frayed at the edges. So he produced the goods and did it efficiently. That kind of efficiency was then rewarded in Rome.

But what would happen when the businessman-bishop found he had a more powerful boss and one nearer home than the boss in the Vatican? St. Thomas Aquinas says a man may desire to be a bishop if he is prepared to be a holocaust; he must be ready to suffer for his sheep. That does not necessarily mean having to die for them. After the Council it began to mean a range of lesser unpleasantnesses: being misrepresented and lied about in Rome, snubbed by his brother bishops at episcopal conferences, sneered at by theologians, attacked in the Catholic press, tricked by his diocesan officials, bullied by his parish priests, insulted by some sharp-tongued reverend mother wearing trousers and earrings and running a revolutionary workshop. Love of God and love for his flock will raise a man above fear of such things, and that the faithful bishop has.

But the bishop businessman or executive, even while still believing, will not want to be a holocaust. (No one naturally wants to be; only grace makes it possible). Not loving his sheep with a deep supernatural love, he will not be prepared to suffer even the minor trials just outlined. Men do not have to be threatened with physical violence before they abandon their duty – a truth well known to governments. The threat of discomfort or unpopularity is enough, especially with men over fifty.

So when the businessman-bishop found that standing up to his rebellious clergy was more disagreeable than defying the Pope, his orthodoxy and loyalty began to evaporate.

Another weakness could be faith and piety without an adequate depth and breadth of theological understanding or of current theological speculation and problems. That a bishop should be orthodox and devout is a primary requirement, certainly. But a bishop is above all a teacher, a "doctor". If his theological knowledge is underdeveloped he is like a university professor with a high-school grasp of his subject. He may get along all right with the docile pupils. But he will be lost when challenged by the brighter rebellious ones. In the past it was enough to tell the bright and rebellious to keep quiet. But when the style of ecclesiastical government changed, he found himself having to justify his commands with reasons and references, which he was ill-equipped to provide.

He was just as ill-equipped, it seems, to meet the flood of new ideas which he met for the first time at the Council. Shaken in his old certainties, his tendency was to surrender to them wholesale or swim with the tide. This is why, in many places, theologians have become the primary teachers in the Church, bishops merely their echoes.[2]

Another figure from the past, the bishop autocrat, also turned out to have feet of clay. Although he looked rock-like, he did not prove so. He knew how to command obedience, but not how to win men's hearts. He has been partly responsible for the present outcry against legalism and authoritarianism. Too many, it seems, were not proper fathers to their priests.

That there were many good and holy bishops before the Council is not in doubt. In all this I have been talking about types, temptations and tendencies, not individuals. But that such tendencies were embodied in not a few individuals seems to be confirmed by the Council's insistence that bishops be more pastoral and see themselves as servants.

However, what the Council means by service is not quite what people today with a hang-up about authority think it means.

In every day speech "a servant" means someone who does the will of another, not his own. Our service of God is always of this kind. We try to make his will ours. Between men, on the other hand, service should mean first and foremost attending to the good and needs of others, not primarily to doing their will, because men do not always will, or perhaps know, what is good. Service between men, therefore, can and often must consist in not giving people, or some people, what they want, if only because in the end they would be losers by it. This is the kind of service given by parents, doctors, and rulers. And still more is it required of Catholic bishops.

As guardian of God's idea and plan for man, a Catholic bishop's first and supreme service to his flock is to remain faithful to that idea and plan, even when it conflicts with the wishes or whims of a part of his flock. So in talking about bishops as servants, the Council was simply reminding them that their position was not for their personal aggrandisement, and that they must keep in mind the dignity and humanity of their flock when exercising authority over them. It did not mean that bishops are meant to serve in the same way as waiters or shop assistants.

Misconceptions about the right way of being a servant have unfortunately resulted in the autocrat too often being replaced by the bishop who wants to be loved. The bishop who wants to be loved is frightened of losing his reputation for being "caring" and "compassionate" by doing something unpopular even when this is what real love demands. Or he tries to "serve" like a politician. When his flock goes into apostasy and heresy, he keeps it together by saying contradictory things to please all shades of opinion, or when the going gets tough, hides behind his diocesan bureaucracy. Or he becomes a kind of religious salesman. If he wants to attract communist voters, he makes the faith sound as much as possible like Marxist Leninism. If, on the contrary he is aiming at prosperous or hedonistically inclined sheep, he will refrain from speaking too harshly or too much about vice.

All this is symptomatic of a slow slide from the level of supernatural faith to the level of natural religious belief. When this happens, the shepherd is tempted to feel that, provided people can be persuaded to believe in God, come to Church on Sunday, pray and keep the commandments (at any rate those that forbid murder and theft), his most important work has been done. He may not consciously doubt any truths of the faith, but they are gradually coming to seem a not absolutely essential extra.[3]

If preaching the truth fails to fill churches, three conclusions can be drawn. There is something wrong with the preacher; there is something wrong with the audience; or there is something wrong with the message. Since it is much easier to alter the message than to alter the preacher or audience, adapting the message will be the method of renewing the Church that will appeal where a supernatural outlook is in decline. But you do not correct past defects by embracing those of an opposite kind.

★   ★   ★

Turning to the rest of the clergy, some of the temptations for priests were the same as for bishops.

If he was not truly a man of prayer, the president of a great Catholic university, the superior or provincial of a major religious order, or the monsignor in charge of a large parish with half a dozen curates under him, could easily turn into a businessman or autocrat too. When the crunch came, how many of them would care what was taught in their university, province or parish?

But there were also, as there always are, difficulties and temptations which were peculiarly the priest's own. These chiefly affected priests who were not in worldly terms "a success"; those with the smaller unimportant parishes. Apart from strictly priestly duties, such priests had much less that they absolutely had to do. It was therefore harder to hide from themselves the real nature of their vocation under a pile of office work. They were, as they still can be, faced with a stark alternative: being priests or suffering boredom.

But being a priest means dealing with mainly invisible realities: offering the God-Man present under the appearance of bread and wine in sacrifice for sin; teaching mysteries for whose truth we only have God's word; applying the intangible, insensible gift of grace to men's souls in the sacraments. To believe in the reality and importance of such things requires faith – for a priest living in an isolated parish, or one where few people came to Mass, a lot of faith.

On the other hand, a priest whose parishioners were mostly comfortable and prosperous perhaps needed even more faith. Unless his faith was strong, supernatural things began to seem unreal to him too. Did they really do much good? Lots of people seemed to get on quite well without religion. The priest glances at the local doctor or lawyer. Weren't their lives more useful? No, of course not. The priest still believed. But all the same . . .

As religion became more and more lacklustre, the danger for such a priest was to turn into a kind of spiritual technician. He serviced the souls of his people to keep them on the road. But he looked elsewhere for his real interest in life; some hobby, or repairing the presbytery, or perhaps the golf course. The curate in the big city parish was exposed to these temptations when the parish priest was not the father he should have been.

If a priest was reasonably well-trained and self-disciplined and also in awe of his bishop all this took place without his parishioners noticing very much.

But it was a seed-bed for disaster. The bored, unhappy or de-supernaturalised priests of thirty or forty years ago were quickest to abandon belief and plunge into promoting the new, less demanding beliefs in order to make life vivid and interesting.

With members of religious orders, when faith was no longer something vital, there were two special temptations.

The first was to make a fetish of rules and regulations.

Rules are not to be despised. According to the great teachers (male and female) of the spiritual life, faithful observance of the order's rule is for religious a first step on the path to sanctity. Rules make the common life possible. Properly applied they give stability of mind and heart, help to curb self-will, promote unity, and enable those subject to them to love God more intensely by releasing them from having to make a multitude of minor decisions.

But they are only a first step. Some people get a purely natural satisfaction out of keeping rules. If rules loom too large, those for whom they have no natural appeal will find them stifling rather than stabilising and liberating. No longer accepted for love of God, they can end by generating weariness of spirit or dull dislike.

That a preoccupation with minutiae was weighing down the life of many religious orders is indicated by the number of men and women religious who, when not abandoning their monasteries and convents altogether, have interpreted the Council's decree on religious life as meaning they could live more or less without rules – the fewer the better.

The second temptation for the bored religious is to use scholarship as a distraction. The danger here lies in scholarship's being a presentable activity. If the members of a religious order are living in luxury or acting immorally everyone can see they are going off the rails. But no one can see the decline of faith, hope and charity in the soul of a religious sitting behind a pile of learned books. A well-known biblical scholar has described how he started studying Scripture because he found his fellow religious too boring to talk to. But in this frame of mind, what is the use of studying Scripture which is so largely about loving one's brothers, boring or not? But here I am touching on the subject of the next chapter.

Notes to Chapter Five

[1] At the request of the Council, Pope Paul had set up a commission to see if the teaching about contraception could be modified. After a first report he enlarged the commission. Both times, the majority recommended a change. The deliberations lasted four years. The final report was leaked to the press. With great courage, the Pope upheld the perennial teaching against his experts' advice and in the face of a hostile world press campaign. It is not possible to go into all the grounds for the Church's decision here. Ample philosophical, theological, sociological and other reasons can be found in the writings of Pope John Paul II. (See his general audience addresses 1979–1984, published as *The Theology of the Body: Human Love in the Divine Plan*, Pauline Books, Boston, 1997.) However, it is, I think, much easier than it was before the "sexual revolution" to see the link between contraception and the collapse of marriage and the family with all its disastrous social consequences. Contraception creates a climate in which children, no matter how much wanted, come to be seen as accidental to marriage instead of its main meaning. If, on the other hand, the main meaning is love, one can fall out of love, so why bother with marriage? It is also easier to see the link between contraception and unnatural sex. If sex is just another pleasurable physical activity, liking eating, drinking or swimming – "recreational sex", as it is now called – why shouldn't unnatural sex be socially acceptable? There is no argument against unnatural sex, if sex has no deeper meaning than the pleasure of the participants.

[2] This reversal of roles was lamented by Fr. Rosmini as far back as 1846. In his passionate plea for certain reforms, *The Five Wounds of the Church*, he repeatedly recalls that in the first six centuries most of the greatest theologians were bishops.

[3] The influence of deism in the 18th century had had similar consequences. Daniel-Rops quotes a French bishop who survived the revolution. "May God forgive us," he is reported to have said. "We almost never spoke about Our Lord Jesus Christ in the pulpit. We only talked about the Supreme Being".

Chapter Six

THE CHURCH LEARNÈD

In this chapter I will look at the Church's intelligentsia.

The work of Catholic thinkers and scholars is of roughly two kinds: presenting, explaining and defending the Catholic faith; and relating it to the naturally acquired knowledge current at a particular time. The first is the easier task and carries fewer temptations. Nevertheless it is not altogether free of them. Officially authorised guardians of the faith can easily become intellectual autocrats. This chiefly means that they will be unwilling to give sufficient weight to the ideas or criticisms of other and possibly rival schools of thought.

Although there were several different schools of Thomism in the preconciliar years, as we shall see later, one in particular had received semi-official approval, and the failings of some of its more autocratic exponents has had perhaps at least something to do with the mauling and near overthrow that Thomism has suffered since the Council. What the autocrat taught was no doubt true, but the manner of saying it could be repellent, because what is holy and mysterious was treated as obvious and self-evident.

Another danger for authorised guardians of the faith was professionalism. The faith had ceased to be a living fire burning in the teacher's "veins and belly". It had become "My subject", "What I am qualified in". The students then received, not something breathing and beautiful which fired their love, but what appeared as either a hyper-ingenious intellectual crossword puzzle, or a heap of bones and dust. In both cases the results would be disastrous. Clever students were tempted to see theology or whatever else they were studying chiefly as a subject to exercise their wits on. The rest were likely to feel, at best, indifference; at worst, dull dislike.

The professional will also be tempted to see all ideas, good or bad, as in the first place interesting products of the human mind. This means that, when heresy makes its appearance, his reaction will be much like that of a doctor towards illness and death. You don't lose any sleep over it. It is all part of the day's work. And if the heretic is a colleague you stay on friendly terms with him.

However, in this chapter I am more concerned with the theologians and scholars whose vocation called them to work of the second kind, those dedicated to reform and *aggiornamento*.

Why did so much of this rampart of the heavenly Jerusalem collapse in heaps of rubble when the modern world marched around it and blew its trumpets? In Part IV, I shall be looking at the intellectual background. Here I will glance briefly at some spiritual and psychological problems.

One of the chief hazards for scholars of every kind is "not being able to see the wood for the trees".

When we look at any of the things God has created, perhaps the most striking thing about them is the contrast between their simplicity and intelligibility when taken as a whole, and their complexity and obscurity when examined in detail. This is why there are biologists who cannot see any essential difference between men and animals, and ordinary folk who can. Peering at the details produces a kind of myopia about the whole.

It is the same with the faith. In its outlines it is so simple that children can grasp it, yet no single library contains everything that has been written about the details. Moreover, here too, studying the details can result in short-sightedness about the totality.

It was for some such reason, according to Newman, that during the Arian crisis of the fourth century, the ordinary faithful often gave a clearer testimony to their beliefs on certain points than theologians, including some of the Church Fathers. The faithful simply gave back what they had been taught, Newman tells us, without their understanding of the grand design having been clouded by complexities and subtleties. Similarly, when the Anglo-Irish Jesuit convert Fr. George Tyrrell started to preach heresy from the pulpit of Farm Street Church in London at the start of this century, the first person to notice was a lay brother.

Another pitfall for learned men of all kinds is the temptation to fall in love with their subject. The archaeologist, Sir Leonard Cottrell, commenting on this weakness, remarked good-humouredly that he had known Assyriologists who thought the ancient Assyrians, as depicted on their bas-reliefs, handsome.

When a Catholic scholar falls too deeply in love with his subject – whether Buddhism, Protestantism, palaeontology, or sociology – it will come to rank higher in his heart than the faith. He will then be tempted to adapt the faith to fit in with the exigencies of "my subject".

Nationalism can also distort a scholar's or thinker's judgement. A famous national figure will be overvalued just because he is a compatriot. We can see this, yesterday and today, in the pressure from German Catholics to have the Church baptise Kant and Hegel, and from the French to have her give her blessing to Descartes and Bergson.

It is strange, when one comes to think of it, that Catholics are not taught to be more concerned for the spiritual welfare of "the Church Learned"; that there are not religious orders specially devoted to praying and making sacrifices for its members, since their work is so necessary and they occupy what, in regard to faith, is one of the most exposed positions in the Church. The world of speculative ideas and massive accumulations of fact is the place where it is easiest to fall into a pit or be swept over a cataract, the implications of new ideas and facts not usually being apparent until quite some time after first appearance. Or we can compare them to soldiers in an observation post continually under heavy shell-fire.

As they study new books and learned publications, they live (often without realising it) under a barrage of temptations of a kind most of the faithful never experience. "Oh, what a brilliant idea! But what happens to the doctrine of grace? Perhaps I should pray before reading further. No, I haven't time. It's more important to get on with my work. *Laborare est orare*. The Church could be wrong. It's never been defined. How could a stupid bishop without a doctorate be expected to understand such a subtly nuanced concept?"

The danger is not so much that they will take a wrong path — anyone can make a mistake — but that, having taken it, they press ahead ignoring warnings.

For Catholic scholars, their unfailing protection is, of course, readiness to submit their conclusions to the Church's teaching authority.

Part of the mystery of the Church is that, in arranging how his truth is to be handed on, God made Greek philosophers, or anyone resembling them, subordinate to Galilean fishermen. The three wise men kneeling before Divine Wisdom made visible as a baby provides a prototype. A Pope or bishop may be personally learned, but his learning does not add anything to his authority as pope or bishop. His authority to pass judgement on the ideas of even the most brilliant thinker, where those ideas touch on faith and morals, comes solely from the fact that he is a successor of one of Our Lord's little-educated working-class apostles. St. Paul the brilliant "university type", was brought in later, but only after a big dose of humiliation.

For Catholics, the purpose behind this plan is not difficult to see. Everything in God's designs is directed to keeping us small in our own esteem, since this is the only way into the kingdom of heaven, and no one needs more help in this matter than clever men and women. (Over the entrance to every Catholic university could well be carved St. Thérèse of Lisieux's words: "God has no need of any human instrument, least of all me.")

But this ultimate subordination of "philosophers" to "fisherman" is not something the clever find naturally easy to accept. With a strong sense of the supernatural they will. But if faith starts to decline it starts to stick in the throat. Then, instead of seeing themselves as servants of Christ and his Church, they become, without realising it, servants of worldly powers – like William of Ockham in the 14th century when he fled from Avignon to the court of Louis of Bavaria – of the spirit of the times, or of their own opinions and ambitions.

One of the most revealing things about some of the theologians who have come to fame since the Council is their apparent indifference to the confusion into which they have plunged the simple and lowly. As long as they can write what they please, they do not seem to care what the consequences are. If doctors had acted like this, leaving behind a trail of corpses and invalids, they would have earned not reputations but infamy.

But, of course, they do not accept God's plan for the Church. The world having entered the age of the expert, they imagine they should be running it, the way many secular experts seem to think they should be running civil society. It is the great dream and illusion of intellectuals. Real intellectuals almost never rule – except briefly in periods of disaster and chaos. The nature of their gifts incapacitates them for it. Thinkers who are also natural rulers, like Calvin and Lenin, are rarities (thanks be to God), and the world usually sighs with relief when they are taken away.

The second fact Catholic scholars easily lose sight of if their outlook becomes de-supernaturalised under the influence of their studies, is the unique nature of divine revelation. Coming as it does from God, it cannot be the subject of uncontrolled debate like black holes or nervous diseases. It is true that in helping the magisterium expound and develop it, Catholic scholars need sufficient freedom to do their work properly, and that the Church recognises and encourages. In his encyclical *Divino Afflante Spiritu*, Pius XII defended this necessary freedom; the faithful, he said were not to assume that every new idea a theologian or scholar put forward was suspect just because new. Nevertheless, when it comes to the faith, Catholic scholars cannot enjoy the unrestricted academic freedom enjoyed by their secular counterparts, however much they long for it. It would be equivalent to saying either that God could not be trusted, or that he had not guaranteed the Church against error. Actually, secular scholars do not enjoy unrestricted academic freedom either. Would a scientist who taught Ptolemaic physics keep his job at Harvard or Cambridge?

Here the Catholic scholar is exposed to temptation of a special kind; fear of his non-Catholic colleagues, of the raised eye-brow, the amused little laugh at the learned meeting or in the university common-room. "Oh, I apologise,

Father. I was forgetting you have to ask the Pope's permission before you agree to that ..."

Father, instead of answering courteously but firmly that he is happy to submit his ideas on any subject impinging on faith and morals to the judgement of his bishop or the Holy See, since if God has made a revelation he will obviously have arranged for it to be protected from human vagaries, wilts interiorly. Why should he have to take into account the opinions of a local prelate with the cultural sensitivity of a pneumatic drill, or a lot of Italians in Rome who know nothing about science? What a burden it is, having to cart the faith about in these civilised surroundings like a shabby old trunk filled with worn out clothes.

If Catholic scholars are to remain faithful today, they are going to need an extra strong formation in detachment from human respect.

Revelation differs from other kinds of knowledge in yet another way. In other kinds of study, intelligence, imagination and hard work are usually enough. Philosophical errors and defects of character will certainly affect results to some degree. Freud's pride, for instance, blinded him to what was obvious to the humbler Alfred Adler. Nevertheless, natural gifts and qualities by themselves can achieve striking results. However, for the study of theology, the Bible or Church history, other things are necessary.

First, to understand fully, one must believe. Unbelieving historians who study the Church know far more about its life and teachings than most Catholics do, but in a deep sense they miss the point about what they know. The same begins to be true of Catholic scholars when doubts set in. They must be men of prayer, their hearts set on advancing in virtue.

When, instead, a Catholic scholar allows himself to become proud, cynical, sardonic or dried up, something the nature of scholarly work easily inclines men to, his understanding of the Church and the faith is certain to be flawed, no matter how wide-ranging his knowledge. An exceedingly lofty opinion of his scholarly powers seems to have been what carried the 19th-century German historian Döllinger out of the Church and made the English historian Lord Acton a very restive member within it. How many Catholic scholars today really believe that faith is a gift they can lose, or a virtue they can sin against?

No doubt most of these remarks about the temptations and natural difficulties besetting Catholic scholars are fairly obvious. But if they are not kept in mind it will be much less easy to understand why this century has seen not only a movement for reform but also a great rebellion of scholars and theologians. As the period of the Councils of Constance and Basle shows, few things are so dangerous for the Church as a reform, or attempted reform, in which a large part is played by insufficiently spiritual men. In these disasters, the causes are always moral and spiritual before they are intellectual.

Chapter Seven

THE FLOCK
PART I

The last two chapters may have laid me open to the accusation of seeing the motes in my brother's eyes rather than the beam in my own. I will therefore begin this chapter by admitting that, in examining the shortcomings of the laity before the Council, I have often had myself in mind as much as my fellow Catholics as I then knew them.

Taking the laity as a whole, we can, I think, for the purposes of our inquiry, divide them into four groups. I will call them the happy, the frightened, the law-abiding and the discontented.

Again I am dealing with types and tendencies, not individuals, and again I am leaving out the outstandingly good and holy. They always exist in the Church. They are one of the marks by which men can recognise her for what she is. Though their numbers go up and down from period to period and place to place, it is largely by their prayers and selflessness that the rest of us are kept spiritually afloat.

Starting with type one, then, we can say that the happy laity, believing and devout, like the happy clergy, loved their religion and enjoyed it. They saw the Church as a family (which it is), they believed that all the Church's teachings were true (which they are), and they welcomed every authorised practice (as was fitting they should). All this was good.

Less good was the fact that in not a few of them happiness often seems to have bred a kind of cosy contentment. It is possible for people to get a purely natural enjoyment out of religion. When that is so, religion comes to be loved more for the comfort and satisfaction it gives than because it expresses the mind and will of God, which may require something different. The disturbance of spiritual comfort, I think, explains at least some of the opposition to liturgical and other change.

The Church was also seen too much as "ours", something for "us". It was delightful if outsiders asked to come in, and they were usually, though not always, warmly welcomed. But there was not much effort to take the initiative and personally invite them to come in. After all, if people felt attracted to the Church, they could always ring the presbytery doorbell.

This attitude, among priests, produced what could be called the "chaplain mentality". The chaplain exists to satisfy the spiritual needs of a family. When he has fulfilled those duties, he can, with a quiet conscience (supposedly), put his feet up and read a thriller. The chaplain mentality, like cosy contentment, saps the missionary spirit and strangles the evangelist.

When cosy contentment went a stage further, the Church and the faith tended to become confused with something not quite identical – the local Catholic way of life. This embraced a whole lot of things from the feasts and ceremonies of the Church to the way the parish fête had always been run. It was "what we are all accustomed to", and contained, in addition to essentials, elements that are changeable and others (like the Christmas tree) not necessarily Catholic.

In its aggravated form, attachment to the "Catholic way of life" turned into a kind of "Catholic nationalism" which bred belligerent priests and lay-men, who sometimes mistook belligerence for apostolic zeal, and confused attachment to the Catholic way of life with love of the Church. It is not always easy to see the difference. "They", the non-Catholics, from being regarded with benevolent unconcern, were then seen more as a threat. Catholics must keep up a united front in face of "them" – Protestants, Freemasons, Jews, or whoever "they" might be. Anyone who let down the side in front of "them" was a "dirty no-good Catholic".

Where this attitude took root, sins were graded less according to their seriousness than according to the amount of public attention they attracted. A Catholic who got his name in the papers by going off with another man's wife was automatically worse than a businessman who underpaid his staff or made money in dubious ways but gave handsomely to Catholic charities.

Belligerence had another aspect. The faithful know they possess the full-ness of revealed truth. This knowledge sometimes generated an unconscious intellectual arrogance, especially in their manner of presenting their beliefs. The temptation was to present them as though their truth were self-evident, something even a fool ought instantly to see the force of, whose non-acceptance could only be accounted for by bad will.

All this is quite different from valuing the faith above all things and being resolute in defending and preserving it, or rejoicing in the Church's beauties, glories and spiritual triumphs. Belligerent Catholics of this kind tended to forget that they owed their knowledge of the truth first and foremost to grace, not to their intelligence or merits, and that whatever the reasons for non-Catholic disbelief it was not in the ordinary sense stupidity.

It is easy to poke fun at this belligerence, and I do not want to make more of it than is fair. To a great extent it was, as is so often the case, the reaction of the weak in the face of the strong – of the socially, educationally and culturally weak in face of the socially, educationally and culturally strong. It flourished in countries where Catholics were in a minority or the surrounding non-Catholic culture was felt as a threat. Who today with an ounce of common sense left will say it was not?

In the once Catholic countries of Europe, belligerence was a side-effect of the battle going on since the French revolution between Catholics and the various kinds of organised unbelief, as Catholics tried to hold on to or recapture control of the state, and the forces of unbelief tried to outwit them.

The struggle, about which I shall be saying more later, has been a confused one in which differences about politics, economics and social change have been as important as the defence of religion or its overthrow. In the heat of it, Catholics sometimes forgot they could not always use the methods and language of their opponents; that returning abuse for abuse and giving way to vindictiveness or hate were forbidden. The struggle was hottest in France, where vitriolic classical rhetoric and revolutionary oratory are part of the national literary tradition. Unfortunately, Catholic writers elsewhere tended to copy the French polemical style. It does not always mean all that it seems to mean, but Pope Paul seemed to have had it in mind when he wrote: "the right-minded Catholic detests malicious and indiscriminate hostility and empty boastful speech".

The battle is now over, the Catholics having lost.

Happy Catholics, who were to be found in all classes and callings, were not as yet troubled by intellectual questionings. Though often well-informed about the faith, they did not read adventurously. Yet many uncatholic points of view had nevertheless begun to colour their religious outlook.

The much put-about idea that Catholics before the Council had not met the modern world does not bear examination.[1] They were part of it. They earned their livings by it. Most of them thoroughly approved of it – in some ways too much. Pope Pius XI (1922–39) called this over-ready approval of existing things "social modernism", by which he did not mean flirting with socialism. He was referring in particular to the attempts by certain influential French Catholics to prevent one of his social encyclicals from being read from the pulpit. But he also had in mind any wrong conformity or falling-in by Catholics with standards and practices out of keeping with their beliefs.

The point is not that Catholics failed to appreciate the modern world, but that they did not bring a fully informed Catholic judgement to bear on its complex manifestations. They seemed to see only two alternatives; trying to hold the world at bay, or a close embrace. The usual result was an uneasy synthesis of both approaches. Religion was for church and the home. Outside these two oases, they felt they could approve or take part without qualms in more or less anything that went on in society except sexual indecency and flagrant dishonesty. In fact they were simply accepting the classical 19th-century liberal position that religion is a purely private affair; it and the rest of life should exist in separate compartments.

By tacitly consenting to this division (by keeping their religion for Church and upstairs with their rosary beads), one could say that they prevented the modern world from meeting the Church in which it would find Jesus Christ living and reigning in the here and now. If they lived in a "ghetto", or had a "ghetto mentality", it was in this sense that they did so.

With the moneyed and employing classes, "social modernism" usually meant a too ready toleration of low wages and bad working conditions for the majority; in their social and economic attitudes most were unreflecting *laissez-faire* liberals.[2]

Seeing a rising standard of living as God's greatest blessing was to be another form of social modernism. So was the largely unqualified welcome given to television when "the box" entered Catholic homes, presbyteries and convents in the late 1940s.

The part played by affluence and television in the collapse after the Council has yet to be assessed. Should bishops have forestalled their effects with penitential processions? How many of St. Paul's converts would have survived if they had been nightly exposed to the more sophisticated goings-on – cultural, social, theatrical – of Rome, Antioch and Alexandria?

These were the main forms of social modernism before the Council. In the middle and upper classes the result could be an unattractive blend of piety and worldliness or social selfishness, which is what the politically radicalised French clergy are talking about when they castigate "bourgeois Catholicism".[3] However, the French Catholic bourgeoisie being in other respects orthodox (the failure was one of charity rather than faith), the wholesale assault on "bourgeois Catholicism" in France has also involved an assault on essential Catholic beliefs and legitimate religious practices, which were equally part of the Catholic "bourgeois" way of life.

I will end this section with a look at two notions current in the West which the faithful had begun to absorb on the semi-conscious level, their influence being quite out of proportion to their value as ideas. We can summarise them thus: "When people die, they all go to heaven – if there is a heaven", and "Everyone is basically good, provided they are clean and behave decently".

Of the first we can say that, leaving aside the question of whether we all get to heaven eventually (which one would certainly like to think), the idea that heaven is more or less a certainty hardly makes spreading the Gospel seem a matter of urgency.

The second, the idea that everyone is "basically nice" provided they are clean and reasonably well-behaved, inclined Catholics to equate decent behaviour and pleasant manners with supernatural goodness. Decent people, it was felt, cannot be guilty of serious sin. In fact these are natural virtues, good in themselves, which are very much a matter of upbringing. By the power of habit they can survive when a man has turned his back on God.

From here, if they practised their religion and behaved well, it was easy for Catholics to slide into thinking of themselves as "good" too. In this they were often unintentionally encouraged by priests who talked too unreflectingly about good Catholics and poor Catholics – the "good" being those who came often to Church and did what the parish priest wanted, while the "poor" were those who came rarely, even when they came as much as the Church's law required.

Strictly speaking, all Catholics in a state of grace are among those whom Scripture calls "the just". But Catholics, even in a state of grace – the first necessity – are still meant to think of themselves as sinners. When the great apostle of counter-reformation Rome, St. Philip Neri, was told by a tactless simpleton how holy he was, he retorted vehemently "I am a devil". He was not putting on a pious show. He meant that he knew what he was capable of being and doing if for an instant God withdrew his grace. St. Francis of Assisi gave a similar reply to a similar simpleton. So did Cardinal Newman.

Christians, heaven knows, should prize the state of grace above all things. But if they become unaccustomed to thinking of themselves as sinners and accustomed to valuing the feeling that they are nice and good, they will be tempted, if they do fall into serious sin, instead of being sorry for having offended God, to be angry at no longer being able to think well of them-selves.

This attitude of mind has, I think, not a little to do with today's drive by lay people to have the Church alter its moral teaching. It would also explain the anxiety of so many European and American bishops to accommodate them. The Church must allow contraception and divorce, one hears it argued, because "so many of our best Catholics want them." As far as one can see, the only reason why the prelates in question regard these particular Catholics as the best is that they are well-off, well-educated and have the right table man-ners.

This is very much a middle-class phenomenon. When the poor decide to break a law of God, they don't normally expect the Church to alter her teaching so that they can continue to think well of themselves. They are not astonished at finding themselves sinners. In this they have more in common with the rich and the grand who, whatever their other failings, are not usually interested in a reputation for moral rectitude either.

Notes to Chapter Seven

[1] What those who make the charge seem to mean is that Catholics as a whole had not read the non-Christian writers and thinkers who have increasingly been shaping the mind of Western society.

[2] Pius XI called the loss of the European working class the great tragedy for the Church in recent times. There were two other tragedies. One was the departure of so many of the new middle class of industrial managers and business and professional men (converted in large numbers to scepticism and free-thinking during the 19th century) who thus fell outside the Church's influence. The other was the failure to instruct the bulk of those who remained in the Church in their duties as employers. The development of the Church's social teaching, the work of a minority of apostolic bishops, priests and lay people in collaboration with the Holy See, was an attempt to remedy the situation.

[3] François Mauriac's novels *Le Noeud de Vipères*, *Le Désert de l'Amour*, and *La Pharisienne* give a good idea of what they had in mind. It wasn't confined to the bourgeoisie. However it is worth recalling that St. Thérèse of Lisieux, now a Doctor of the Church, was nourished on a piety that would have been classified as bourgeois.

Chapter Eight

THE FLOCK
PART II

Our remaining three types are the frightened or fear-filled, the law-abiding, and the discontented.

The "fear-filled" were of two sorts: those with a wrong kind of fear of God and his Judgements; and those who were afraid that if they looked too closely at their beliefs, they would not stand up to the test.

Those with the wrong kind of fear of God, of whom there were considerable numbers, were suffering from the last traces of Jansenism – Calvinism in a Catholic guise, which entered the Church in the 17th century. Fear of God is the beginning of wisdom. But if we are trying to serve Him, our fear should have the quality of filial awe rather than slavish dread.

As a heresy, Jansenism was driven out in the 18th century; but as a spiritual taint or predisposition it survived well into the 20th. France was its home, and from France, through Ireland, it got a firm hold in the English-speaking world. God's chief remedies were devotion to the Sacred Heart, St. Thérèse of Lisieux's doctrine of spiritual childhood, and the introduction of frequent Holy Communion by St. Pius X. But the remedies had not been applied as widely as they should have been.

With its one-sided emphasis on God's justice and punishments, Jansenist spirituality tended to chill love, cramp generosity of soul, and encourage scrupulosity – a preoccupation with spiritual trifles. It was also responsible for uncatholic ideas about marriage and sex, and so to some extent for the violent rejection of any kind of restraint in this area. Calvinism has produced similar reactions within Protestantism.

The romantic movement, with its love of the sombre, the sinister and the lugubrious, had also influenced Catholic thinking and attitudes in a way that contributed to making the Church appear overly preoccupied with sin, sadness, evil and death. Priests influenced by Jansenism tended to be moral rigorists. Moral rigorism is an inclination to see most sins as serious ones. There is nothing to be said for it – except that moral laxity or indifference is worse. All sin matters; but not all sins are of the same gravity. The temptation for the rigorist, if faith starts to decline, is to weary of his exacting work and swing to the opposite extreme. What a relief from the strain of seeing and fighting sin everywhere to see practically no sin anywhere!

From the world of moral rigorism have come some of today's leading moral revisionists. The late Fr. Bernard Haering, a Redemptorist and *peritus* at Vatican II, is an example. Priests of the Redemptorist order used to be renowned for their strictness (though their founder, St. Alphonsus Liguori, was an apostle of gentleness in the confessional). After the Council, as he travelled the world explaining to Catholics on which points they could qualify their adherence to the Church's teaching about the use of their procreative powers, Fr. Haering's expenses must have been a considerable item in his order's budget.[1]

The reaction against Jansenist spirituality partly accounts for the present rather desperate insistence on God's love (as though it had never been heard of before), on the Resurrection in contrast to the Passion (even by people who doubt the Resurrection's reality), and on the idea that every religious occasion ought to be a "celebration" (even Lent is to be seen as a season of rejoicing). Though other things have played a part, with many Catholics these particular shifts of emphasis represent a confused attempt to recover a proper balance between what ought to be two fundamental Christian attitudes – joy and gratitude for the blessings of this world and the next, and sorrow for what we do along the way. In deeply Catholic countries, I would say, the balance had never been seriously disturbed.

Catholics frightened of looking too closely at their beliefs, belonged mainly to the professional classes. Not intellectually inquiring outside their own special fields, they were busy all day earning their livings, and by the evening were tired and wanted diversion.

What they feared was finding that the Church was asking them to believe "the impossible". They did believe, and they wanted to go on believing. But the only way they felt they could hang on to their beliefs was to keep them in a state of arrested development. Instead of informing themselves about their religion and facing up to any problems, they hid from them. They allowed their knowledge of their religion to remain at school catechism level, a condition deplored by Pius XII in the 1950s. Every Catholic's knowledge of his religion, he said, should be at the same level as the rest of his education. They were in a true sense in need of a mature or adult faith.

There is less to say about the law–abiding. Many were perhaps barely hanging on to the faith. For these, religion tended to be a matter of painfully keeping the moral law by their own efforts; they were all but Pelagians without knowing it. God, an unpredictable taskmaster, had few if any attractions; and heaven, where they expected to feel out of their element, was scarcely looked forward to either, except that it was preferable to hell. Habit helped to keep them in the Church. When habit was disrupted, the links with the Church were easily snapped.

Others in this category had a better understanding and greater appreciation of the faith, even if it contained a strong dash of stoicism. Their religion mattered to them and they practised it faithfully, if without great joy. Wise priests recognised their merits. In the present crisis, they have often held on to their beliefs better than more conspicuously religious types. But because they did not usually take much part in parish activities, they were not always valued as they should have been. Also, having been brought up at a time when every parish priest taught more or less what the Church taught, so that opposing the priest on faith or morals seemed equivalent to disagreeing with the Pope, they have tended to stay in the background in a state of perplexity. The thought of having to oppose a bishop would seem even more horrendous. Better instructed, they might have developed into fervent joyful Catholics equally good at commending and defending the faith – joyful, moreover, with the real spiritual joy of the saints and holy Italian chambermaids, not the rather self-conscious worked-up joyfulness which is often such an embarrassing feature of the present religious scene.

I come fourthly and lastly to the discontented.

Again we can speak of two kinds. Some were discontented because they were finding the laws of marriage too great a strain. The pressure on the clergy to allow birth control did not begin in the 1960s. "Father, you don't know what it's like. If you were married and had six kids . . ." It was not always the penitent who was on the receiving end in the confessional when unpleasant things were said. If in the past the clergy at times complained about having to hear confessions, as some did, this was no doubt one of the reasons.

What was the priest with the outlook of a spiritual technician to do in circumstances like these? It was then principally that he failed his sheep. He had nothing to offer them. How could he persuade them that grace and prayer can be all-conquering, or that the acceptance of suffering is part of the Christian vocation, when these things meant so little to him personally? He could only lay down the law, angrily or half-heartedly. In this encounter in the confessional, priest and penitent unconsciously administered a dose of scepticism to each other about the wisdom and certainty of the Church's teaching. When the revolution breaks out, the spiritual technicians will be the first and loudest in their complaints that the Church had turned the faith into a set of rules, though they themselves will have had a share in making it appear like that.

The discontented of the second kind came from a very different world – that of cultured Catholics interested in literature and the arts. They represented only a section of that world, but it was to become a highly influential and vociferous section. They were exposed to many of the same temptations as the Catholic scholarly world. They were beginning to feel the tension between Catholicism and modern culture in a conscious and direct way.

The difficulty for cultured Catholics of any period is that culture – or the enjoyment of its fruits – can become a rival religion pulling the heart in opposite directions. In a way, any strong interest can do it; gardening or stamp-collecting. But a love of art, literature and ideas poses special problems because they often impinge directly on religious belief. Many educated Christians in the last centuries of the Roman empire, like St. Basil and the Gallo-Roman poet Ausonius, felt this two-way pull between their faith and a great culture whose foundations were not Christian. The foundations of contemporary Western culture are partly Christian, partly not. The same can be said of what has been built on top of them, and I shall not try to determine here which is the greater part. The fact remains that unless today's cultivated Catholic has, like St. Basil, a strong faith, culture is likely to be the stronger attraction, as it was for Ausonius.

When that happens, the cultivated Catholic comes to feel more in sympathy with the ideals and aims of his cultivated non-Catholic friends than with the mass of his fellow Catholics, and starts looking at the Church through the critical eyes of those friends as though he were himself an unbelieving outsider.

Why, he wonders fretfully, does his religion contain so much that he finds embarrassing: reactionary cardinals, conservative bishops, ignorant peasants, negative attitudes, miracles, indulgences, Latin-style devotions, things like holy water obviously connected with magic? Why is the Church not more progressive, less anti-communist, more anti-fascist, less frightened of sex and science, more in favour of modern art . . . ?

It is true that Catholics of this kind recognised the need for a more discriminating approach to certain contemporary ideas and problems, and that was to their credit. Their criticisms of some of the attitudes I have been describing were also just – the narrow-mindedness of Bishop X, the belligerence of Fr. Y, the pettiness of Reverend Mother Z. But neither the defects of individuals or groups were, I believe, the fundamental cause of their discontent. Later events suggest the fundamental cause lay in the nature of the Church and its teachings: the fact that the Church is a monarchy, though of a very special kind, in an age of democracy – God three-in-One, is a monarch (should one say "unfortunately"?); that in an age of science the Church teaches mysteries which cannot be proved by experiment – the mind has to humble itself to accept them; that in the area of faith and morals the Church asks for obedience when all around are insisting on unrestricted liberty. How were these things to be explained away to cultured non-Catholics over the dinner table or at the literary cocktail party?

Discontented cultured Catholics were like a field newly ploughed and raked, waiting for the revolutionary theologians to sow their seed.

When with the election of Pope John, the subject of reform is broached, they will immediately interpret reform as getting rid of these "embarrassments".

★ ★ ★

Such, it seems to me, were the principal shortcomings of the Catholic people in the West on the eve of the Council. Nothing sensational. At every period of the Church's history there has been a fair degree of social conformism, complacency, tepidity, minimal practice, lack of apostolic zeal, and the spirit of routine. How, then, could these things have done so much damage without anyone noticing? The effects seem out of all proportion to the causes.

At least before the Reformation, and again before the French revolution, symptoms of decadence – absentee bishops, clergy with concubines, sale of ecclesiastical offices, the revenues of monasteries and convents diverted into the pockets of laymen – had been visible to all and a catastrophe expected for a long time.

On the other hand, as Pope Paul remarked, before the Second Vatican Council there was little if anything of that sort to complain about. Order and regularity of life prevailed. The irregularities and disorders – sacrilegious masses, priests and nuns cohabiting, clergy wielding sten-guns – have followed the reform. The normal sequence of events has been reversed. This is what many people find so perplexing.[2]

What then is the explanation?

We can perhaps find the beginnings of one in the social climate of post-renaissance Europe. Through the influence of Protestantism and the rise of modern science, increasing importance came to be attached to the spirit of system and orderly public behaviour. As a result, in addition to their real and great achievements, the Counter-Reformation and the 19th-century religious revival had an unexpected side effect. Large numbers of Catholics in the culturally dominant countries of northern Europe and North America were, for the first time in history, made respectable. It took four hundred years and considerable effort. Respectability is a very un-catholic thing. Much of it was the result of not wanting to let the side down in front of the separated brethren and non-believers. But at last the work was done. Most of the grounds for non-Catholic criticism of Catholic nations that had been such a cause of inferiority complexes – tumble-down presbyteries, gravy-stained cassocks, beggars crowding the church porches, general irregularity and apparent inefficiency – had at last, it seemed, (if you forgot about Sicily and such like blots on the landscape) been done away with or swept under the rug and we were proud of it.[3]

In France, Germany, the Low Countries, North America and Australia, if nowhere else, a Catholic could hold up his head with the best of his Protestant and unbelieving neighbours. But our hard-won respectability had disguised from the greater part of the world and ourselves the essential fact; how much less most of us cared about God than we appeared to.

The new theologians, however, were not among those bemused by the grand façade. So it is now time to look at the Council's "new orientations" and developments which were to remedy the defects just described and, it was hoped, close the "gap between faith and life". They affected five areas of belief: the nature and mission of the Church as a whole; its government by Pope and bishops; the role of lay people; the relationship of the Church to other Christians and other religions; and finally the relationship between the Church's mission of salvation and men's earthly activities, or between the history of salvation and the history of civilisation and progress.

Notes to Chapter Eight

[1]   That the way some manuals of moral theology presented their material was open to criticism may have been true. A much used manual before the Council has been blamed, for example, for hardly ever quoting Scripture – though the same charge can be brought against Fr. Karl Rahner. However, revising the method of presentation does not justify trying to revise the content. The tragedy in Fr. Haering's case is that his *The Law of Christ*, written before the Council, is widely considered to have given a valuable "freshening" to moral theology. A decade or so later in his *Morality is for Persons* (Farrar, Straus and Giroux, 1971) he was writing "If . . . we offer youth only a 'holy rule' that remains forever 'as it was in the beginning' having no pertinence here and now, then our appeal will only be to sick people suffering from a security complex." Reviewing the book for the U.S. Catholic monthly *Triumph* in November 1971, Fr. Vincent Miceli S.J. attributed the transformation to an overdose of Heidegger, Teilhard de Chardin, Sartre and Bultmann.

[2] It is curious in a way that dissenting theologians should have taught Catholics to deplore everything supposedly emanating from the Council of Trent and the Counter-Reformation, seeing that it was Trent which, by tightening up ecclesiastical discipline, put an end to most of the irregularities and scandals which are supposed to have provoked and justified the Protestant revolt.

[3] For Newman's riposte to Protestant criticisms of Catholic nations see his *Difficulties of Anglicans*, Vol. I, Part II.

PART III

THE NEW ORIENTATIONS

Chapter Nine

THE CHURCH:

FROM PERFECT SOCIETY TO MYSTICAL BODY

The Church, the followers of Jesus Christ united with each other and their Head by baptism and belief, is not something that has to be discovered, invented, made or remodelled. It simply *is*. But what it is contains a large element of mystery.

To describe that mystery, the Bible, the Fathers and the Church herself through her official teaching and approved theologians, have used many images, some of which in the course of her history have received more attention than others. But all are part of her general understanding of herself. None on its own says all that can be said. The attempt to explain the Church in terms of one image alone results in distortions. Many of the present troubles are the result of this kind of selectivity.

Among the images of the Church mentioned by the Council are: Christ's Body, Bride and Spouse; a sheepfold to which he is the entrance and a flock for which as Chief Shepherd he has laid down his life; a field where wheat and weeds grow together until the harvest; a vine to which branches, twigs and leaves must remain attached if they are to live; a temple made of living stones; God's family or household; God's people, the second Israel or the new chosen race making its way as an exile and pilgrim in this world towards its heavenly homeland; the new or heavenly Jerusalem.[1]

The element of mystery is due to the fact that this unique social body exists outside as well as inside time and space – in heaven and purgatory as well as on earth – and has a mainly supernatural purpose and end. In other words it has invisible as well as visible dimensions.

To the outward eye, the Church on earth looks much like other organised bodies of people with rulers, laws, institutions and customary practices. That is how the world sees her. And as far as it goes, the world is right. God meant the Church to be like that. Indeed, in her own realm, according to an age-old definition, the Church is "a perfect society": that is, she has everything in herself necessary for her life and mission; she has recognizable boundaries; she is not dependent on any other society (she is not, for instance, as so many emperors, kings and statesmen have tried to make her, a department of state).

75

Of course the style of the Church's government, not its essence but the way it is exercised, can be coloured by contemporary secular styles. In this sense the age of absolutism and princely grandeur did leave some marks on the Church's skin in a fashion of which I gave examples earlier. They have been easily erased without touching the substance of the papal and episcopal offices. It was largely a matter of changing a mode of authority and living, and removing a few yards of watered silk on state occasions.

Such is the Church's visible component.

But this naturally organised and governed society is also a community of believers who, rulers as well as ruled, when not separated from God by sin, live by the divine life of habitual or sanctifying grace as well as natural and biological life, and act under the impulsions of the Holy Spirit – not all the time of course, but when and as they let Him. The Holy Spirit is the soul of the Church.

This is the aspect of the Church that only believers can recognise. Whether or not they appear so to outsiders, and however improbable it may often seem to themselves, the faithful really are in the words of St. Paul a "new creation". All have spiritual gifts and charisms of some kind, even if they frequently fail to use or develop them as they should.

However, the visible society (or "institutional Church", as dissenters like to call it) and the Spirit-guided community are not two separate realities artificially joined together like blocks of stone with cement. Nor are they opposed to each other (as in *Concilium* theology) with the Holy Spirit making war on Himself through the two parts. The Holy Spirit acts through the institution (the shepherds, sacraments, laws, and governmental forms) as well as directly on the individual soul, with the latter subordinate to the former. Institution and spiritual community are one and the same reality. The institutional features may be destined to vanish at the Last Day, but until then they are instruments of the Holy Spirit.[2]

Such is the understanding of the Church, that Catholics ought to have, and which for the most part, I think, implicitly always have had. However, for various reasons, one aspect, the visible or invisible, the human or the divine, can be emphasised at the expense of the other. When that occurs one of two things may happen.

Too much emphasis on the organisation leads to a veiling of what is heavenly by what is earthly, and to the faithful identifying the Church mainly with her rulers. To some extent this is inevitable since the Pope and bishops are the Church's visible matrix. It was through the apostles that God summoned the community of believers into existence, and it is through their successors that he continues to hold it in being. The hierarchy preceded the community; it did not emerge from the community later under the pressure of necessity. It is in the hierarchy that Christ's threefold powers of prophet, priest and king are vested in the first place.

Nevertheless, the identification of the Church largely with her rulers does tend to distort the faithful's understanding of the Church and their role in it. A sort of separation comes about in their minds between themselves and the Church (I am talking, of course, about unconscious or semi-conscious ideas and attitudes). The Church tends to appear as something external, like a hotel or department store, to which they resort from time to time to get certain spiritual goods and services, without having any closer connection with the business than that of being habitual customers.

Even if this is a caricature, it contains a likeness. How often even today, after all that has been said about everyone "being Church" does one hear the same people say "Why does the Church do this or that?" as though they themselves were external to it. What they are talking about is not the Church but the magisterium or the episcopate.[3] Even the Council documents do not always avoid making the identification.

Such a state of mind encourages the individualistic approach to religion so deplored by the new theologians and reform party. Religion is getting to heaven by avoiding grave sin, with the clergy providing the means. The faithful are the passive recipients of the clergy's ministrations. Spreading the faith is the clergy's business, while large-scale works of charity are for the religious orders.

Alternatively, the faithful can see their relationship to the clergy in military terms. The clergy are the officers; the faithful, the troops. The officers give the orders, the troops obey, often without having much understanding of the reasons for the orders. Orders are concocted far away at headquarters, and who on earth knows why.

This way of looking at things was less far from the mark than the hotel or department store view, since in an army officers and men are at least conscious of all belonging to one corps with a single collective purpose (defeat of the enemy). And, as we have seen, many of the faithful were contented troops, attached to their officers and happy to be led by them. They had a strong sense of belonging, if not of taking the initiative.

Even so, the military analogy does not give a fully accurate picture of what the clergy-laity relationship should be. Besides weakening lay initiative, it makes religion seem too much a matter of "keeping the rules".

In saying all this I am decrying neither concern for personal salvation –

ultimately nobody can save a man's soul but himself with God's help – nor the importance of keeping the law. No Christian holiness can be built without them. The commandments are like a concrete launching pad without which the rocket of the spiritual life cannot get off the ground. But if personal salvation and keeping the law are seen as the sole substance of religion, the result is an impoverished idea of the Christian vocation, which is essentially incorporation into a supernatural mystery.

It would also be a mistake to think that many of the faithful did not have a strong practical appreciation of the Church's supernatural dimension. They had a firm faith in the reality of miracles and the appearances of Christ and his Mother to holy people – "religious experiences" which, unfortunately, too many of the reformers were anxious to have played down on the grounds that modern man could hardly be expected to believe in them. Christ, his Mother, the saints, and souls in purgatory were as real to them as their own families and friends. They knew, too, that as sources of grace the sacraments really "worked". What they would seem to have needed was a more theologically integrated understanding of the two dimensions.

On the other hand, emphasis on the invisible dimension at the expense of the visible, has usually been the first step on the path to heresy. This was the road Tertullian eventually took, followed by the founders of a number of medieval sects and eventually by Luther.

The Church for Luther was "nothing else than the congregation or assembly of the saints, that is pious believing men on earth, which is gathered, preserved and ruled by the Holy Ghost." The Church has no visible boundaries, only the virtuous belong to her and all her members are equally priests. The appointment of special ministers to lead or rule the congregation is a man made convenience. The clergy have no powers not possessed by other members of the assembly. As for what is to be believed, the Holy Spirit makes it known through the consensus of the faithful. That at least was the theory. In practice, the belief of each "confession" was determined by its founder or its dominant members.

Another idea often found in movements of this kind is that of a coming new "age of the Holy Spirit". The Old Testament period belonged to God the Father; New Testament times and the reign of the Church belonged to God the Son. But the reign of the Church is now over. The future belongs to the Holy Spirit, who is about to inaugurate an age of perfect spiritual liberty in which Church government and institutions will be unnecessary. The most famous exponent of this theory was the 12th-century Calabrian abbot, Joachim of Flora. Ghostly reincarnations of all these ideas began to appear again after the Council, particularly among the more extreme forms of Protestant Pentecostalism's overgrown child, the charismatic movement.

Such can be the consequences of one-sidedly emphasising the Church's invisible dimension.

At no time in her history did the Church fail to speak about both dimensions, but in the post-reformation period, the need to defend herself against Luther's theories led her to place special emphasis on her existence as an organised society with recognizable boundaries whose leadership, laws and institutions have their source in God. Only those who accept her authority and believe as she does belong to her, and they include sinners as well as saints. The 16th/17th-century Jesuit theologian and cardinal St. Robert Bellarmine did not coin the term "perfect society", but he was mainly responsible for its becoming the primary definition of the Church for the next two and a half centuries, with some of the consequences I have described.

To highlight the invisible dimension was therefore one of the reform party's first concerns. In this they were not doing anything new. Restoring a proper balance had been one of the aims of the movement for theological reform, which began in the wake of the revolutionary and Napoleonic wars.

The endeavour started in Germany under the leadership of the Bavarian theologian Michael Sailer, a professor at the recently-founded university of Landshut, and his more famous pupil Johann Adam Möhler (1796–1838) who taught at Tübingen and later Munich, where the University of Landshut had meanwhile been moved.

Möhler's earliest writings about the Church were cast in a Gallican mould. He put the customary stress on the Church as a visible society, but with the Pope ultimately subordinate to the majority vote of the bishops. Then, partly under the influence of German romanticism with its interest in folk culture, partly as a result of his studies in Protestant theology, undertaken with a view to arriving at a deeper understanding of the points of agreement and disagreement, he swung the other way and made the action of the Holy Spirit in the community as a whole the all-important factor. According to him, it is the Holy Spirit who brings the community into existence. The faith and charity that the Holy Spirit imparts to individual believers provides the inner impulse towards unity which is personified locally in the bishop, and throughout the Church as a whole in the Pope. Ordination is a sign that a particular member of the Church has become capable of representing the love of a certain number of believers.

This second stage in the development of Möhler's thinking about the Church found expression in his book *Unity in the Church* (1825). Here the

Church's hierarchy seems at times to owe its origin more to the community's impulse towards unity than to its descent by succession from the apostles.

Eventually, however, by putting the main accent on Christ and the Incarnation, he achieved a balance which did justice to both the Church's dimensions – the action of the Holy Spirit and the visible organisation. The Church, the Body of Christ with the Holy Spirit as its soul is an extension of the Incarnation in space and time. It is a visibly organised body because Christ had a body. He also got the pope and bishops into the right relationship.

This final vision of the Church was expounded in his *Symbolism: or the Exposition of the Doctrinal Differences between Catholics and Protestants* (1832–1838).

About the same time in England, John Henry Newman, Möhler's younger contemporary, began contributing to the growth of a more "biologised" spiritualised theology of the Church with his *Development of Christian Doctrine*.

Writing while still an Anglican, Newman was looking for an answer to the question as to why in the Catholic Church of his day he found practices as well as teachings in a form not explicitly mentioned in the New Testament and earliest Fathers. Roughly, his answer was the Scriptural one. The mustard seed was not destined by the divine planter to remain in a seed-like state. It has a principle of growth. Growth, however, does not mean change or transformation of nature, any more than development of doctrine means change or transformation of belief, or growing-up means turning into a different person.

Between them, Möhler and Newman began the revival of a way of thinking about the Church which led to the study of the Church as Christ's "Mystical Body" – with the works of Kleutgen and Mersch among the outstanding milestones – culminating a hundred years later in Pius XII's encyclical *Mystici Corporis Christi* (1943) and twenty years later in the Second Vatican Council's dogmatic constitution on the Church, *Lumen Gentium*, whose first chapter is entitled *The Mystery of the Church*.

Lumen Gentium, which satisfied the aspirations of the more moderate reformers and new theologians, together with *Dei Verbum*, the dogmatic constitution on divine revelation, is the heart of the Council's teaching about the Church and its message. All the other Council documents can be considered as radiating from these two as spokes from a wheel's hub, or rays from a star and are to be understood in relation to them.

Notes to Chapter Nine

[1] Other scriptural or traditional images represent her as: a ship sailing the seas of history with St. Peter as the chief steersman, a fishing net holding in its mesh a mixed catch only to be sorted out on the last day; the ark of Noah in which alone there is safety from death by drowning in the floodwaters of sin; a mother conceiving and forming in her womb the new Christian man.

[2] "Among (the Spirit's) gifts", says the Council, "the primacy belongs to the grace of the apostles to whose authority the Spirit subjects even those who are endowed with charisms." (*Lumen Gentium*, Art.7). Saints like St. Brigid of Sweden and St. Catherine of Siena, raised up by God to rebuke popes and bishops, are never found challenging their authority, only their failure to live up to its demands.

[3] Technically, the word "magisterium" is used for the episcopate's teaching, not its governing office. But popularly, it tends to be used for both.

Chapter Ten

PETER AND THE TWELVE

In Chapter Three, I mentioned the Council's teaching about "collegiality", which has to do with the relationship between the pope and bishops as rulers, individually and collectively, of the universal Church. In other words, it is about the government of the Church at the highest level, and a short excursion into the past is, I think, the best way to show why this subject was thought to need clarification.[1]

Collegiality is not a new doctrine in the sense of describing something that was not implicitly there before. Everything the Church teaches has always existed either in her public practice or her conscious or sub-conscious mind.

The two things about the papal-episcopal relationship understood from the beginning were, first, that Christ did not mean the government of the Church to be an absolute monarchy of the 17th/18th-century kind with the Pope as a king able to alter things at will and the bishops as Versailles-like courtiers saying "Yes" to his every whim; secondly, going to the other extreme, he was not setting up a federation of petty independent "principalities", like the medieval German empire, with each bishop reluctantly surrendering some of his power to a central authority for the sake of collective security. He intended something quite different.

The Church's constitution could perhaps best be described as a system of vice-royalties under a supreme viceroy, subject to a Monarch who has "gone away on a journey for a time", or a brotherhood of shepherds teaching and ruling together with and under a chief shepherd.[2] Were this not so, it would be impossible to explain why, the moment Constantine left the Church free to act more or less as she wished, we find, on the one hand, bishops gathering from time to time in general and local councils; on the other hand, recognition of the special position of St. Peter's successor, his right to settle disputes about doctrine and give judgements in matters of discipline. The fact that the recognition was often reluctant and sometimes resisted, only proves that the right was part of the Church's faith from the start. The popes could never have established such a right against the belief of the whole Church if that right had not been embedded in tradition, as well as explicitly stated by St. Matthew. There were no biblical critics in the 3rd, 4th, and 5th centuries to tell people that the words "Thou art Peter and on this rock, etc." did not mean what they seemed to mean, or were a later interpolation.

What was not precisely understood or laid down from the beginning was how far the popes' rights as supreme teachers and rulers of the universal Church extended in all their details, and how they harmonised with the rights of bishops as representatives of Christ in their individual dioceses, or groups of bishops collaborating in particular regions. This was one of those things God willed should come to light over the course of time, as the Church passed from the state of being like a mustard seed to becoming "the biggest of the garden herbs". But it was not destined to be an untroubled growth. God designed the Church to live in a world which not only bears all over it the marks of his goodness and power, but which he allows to be continually disturbed, especially in its human part, by the activities of our chief Enemy, who was to leave his mark on the development of the Church's understanding of the relationship between Pope and bishops as on so much else.

In confusing the issues, the Enemy's most useful instruments were, as always, human frailty. From time to time the cowardice, worldliness, and even in a few cases downright wickedness of certain popes provoked rebellion against their authority, while things like jealousy, ambition and national pride were the pitfalls for less holy members of the episcopate. In any quarrel involving the papacy, the temptation for unspiritual bishops is to take the side of the local government, ever anxious to limit papal authority and set up national churches. Secular rulers, one could say, are almost "by nature" averse to having any outside authority influence the people under their control.

These were the principal factors leading to the schism between western and eastern Christianity in 1054, which became all but total after the fall of Constantinople to the Turks in 1453.

As the Roman empire turned into what we now call the Byzantine empire, the emperors, with the support of bishops for various reasons hostile to Rome, gradually assumed the role, in practice if not theory, of head of both Church and state. Thus was born what historians call caesaro-papism. Caesar was head of both Church and state.

Caesaro-papism did not triumph without a long struggle. In the east itself there was for centuries a strong pro-papal party lead by great saints like Maximus the Confessor and Theodore of Studium. But in the end as east and west drifted culturally and politically further and further apart, the imperial government, abetted by subservient, ambitious or nationalistic clerics eventually alienated the minds of its subjects from the papacy more or less completely.

In the west, understanding of the papal office at first developed more harmoniously. The holy bishops and missionaries who brought the faith to the barbarian invaders had set them on the right track with regard to Peter's authority. Quarrels between Church and state were mainly about practical things. It was not until the early medieval principalities began to coalesce into modern nation states that challenges to papal authority began on the theoretical level.

The first of these challenges in order of time took the form called *conciliarism*.

Conciliarism is the theory that the bishops gathered in general council are the highest authority in the Church. The Pope is bound to obey the council's majority vote.

From the time of the earliest Councils (the fourth and fifth centuries) there had been attempts to hold general councils without papal consent, or to legislate through them in opposition to the reigning pope. But the theory first took explicit shape in the West at the time of the Great Schism (1378–1417) and the Councils of Constance (1414–18) and Basle (1431). The Council of Constance, at which priests outnumbered bishops in the early sessions, tried to bind Pope Martin V to regular general councils; while at Basle ten years later there were attempts to impose similar restrictions on Pope Eugenius IV.

In spite of repeated condemnations, conciliarism was to trouble the Church's life and provide the basis for incipient schisms down to the end of the 18th century.

Gallicanism, conciliarism's sister movement, was simply a western form of caesaro-papism. As a theory it began to take shape under the French King Philip the Fair (1268–1314) who tried to subordinate the papacy to the French monarchy, but it got its name from the four Gallican articles of belief, a special creed for the French, which Louis XIV tried to impose on his subjects in the 17th century. It was no longer possible for the French government to make the Pope a French puppet, as it had in the 14th century. The rival monarchies of Austria and Spain would not have allowed it. Louis' solution was to exclude the pope as much as possible from the life of the local Church, without actually breaking with him as Henry VIII had done.

According to the Gallican articles, the pope is not only subject to a general council, he may not touch the usages of the local church, nor may he criticise or censure anything rulers do in temporal affairs. About faith and morals, his judgements are not final until accepted by the whole Church. In Gallican practice no bull or other papal document could be published without the permission (*exequatur* or *placet*) of the local ruler.

Eventually Louis XIV withdrew the Gallican articles, but they continued to be taught in French seminaries, and in the 18th century, Gallican principles spread throughout Catholic Europe. Outside France its chief proponents were the Emperor Joseph II, his brother Leopold, Grand Duke of Tuscany, and the German ecclesiastical apologist for the theory, Nicholas von Hontheim, auxiliary bishop of Trier, who used the pen-name Febronius. According to Febronius, bishops being equals, the pope had no authority outside his own diocese; the original constitution of the Church was "collegial" not "monarchical".

In spite of this, although there is a widespread notion that papal power was steadily increasing from the early middle ages up to the Second Vatican Council, in fact papal power had been ebbing since the late 16th century, and by 1780 had reached one of its lowest points. It then looked as if a general revolt against the papacy by Europe's Catholic monarchies was about to explode, followed by the establishment of all but independent national churches, when suddenly the whole crowd of Gallicans and Febronians – emperors, kings, statesmen, bishops, priests and theologians – were put to flight, executed or vanished from sight in the turmoils of the French revolution. The Revolution was certainly what would be called today "a negative experience" for the Church, but it did at least do it that much service.

Although the Gallican mentality outlasted the revolution, and in the surviving Catholic monarchies like Austria persisted down to World War I (it will no doubt never completely die), it no longer had the same vigour. Political revolutionaries now seemed to Europe's Catholic rulers more dangerous competitors for the allegiance of their subjects than ever the popes had been. Moreover, after 1850 the popes could count increasingly on the support of the ordinary faithful, with whom the railways and newspapers were bringing them into ever closer touch. Conciliarism and Gallicanism had never been popular movements. Their appeal had always been to members of the ruling classes, higher clergy, haute bourgeoisie and intelligentsia. Why should fine upstanding Frenchmen and Germans (or today, Dutchmen, Englishmen or Americans) have to defer to miserable foreigners, especially Italians?

This then was the background to the First Vatican Council's definitions of papal primacy (the popes' authority as supreme rulers of the universal Church) and infallibility (their protection from error when teaching on faith and morals). The First Vatican Council was not something that happened out of the blue; an unprovoked assertion of papal prerogative. It was the culmination of a long struggle between conflicting views about how Christ intended his Church to be governed at the highest level. Even if at times the failings of particular popes had seemed to give substance to the conciliarist or Gallican case, the vast majority of Catholics had always known "instinctively", when not explicitly, that the pope is not subject to the body of bishops (the Church is not Episcopalian), and that his authority as teacher and ruler is not exercised in a particular region only with the consent of the local episcopate or ruler; it permeates the whole Church. It was this that the First Vatican Council at last put beyond doubt.

The interruption and dispersal of the Council by the outbreak of the Franco-Prussian war (1870) before it had time to deal with the authority of bishops, may have resulted in many of the faithful coming to think that a bishop is merely a kind of papal delegate or representative, like a nuncio. Nevertheless, it is difficult not to see the hundred years' lapse between the First and Second Vatican Councils as providential. Given the long tradition of conciliarism and Gallicanism in Europe, time was needed for the teaching of Vatican I about papal primacy and infallibility to sink in.

However, the rest of the work of Vatican I had still to be done. What then are the range and limits of the authority of an individual bishop, or that of all the bishops together, in relation to the Pope's own authority?

There was no uncertainty about the bishop's authority over his diocese. Once lawfully elected or appointed, and recognised by the reigning pope, a bishop rules his diocese by divine right. Except for matters specially reserved to the Holy See, the bishop does not have to ask the Pope's permission for what he says and does. In each diocese the two authorities, papal and episcopal, interpenetrate. The Pope's higher authority is designed to support, not extinguish, the bishop's exercise of his powers.

The question busying theological minds in the pre-conciliar period was whether and how the bishops in some way share individually and collectively in the government of the whole Church. They unquestionably do in a general council. But what about the rest of the time? And what is the theological foundation for such sharing?

It was to answer these two questions that theologians began examining the idea that all the bishops together, with and under the Pope, form a "college or permanent body" just as the apostles with and under St. Peter formed a college or permanent body.

The difficulty the Council had in shaping its teaching – the full implications and mode of application are still subject of fierce debate – was due to two causes. The first was having committed itself to not issuing formal definitions. The second was the tendency of people today to think about nearly everything in political terms including, it seems, not a few of those taking part in the Council.

The essential point to grasp is that the "college" does not mean the bishops apart from the Pope. The college is not like the U.S. congress *vis-à-vis* the president, or the English parliament in the past *vis-à-vis* the monarch. Without the Pope, its chief member and head, there is no college. Papal primacy and episcopal collegiality are complementary not antithetical notions.

How precisely, then, do bishops share in the government of the universal Church?

The first way of course is by ruling their own dioceses well. After that, "collegial" government is a matter of bishops having an out-turned co-operative attitude rather than of their possessing hitherto unknown rights and powers. The words the Council repeatedly uses are concern and "solicitude". A bishop's interest in the Church is not meant to stop at the boundaries of his diocese. Bishops, it says, should show a concern and solicitude for the good of the whole Church. On the Pope's side, collegiality implies widespread consultation, even if it is not obligatory. It is up to the Pope to decide when to exercise his supreme authority personally or with the help of the rest of the college.

There has always been more co-operation and consultation in both directions than is generally realised. History gives us many examples (St. Hilary of Poitiers, St. Eusebius of Vercelli, St. Boniface; or nearer our own times Cardinal Lavigerie) of bishops acting outside their own diocese to help fellow bishops or the Church as a whole. Just as frequent have been the cases of popes turning to individual bishops for advice or consulting the entire episcopate. Popes regularly consult the college of cardinals.

To make all this clearer, in the years since the Council, the Church has drawn a distinction between strictly collegial acts and expressions of the collegial spirit.[3]

Strictly collegial acts have to be done by the college as a whole. The general council is the most obvious instance. But here too we must realise that, like the college, there can be no lawful general council apart from the pope. To be a true general council, it must be summoned or subsequently recognised by a pope. Nor are general councils intended for the day-to-day government of the Church. They are called to deal with emergencies or particular problems, and only those of its acts ratified by the Holy See have force.

The only other strictly collegial act that Vatican II seems to foresee is a pope asking the whole episcopate to assent to some undertaking or proposition without leaving their dioceses.

On the other hand, when a bishop sends priests, money or other aid to areas where they are in short supply, he is showing a collegial spirit. So are the bishops of a particular country or region when they act in concert. Their actions are not actions of the college. The college is indivisible. A part cannot act for the whole.

This applies to episcopal conferences. Encouraged by Pius XII and made mandatory by the Council, episcopal conferences are an important expression of the collegial spirit, but are not part of the Church's fundamental constitution. The fundamental authorities remain the individual bishop and the Pope, or the Pope and all the bishops together.

In keeping with the spirit of collegiality, Pope Paul gave bishops and national hierarchies powers of decision in an increasing number of cases hitherto reserved to the Holy See. Although these transfers of power are not irrevocable, they necessarily enhance the authority of the local bishop or episcopate in fact as well as in the eyes of his flock.

The internationalisation of the Roman curia was another of Pope Paul's measures to promote the spirit of collegiality. The purpose was to involve bishops and priests from as many different parts of the world as possible in papal government. By 1985 the number of Italians had been reduced from 88% to 44%, and in the lower ranks from 56% to 23%. The Italian component would be lower still, no doubt, if conditions of work were more attractive. Reasonable accommodation in Rome is hard to come by and expensive when found, curial salaries are low, and not everyone likes spaghetti.

However the most significant expression of the collegial spirit is unquestionably the Episcopal Synod, which Pope Paul set up during the last session of the Council (Sept. 1965), and it was officially established by his *motu proprio* "Apostolica Sollicitudo" a few days later.

The Synod provides for the regular meeting in Rome every three or four years of a selection of bishops representing the entire Catholic episcopate for (in the words of Pope Paul) "consultation and collaboration when this seems opportune to us for the general good of the Church". After extensive consultation the Pope chooses the subject for discussion, and about a year later sums up the particular meeting's work in a document (apostolic exhortation) to the whole Church. A permanent general secretariat, supervised by an elected council of bishops, organises the meetings and ties up the loose ends. The Synod is a strictly advisory body, though John Paul II has hinted that he might give a particular meeting deliberative powers like a general council if circumstances seemed to call for it.

Where Vatican II teaching about collegiality is seen as complementary to Vatican I teaching about papal primacy and infallibility, the results will surely be good. Among other things it should make reunion between Catholics and Orthodox easier.

Unfortunately, the doctrines of the two councils were widely interpreted as being in some way contradictory – collegiality can only be achieved by reducing papal authority – and used in the interests of a revived conciliarism and Gallicanism.

At the end of the Council, many had hoped that the Synods could be turned into general councils dictating to the Pope every three or four years. This was particularly apparent at the first "trial-run" Synod in 1967. Before it began, the idea had been put about that the Pope would use the occasion to divest himself of some of his powers. Hopes for this ran high at the Third World Congress of the Laity meeting in Rome at the same time. I have not been able to discover who it was thought it would be a good idea to have this clamorous assembly – imbued with the conviction that authority and infallibility reside in the last resort in "the community" – coincide with the first Synod. But the intention seems to have been to stage a replay of the French Estates General in 1789. The Laity Congress's preposterous demands and attacks on authority were in the best tradition of French histrionics.[4]

In a more restrained way, a similarly anti-Roman mentality prevailed in the Synod hall. The agenda prepared by the Holy See was rejected and the Synod appointed a commission of theologians and bishops "to express the mind of the Synod on theological questions". There were also requests for a permanent theological commission in Rome. In the thinking of some at least, it was to be a rival to the Congregation for the Doctrine of the Faith, which, responsible to the Synod rather than the Pope, could be a base from which to fight "Roman theology" on its home territory. But Pope Paul stood firm. When he set up the International Theological Commission a year later, it was firmly under his authority and remains an advisory body. During the last eleven years of his pontificate he also outwitted the attempts to turn the Synod into a permanent general council, giving it the form it has today. This, in the circumstances, was no mean achievement for which Paul VI deserves more credit as a ruler than he usually gets. The extent of his success can be measured by the annoyance of his opponents. In an interview in 1992, Cardinal Koenig, the retired Archbishop of Vienna, was complaining that "episcopal collegiality is simply not working. The Synod of Bishops is just a makeshift." (*The Tablet*, 17th Oct. 1992)

Meanwhile, as the 1980s progressed and hopes of getting control of the Church at the centre faded, the forces of dissent concentrated on measures to increase the authority and independence of the "local" churches. The term "local" or "particular" church did not here mean the local diocese. It meant the national or regional collectivity of dioceses under the leadership of the local national episcopal conference, only too many of which have proved to be more under the control of bureaucrats than bishops.

Already at the Council, Cardinal Ottaviani had pointed out that, while bishops are successors of the apostles, episcopal conferences have no such precedent, and *Lumen Gentium* (Art. 25) and the 1983 *Code of Canon Law* (can. 455) have drawn out the implications.[5] Conferences have authority when they reiterate universal Church teaching; in all other cases "the competence of each diocesan bishop remains intact." In spite of this, attempts to separate individual bishops from Rome by subordinating them to the dictates of the conference continued, and with the 1980s a move began to enhance the conferences' teaching authority. At the end of the 1985 Synod, the head of the U.S. Episcopal Conference asked the Pope to set up a commission of inquiry into their theological status. This in itself was quite legitimate and the motives of the bishop in question may have been perfectly good. But, with at least some, the idea seems to have been that episcopal conferences should have locally the same kind of binding doctrinal authority as general councils have for the whole Church. John Paul II set up the commission as asked and eventually, 13 years later, on the basis of its investigations, issued his motu proprio *Apostolos Suos*, of which Art. 18. says, "Episcopal conferences with their commissions and offices exist to be a help to the bishops but not to substitute for them."

However, a single papal document cannot check a widespread movement, and neo-Gallicanism is likely to remain a problem for the Church during the 21st century as it was during the 17th and 18th centuries.[6]

Notes to Chapter Ten

[1]   The doctrine is expounded in the two documents *Lumen Gentium* on the Church, and *Christus Dominus*, the decree on bishops.

[2]   The Western democratic tradition's suspicion of monarchy is a mixture of two constituents, one good ands one bad; distrust of a disordered form of monarchy, and aversion to any kind of sovereignty not having its origin in oneself – each man must be his own absolute monarch.

[3]   In making the idea its own, the Council did not use the noun "collegiality", though it has become the accepted term for both forms of episcopal participation.

[4]   "It was appalling", a curial monsignor who had been present once said to me. Without actually blanching, he sounded a bit like someone who had witnessed the Paris mob invading the Tuileries.

[5]   Fr. Congar had also foreseen problems. Such conferences, he maintained, at the time of the Council, "must not obliterate the personal responsibility of bishops by imposing

on them the dictates of an organisation, nor must they even remotely threaten Catholic unity." Wiltgen, *The Rhine Flows Into the Tiber*, p. 90.

[6]   I first became aware of this revived Gallicanism at a U.S. bishops' press conference during one of the Synods in the 1980s. A journalist asked the then head of the U.S. conference what the U.S. bishops would do if the Holy See insisted on their making a really serious effort to preach *Humanae Vitae*. The answer was roughly: "I don't think the Holy See would want to take on a really big episcopal conference these days".

Chapter Eleven

THE LAITY: WAKING THE SLEEPY GIANT

The hundred years between 1860 and 1960 in the Catholic Church was a century of burgeoning lay movements or associations, all in different ways putting themselves at the service of the Church and their fellow men. But they only touched a fraction of the Church's total population. How were the rest of the faithful to be persuaded that the Church is more than a social service agency for getting us safely to heaven?

The Council's principal remedy for lay passivity and individualism was its teaching about the call of all members of the Church to holiness ("Be you perfect as your heavenly Father is perfect" was not said just for priests, monks and nuns), and the fact that the laity as well as the clergy share in Christ's threefold office of prophet, priest and king (if not in all respects in the same way).

Being a prophet means, in the first instance, being a teacher of divine truth. Although in the Catholic scheme of things, bishops are the primary guardians and teachers of that truth, the laity's right and duty to bear witness to it (whether by word or example) springs from their baptism. They should ensure that what they are preaching or bearing witness to really is the faith of the Church, but they do not need any further authorisation. If asked "Why do Catholics worship statues?" they do not have to run to their priest or bishop for permission to say they don't. Baptism makes the layman an apostle from the outset.

It also makes him, if not a priest in the strict sense, a member of a "priestly" people. When St. Peter told the first Christians they were a chosen race, a consecrated nation, a royal priesthood, he was not speaking only of the clergy. The laity, it is true, cannot say Mass, forgive sins, confirm, anoint, or make priests or bishops. The Church insists on the distinction between the "common priesthood" of all the faithful and that of the ordained priesthood; it is a distinction of kind not just of degree. Nevertheless, the laity's vocation is priestly in that they have been called by God to offer him worship, intercession and reparation for sin with and under their priests in union with the God-Man Jesus Christ. God wants the offering of a whole people not just of a priesthood in the strict sense. To the perfect offering brought about whenever an ordained priest says Mass, the rest of the "priestly people" are to unite all their "thoughts, words, joys, actions, and sufferings" at least once a week by their physical presence, and at other times in intention.

The Mass, the sacrifice of Christ perpetuated through time and space in union with his "Body" the Christian people, is the heart of the Christian mystery. It is what activates the mystery. The Mass sets in motion and makes possible the dying to sin and rising to new life which is the essence of Christianity.

This work of worship, sacrifice, intercession and reparation is not just for the benefit of Christians. It is for the whole of mankind. By offering praise to the Blessed Trinity, praying for the world's needs, and, through their acts of penance, "making up for what is wanting in the sufferings of Christ" (Col 1:24), the faithful are the body that exists to draw down the graces necessary for all men, if they so will, to reach the next world safely, and at the same time to keep this one from going rotten. How the members of the Mystical Body act, whether they are more or less faithful to their calling, to a great extent accounts for the state of the world at any given time, as well as the place in the next life of many of their fellow men.

In relation to the world, the Church or Christian people fulfils somewhat the same role as the tribe of Levi did for the other eleven tribes in Old Testament times, while the relationship of clergy to laity within the Church is not unlike that within the tribe of Levi between the priests proper who alone could offer the temple sacrifices and the rest of the tribe dedicated to lesser forms of temple service.

Were it possible for a pagan ruler to understand these truths without himself becoming a Christian – that is recognise that the fidelity or infidelity of his Christian subjects could affect the well-being of his country as a whole – one could imagine him forcing Christians to live up to their vocation under pain of death.

If all this were better understood there would perhaps be fewer Christians asking themselves "What on earth is the Church for?" – the title for a series of Lenten meditations prepared by an English ecumenical committee a few years ago.

The laity share in Christ's kingly power in the first place, according to the Council, firstly by overcoming the reign of sin in themselves, secondly by serving Christ in their brethren (to serve Christ who reigned by serving is to reign too), thirdly by "engaging in temporal affairs and directing them according to God's will" (*Lumen Gentium* 31, 36).

But with regard to this last way of "reigning", the Council warns, the faithful "must distinguish carefully between the rights and duties they have as members of the Church, and those which fall to them as members of human society."

Although "all power in heaven and earth" was given to Christ in reward for his "obedience unto death", nevertheless, in the time between his first and second comings, Christ wills to rule publicly and directly only over his spiritual kingdom, the Church, through the successors of his apostles. "My kingdom is not of this world". The management of this world is given over to men whether they are citizens of his spiritual kingdom or not. Only after his second coming will he rule over all things directly. This is the basis for the distinction between Church and state, which should be recognised even in Christian commonwealths.

The Catholic laity, therefore, as ordinary members of civil society, men like other men, have a direct kingly power over created things, a power deriving from God's command to the first man to "fill and subdue the earth". They govern them by natural right. As members of Our Lord's spiritual kingdom, their power is indirect. They do not derive their power to rule over created things from their baptism. On the other hand, their baptism obliges them to try and order the affairs of this world, so far as circumstances allow, in a Christian direction. In the words of the new code of canon law, they should try to "permeate and perfect the temporal order with the spirit of the Gospel". The laity are the medium through which Our Lord's direct authority in the Church is indirectly brought to bear on or influence the social and cultural life of mankind at large.

In carrying out their earthly duties well, the laity are at the same time fulfilling their prophetic or teaching role. They are teaching by example.

Within the Church, parents exercise a direct kingly authority over their children; so presumably do elected rulers of lay associations. Elsewhere in the Church, authority exercised by lay people would be a delegated authority.

Was all this teaching about the laity new? In the broad sense, No. Nothing fundamental in the Church is ever at any time totally absent from her practice or unknown to her mind, even if not all the knowledge is fully conscious.

Although the Church's constitution is ultimately monarchical, in other respects her life and practice have always been profoundly "populist" (the word "democratic" would be misleading). In every age the priesthood, and so her leadership, has been open to men of every class; everyone starts life as a layman. The law is the same for all – lying and adultery are not less punishable in a bishop than a street sweeper, or if there is any inequality it is in the street sweeper's favour; and most important of all, the highest rank, sanctity, is within everyone's reach.

Few things in the history of the Church are so remarkable as the way popes, cardinals and bishops have been ready to take advice in vital matters from holy lay people of every social class – servant girls, queens, noble women, mothers of families, farm hands, businessmen, artisans. The careers of St. Catherine of Siena and Bl. Anna Maria Taigi, wife of a 19th-century Roman footman consulted by the highest church dignitaries, are unparalleled in the history of civil society. The Church is in a real sense the one classless society and the calendar of saints is there to prove it.

Throughout her history, too, relatively few new undertakings have started from above. The feast of Corpus Christi owes its origin to an orphaned girl from the Low Countries, Bl. Juliana of Montcornillon; the nine first Fridays and Holy Hour devotions to an obscure Burgundian nun, St. Margaret Mary Alacoque; the worldwide Society for the Propagation of the Faith to a middle-class French spinster, Pauline Jaricot. There were laymen among the earliest apologists, for example St. Justin, Lactantius, Minucius Felix. Much of the mind of medieval Christendom was formed by poets like Dante and Langland, and the same can be said of the unknown authors of the medieval mystery plays. The tradition has continued into modern times with writers like Chateaubriand, Görres, Péguy, Gertrud von le Fort, Manzoni, Chesterton, Belloc, Claudel and Tolkien. Their influence on the general Catholic mind has been as powerful in its own way and time as that of theologians. So too has the influence of the Church's great painters, architects and musicians, the majority likewise laymen.

The rise of the "third orders" in the 13th century, of movements like Gerard Groote's Brethren of the Common Life in the 14th and the Company of the Blessed Sacrament in the 17th centuries shows that the call of all members of the Church to holiness, laity as much as clergy, was never lost sight of either.

During the first four or five centuries there can have been few Christians who did not know that their vocation was a calling to be apostles. What brought about the first great change in the laity's outlook was the fact that, by the 7th century, both in the Byzantine east and the barbarian west, members of Church and State had become one and the same. The upshot was not so much clerical dominance as is often stated, but a more clear-cut division of competences. The clergy looked after things spiritual; the laity, sanctified and instructed in their duties by the clergy, took care of things temporal, ordering them according to what they understood as the mind of God. That at least was the theory, however much practice fell short. Even so there was a great deal of interpenetration, not to mention illegitimate crossing of boundaries, as much from the lay as the clerical side. From the moment the Roman empire became Christian, much of the Church's history has been the history of her struggle to free herself from lay control. Her battles with Roman emperors and medieval magnates are well known.[1]

But lay interference or intervention was not confined to kings and nobles. Lay turbulence was among the reasons the Church abandoned popular episcopal elections. At one medieval conclave, when the cardinals had not reached a decision after a year, the local laity took the roof off the building where they were meeting in order to concentrate their minds by letting in the weather. Even in the more decorous 18th century, we hear of the people of Prato burning the books and episcopal throne of their Jansenist bishop when he removed a valued relic from their cathedral and forbade them to light more than 14 candles before a statue at any one time.

I cite these cases simply to correct the picture of a supposedly totally passive laity during the long centuries when Europe was publicly and officially Christian. What chiefly atrophied during these centuries, as I said before, was the laity's missionary spirit, because everyone was in theory a Christian.

However, by the mid-19th century, two things had begun to happen. Where the Church lacked or had lost the support of the state, the surviving faithful tended to look to their clergy as civil as well as religious leaders. Excessive lay dependence on the clergy was a mainly 19th- and early 20th-century phenomenon.

At the same time, some of the laity began awakening to their missionary vocation. There were now "heathens" enough to convert without going outside one's town or village. But they were heathens with a difference. Unlike the unbaptised heathens of foreign lands, they started with a deep prejudice against the Church and Catholic clergy. Far-sighted bishops and priests realised that if these millions of new unbelievers were to be recovered, more of the laity would have to be turned into active apostles. In both cases, laity and clergy, we are talking about minorities, even small minorities. But all really worthwhile things have small beginnings.

They also began to realise that as Europe became increasingly de-Christianised, ordering society according to the mind of God from above through the state was going to be more and more difficult. If it was to be done at all, it would have to be a work of penetration from below and within. All that has come to be called Catholic action − lay movements like the Legion of Mary for spreading the faith, defending the Church, or improving social conditions − whether directly under the control of the hierarchy or not, flowed from this new awareness and situation.

But how was all this lay activity to be justified theologically? The reigning schools of theology did not envisage lay participation of this kind or on this scale in the Church's mission.

Once again Newman was a pioneer. Newman was one of the first to focus attention again on the laity's share in Christ's threefold office, his chief concern being with their share in his "prophetic" office. His essay *On Consulting the Faithful in Matters of Doctrine* is the clearest expression of his mind on the subject.

By "consult", Newman was careful to explain, he did not mean taking the kind of expert opinion which settles a question. Nor was he suggesting that the Church's beliefs or practice should be settled by majority vote. By "consult", he said, he meant "making inquiry" into the belief and feelings of the Christian people, and that for two reasons. The first was to make it easier for them to accept the decisions of the magisterium. The second was because the faithful as a whole are one of the sources (or theological *loci*) by which the Church's beliefs may be known. As prophets they are meant to think about the beliefs they have to bear witness to, and in thinking about them, when they really are faithful, they have what is called a *sensus fidei* (or the Council described as "a supernatural appreciation of the faith") to guide them. However, the laity's beliefs are only one of several theological *loci*, and not the primary one. Moreover, to be of any value, their "insights" have to be in accord with what has been believed always and everywhere.[2]

How little reliance Newman placed on current opinion in this or that section of the Church at this or that time can be seen when he writes: "Throw up a straw in the air and you will see which way the wind blows; submit your heretical or Catholic principle to the action of the multitude, and you will be able to pronounce at once whether it be imbued with Catholic truth or heretical falsehood". For Newman, consulting the faithful was a matter of what is fitting rather than what is obligatory, and presupposes in the first place the power of discernment in bishops.

Fr. Rosmini, another pioneer, wanted the laity to have a better understanding of their priestly role. In his *Five Wounds of the Church* he sees the first wound as "the excessive separation of clergy and faithful in worship". The people should be actors in the liturgy as well as hearers. He also wanted lay people to be more aware of their dignity as members of the Church. This too would help to bring clergy and laity closer together. After all, "to be a Christian is the first step in the priesthood". Because enough was not made of the laity's baptismal dignity, too many of both clergy and laity saw becoming a priest as joining a privileged caste.

After Newman and Rosmini, there was much writing about lay activity, but more about the forms it should take than its theological significance. The 1917 code of canon law contained few references to the laity's role. Fr. Congar's *Jalons pour une théologie du laïcat*, (1953: English translation, *Lay People in the Church*, 1957) was the first attempt at a full-scale theology of the laity.

In Fr. Congar's opinion, there could be no proper thinking about the laity without a full-scale rethinking about the Church (ecclesiology). A proper theology of the laity could not just be tacked on to the reigning ecclesiology. So the development started by Möhler and Newman must be carried a stage further. The definition of the Church as the Mystical Body of Christ was satisfactory up to a point. At least it did justice to the Church's invisible dimension. But according to Congar, there was too much insistence on hierarchical order or levels of authority and responsibility, even if only by implication. For the Church to attract modern men, the accent must be shifted from the notion of hierarchy to the notion of community. Ecclesiology must begin with what is common to all members of the Church. All this led Fr. Congar and his fellow Dominicans and comrades in arms, as he calls them, Frs. Chenu and Feret, to choose "people of God" as the best primary definition of the Church.

It was not a new term. The liturgy is full of references to God's holy people and visitors to the basilica of St. Mary Major in Rome can read the words in the 5th-century mosaics over the high altar. The inscription runs "Sixtus, Bishop of the People of God" (*Xstus. Epis. Pop. Dei*). But neither in theology nor ordinary speech had the term ever been widely used. It only started to attract attention after World War I, when theologians became interested in the idea of the Church as first and foremost a community of believers. The hatreds of the war period had, by way of reaction, generated a climate favourable to ideas of universal brotherhood, democratic egalitarianism and popular social action.[3]

In the preface to his *The People of God* (1937), Dom Anscar Vonier, abbot of Buckfast Abbey, England, described it as "a modest attempt to add my voice to many others, immensely more powerful, to rally Catholics to a fervent realisation of their corporate existence".

The more powerful voices would eventually include those of the German Dominican Fr. Kosters, whose work on the Church as the people of God, *Ekklesiologie in Werden* appeared in 1940; of the Redemptorist Fr. Eger and the Benedictine Fr. Schaut, whose studies on the same theme appeared in 1947 and 1949; of Fr. Cerfaux, whose *La théologie de l'église suivant St. Paul* emphasised the influence of the notion on early Christian thinking. A decade earlier, a Fr. Robert Grosche had drawn the attention of theologians to the notion of the Church as a pilgrim people en route to a promised land, an idea long popular with Lutheran theologians.

But on this as well as other matters, Fr. Congar's voice was eventually to be the most powerful. *Lumen Gentium*, the Council's document on the Church, after dealing in its first chapter with "The Church as a Mystery", devotes the second chapter, under the title "The People of God", specifically to what all the members as a community have in common. Only in chapter three are the rights and duties of the hierarchy explained.

Giving greater attention to a neglected or under-emphasised part of the Church's teaching does not or should not, as explained earlier, mean denying the importance of its complementary opposite. With this proviso, one can say that in its teaching about the laity the Council shifted the emphasis from the laity's duty of obedience to the teachings and authority of the hierarchy to their obligation to participate in its mission.[4]

Notes to Chapter Eleven

[1]   Around the time of the Council, the forces of dissent launched the term "the Constantinian Church". The idea behind it was that with Constantine the Church entered into a permanent alliance with the State – any and every state apparently – in order to keep the laity in a condition of childlike subjection politically and religiously, a situation that was supposed to have lasted without interruption from 313 A.D. to 1958. At one stroke and in three words 1600 years of the Church's life were impugned. The most expensive public relations agency could not have done better. One regrets that a famous "reformist" member of the sacred college was not above giving countenance to this historical fiction.

[2]   The same idea is expressed today, e.g. by Cardinal Ratzinger, by saying that we know what must be believed from what has been believed diachronically (across time) as well as what is believed synchronically (everywhere today).

[3]   However, Cardinal Ratzinger has pointed out that although the term "people of God" appears in the New Testament, only in two places does it refer to the Church. Elsewhere it means the people of the Old Covenant. (*The Church, Ecumenism and Politics*, German original 1987; English translation, St. Paul Publications, 1988, p. 18.)

[4]   The mode of that participation has been widely misunderstood. Modernist theology regards the roles of clergy and laity as more or less interchangeable. The conciliar teaching is that they are complementary: the clergy sanctify the laity, and the laity in their turn go out and endeavour to sanctify society or the world. This, fundamentally, is how the laity are to be involved in the Church's mission. Unfortunately, many of the clergy, the majority perhaps quite innocently, understand the teaching in a modernist or

semi-modernist sense. They think that it means co-opting as many lay people as possible into strictly church activities, while there has been a growing tendency on the part of some priests to interest themselves chiefly in social and political agendas. The 1987 Synod on the Laity referred to this as "clericalising the laity and laicising the clergy", and the Fathers who used the expression did not mean it as a compliment. Of course, there is always a need for lay people to help with parish work, and very worthy work it is. But it is not the essence of the lay vocation or the lay contribution to the Church's mission. If it were, the bulk of parishioners would be without a vocation. There is never enough strictly church work to occupy more than a small percentage of the total parish population.

Chapter Twelve

THE CHURCH AND OTHER CHRISTIANS

I   The Circles of Dialogue

The adjustments in the thinking of the faithful, which we have so far been looking at, have had to do with the Church and its internal life. The next three concern the meaning and mission of the Church in relation to the rest of mankind, to its history, and to creation as a whole.

The long centuries during which Christendom had had to defend itself from outside attack, whether from Vikings, Arabs, Mongols or Turks, followed by the period of Catholic-Protestant conflict, and after that by the struggle to preserve the Catholic character of Catholic Europe against the assaults of organised unbelief, had inclined many of the faithful to see the Church and the rest of mankind as two opposed blocks, which if not permanently at war with each other must at best live in a state of armed neutrality. Religiously, people outside the Church were seen either as objects of missionary effort or adversaries of some kind, all in a darkness sufficiently deep for variations and degrees not to matter much.

It was an attitude not unlike that of the Old-Testament Jews towards the Gentiles. It was also a simplification or rather a caricature of the great St. Augustine's doctrine of the "two cities", a doctrine enshrined in his masterpiece *The City of God*, the first theology of human history.

In St. Augustine's doctrine, the heart of human history is a spiritual contest between the forces of good and evil, involving individuals and nations and lasting till the end of time, in which the headquarters and higher generalship on both sides are out of sight, and the central issue is the salvation or loss of souls, with the creation, the fall, the life, death and resurrection of Christ and the last judgement as the decisive moments.

What a man loves will determine to which city he belongs. There are only two loves that really matter. The first puts God and neighbour before self. The second puts self before God and neighbour. The first is essentially a social love. The second is individualistic and anti-social; it sees everyone and everything as existing solely or mainly to minister to its pleasures, pride and lust for domination. Abel and Cain are the prototypes of these two loves. Those moved by the first kind of love belong to, or are at least potential members of, the city of God, those moved by the second belong to the city of the world or the evil one, the world in this context meaning men in so far as they are organised in opposition to God, or living as though he did not exist. It is in this sense that "the things men hold in honour are an abomination in the sight of God".

However, with most men, neither love predominates absolutely. Therefore in this world the boundary between the two cities is not always clearly discernible and the struggle is a confused one. The contending troops frequently change sides, work a bit in both causes simultaneously, fraternise with each other, or sit down and do nothing. This applies inside as well as outside the Church. So while the Church on earth can rightly be seen as the advance headquarters of the City of God, everyone and everything outside the Church does not constitute the City of the World or the Evil One, governments included. The opposition is not between Church and State. For St. Augustine, states and governments are necessary because of original sin, even if he sometimes castigated them as groups of robbers. Without government, things would be far worse. Therefore, unlike the City of God, the city of the world has no permanent visible centre on earth, however much certain governments, political parties or ideological movements may have seemed at times to be competing for the title.

From this it will be seen how St. Augustine's view of the relationship of the members of the Church to the rest of mankind differs from the caricature just mentioned. Once again it was a question of half-conscious attitudes and unthought-out assumptions rather than of consciously held beliefs, and they were beginning to dissolve. But no adequate alternative had replaced them. Where they did survive they were responsible for the combative mentality described earlier.

The reformers had two remedies, one practical, the other theoretical. The practical remedy was the use of dialogue or friendly discussion as the best way of spreading the faith. Dialogue should replace apologetics, controversy or polemics. They regarded controversy and polemics as mostly an obstacle to understanding. They can obscure the real issues. Dialogue, on the other hand, by dissolving prejudice and breaking down unnecessary distrust, enables opponents to see better where the real areas of agreement and disagreement lie. This was especially true today. To go on addressing other Christians, non-Christians or unbelievers, whether in official or unofficial writings, as though they were all lapsed French, Spanish or Italian Catholics who ought to know better, was self-defeating. Apologetics, controversy or polemics presume an audience that is at least paying attention. But modern man is just not listening. So the first thing to do was to stimulate interest by getting him talking.

The theoretical remedy was what Pope Paul in his encyclical *Ecclesiam Suam* called "the circles of dialogue".[1]

As a way of looking at the Church in relation to the rest of mankind, the circles of dialogue emphasise what Catholics have in common with their fellow men rather than what distinguishes or separates them. In the words of the Council, constantly repeated by John Paul II, Christ, in taking a human nature, "has in a certain sense united himself to every man". There is no qualification to his injunction, "if you did it unto one of these the least of my brethren, you did it unto me". Before helping a beggar or prisoner, we do not first ask whether he is a Christian.

With this as our starting point, we are then asked to envisage the Church as the religious centre of mankind with the rest of humanity ranged round her in a series of concentric rings. Those having most in common with her (other Christians) will be in the innermost rings, those having least (unbelievers) in the outermost. But all are in some way related to her because all are made in the "image and likeness of God"; all are potentially redeemed even if all have not taken advantage of their redemption by implicit or explicit acceptance of Christ; and all can be presumed to have some glimmering of truth.

St. Augustine's teaching about the "two Cities" and Paul VI's about the "circles of dialogue" should be seen as complementary, not contradictory doctrines. The "two cities" is concerned primarily with the state of men's hearts; how far as individuals are they turned towards or away from God? The "circles of dialogue" concentrates on their beliefs or philosophical views as groups and collectivities in order to show how much or little they contain of natural and revealed truth. It tells us little or nothing about how near or far from God they are or how close to the Church as individuals. A Muslim believing in one God is neither more nor less likely to become a Christian than a Hindu believing in many. The Church is at any time as accessible to members of the outermost circle as to the innermost.

However, the boundary between Catholics and other Christians is clearly different from the boundary separating Catholics and other Christians from the rest of mankind, so I will look at this relationship first. How does what the Church is now saying about her relationship to other Christians harmonise with what she has previously said; and why was there not a movement for Christian unity sooner?

Again a little history will throw light on the question.

II   Christian Unity and Disunity

The Acts of the Apostles tell us that immediately after Pentecost, the baptised were all "of one mind and heart". Christ had given the apostles with St. Peter at their head, authority to teach, rule and sanctify his people; and his people, responding to grace, believed what they were taught and obeyed the apostles' instructions. The three basic requirements for unity were fulfilled: fullness of belief, baptism and obedience to the apostolic authority. So, ideally, things should have remained.

But God did not take away free will. So almost from the start we find groups of the baptised leaving the unity of the Church and setting up rival communities, each claiming that it, and only it, gave the true teaching. For Catholics, therefore, not only has the oneness willed by God always existed (in the Catholic Church), so too have groups of Christians separated from that oneness.

Moreover, these departures have always taken one of two forms. Either the seceding body wants to alter belief, or, going to the opposite extreme, it repudiates the Church's right to make practical changes — it refuses to obey rather than refusing to believe. People leave, one could say, by opposite doors: the first by the door of doctrinal innovation or heresy, the second by the door of excessive attachment to custom, ending in schism.

From this we can, I think, see better what ecumenism is and is not about, or should and should not mean. Since neither theological jugglery nor ecclesiastical engineering are capable of ensuring that Christians will agree or be obedient for evermore, the object must be to enable as many men and women as possible to find the source and centre of unity.

If there is not a centre of unity where belief in the entire revelation has been preserved, with authority to settle disputes about its meaning, unity must always be ephemeral. What is agreed today can be undone tomorrow. Either the oneness willed by God has always existed, or it can never exist.

Over the course of the centuries, groups and even large bodies of separated Christians did from time to time rediscover the centre of unity. By the end of the eighth century, most of the Arians of Italy and Spain had found their way back. Efforts to heal the breach between Rome and Constantinople went on throughout the middle ages. But the circumstances of the past — slow travel, rudimentary postal services, cultural and political isolation — made contacts and understanding difficult. Moreover, the separated Christians, like the Catholics, held two perfectly sound ideas. The truth revealed by God at such great cost (the passion and death of his Son) could not possibly have been lost. On the other hand, only one of the versions of that truth could be completely true.

By the beginning of this century, however, these certainties were being shaken in the mainline Protestant churches. Doubts about the reliability of the Bible, experiences in mission lands (where their missionaries found themselves competing not only with Catholic missionaries but with each other), and the chill winds of the on-coming religious ice age, inclined growing numbers of mainline Protestants to look at each other more sympathetically. The age-old question re-presented itself ever more insistently: is my version of Christ's message really the authentic one?

The result was the modern movement for Christian reunion, which started with the Protestant World Missionary Conference in 1910, and can be seen as a reversal of the trend towards increasing fragmentation set in motion at the reformation by private interpretation of the Bible. The movement's underlying idea was that no one has the whole truth. There is no centre of unity. Unity has been lost. This approach had already given rise to the branch theory of the Church. Each church, possessing part of the truth, is no more than a limb. By coming together the branches can bring the tree back to life even though the trunk has disappeared.

Very quickly, however, two conflicting tendencies appeared. Traditional Protestants, who continued to regard the Bible as a reliable source of knowledge, were not willing to purchase unity, however important, by watering down the word of God as they understood it. Beliefs still mattered. Unity meant in the first place agreement about belief. The rest gave first place to "Christian action". (Among intellectually sophisticated Protestants modernism was already widespread). No longer believing in a trustworthy source of revelation, they saw joint action, joint worship, baptism and the love of men as the only practicable bases for unity. In regard to belief, it was enough for a man or woman to affirm that "Jesus Christ is God and Saviour". This was not explicitly stated, but increasingly became the accepted view. Moreover, as certainty about Christ's divinity waned, the more ambiguous "Jesus Christ is Lord and Saviour" was put forward as an alternative basic affirmation.

These conflicting approaches were reflected in the movement's two original organised bodies; the Faith and Order Movement started by the U.S. Episcopalian Bishop Brent, and the Life and Work Movement founded by the Swedish Lutheran Archbishop Soderblom, which held their first major assemblies in 1925 and 1927.

To begin with, they were more or less evenly balanced, or if there was an imbalance it was in favour of the traditional Protestants. But as the century wore on and agreement about belief seemed as far away as ever, the drive for unity came more from the modernist or semi-modernist side, with the tradi-tional Protestants putting on the brakes. Various eastern-rite churches and bishops also took part, but it was a cautious part because they did not believe the truth in its fullness had been lost. Bible-based Protestant sects usually held aloof from the movement altogether. It is worth noting that the failure of the participating bodies to reach agreement over the fifty year period from 1910 to 1960 had nothing to do with "Roman intransigence". Rome at this time was not a party to the movement. Theoretically there was nothing to prevent the Protestant members uniting. Yet with all that they had in common, they found it impossible.

Meanwhile, Rome watched the movement grow, allowed some unoffi-cial contacts, took some initiatives of her own, but played no official part in the movement which, up to 1960 remained a mainly Protestant enterprise. The Church's caution was not motivated by pride, indifference or ill-will, however much individuals may have sinned in those regards. She had a more difficult course to steer. Public participation in the movement might be misunderstood as acceptance of the underlying idea (that there is no centre of unity where fullness of belief has been preserved) and therefore as implying doubts about her own claims. She also had to consider the faith of her children.

However Pope John considered the time had come for a change of policy, and for closer Catholic participation in the movement. As we have seen, he regarded Christian unity as one of the prerequisites for a successful apostolate to the modern world. Any risks would therefore be outweighed by the ad-vantages. His first interest was reunion with the Orthodox. Between 1934 and 1944 he had been a papal diplomat in Greece and Turkey.

III The New Policy

The handling of the new policy naturally fell to the ecumenists in the reform party, who, in addition to practical initiatives, wanted a theological re-thinking of the relationship between the Church and other Christians. During the 1930s, '40s and '50s, Catholic ecumenists had produced a considerable litera-ture on the subject. Among the best known, we can name Frs. Karl Adam, Lambert Beauduin, Max Pribilla, Augustin Béa, Georges Tavard, Louis Bouyer. But as in ecclesiology and the theology of the laity, Fr. Congar was again destined to play the leading role. His two books *Chrétiens désunis*, Paris 1937 (*Divided Christendom*, London 1939) and *Vraie et fausse réforme dans l'église*, Paris, 1950, gave the most wide-ranging treatment of the problems.

His first concern was to show that the separated Christians are in some way attached to the Church, if not in the full sense members. This meant shifting the emphasis from what the Church regards as their material errors to the implications of their baptism when those errors are held in good faith.

Since at least the third century, the Church has regarded the baptism of separated churches and bodies as valid, and when valid, its effects, with one exception, though a crucial one, are the same for all. "When baptism is duly conferred and accepted with the right dispositions it really incorporates a man in Christ", says the Council. But for full membership of the Church he must also make, or have made for him by a godparent, a full profession of faith. "In itself baptism is oriented to the complete profession of faith." "Only those are to be accounted really members of the Church who have been regenerated in the waters of baptism and profess the true faith." (Pius XII, *Mystici Corporis Christi*, art. 21).[2]

So the non-Catholic Christian, without being a full member of the Church is somehow linked to Christ in a way that only a deliberate rejection of Christ will break. But his defective or incomplete knowledge cannot constitute such a rejection because he has never recognised the Church as speaking in the name of Christ. It is assumed that without an additional grace enabling him to see the Church in this light, such things as training, custom, habit or cultural and psychological factors, for the time being, form obstacles to full belief for which he is not to blame.[3]

On the other hand, a man who has once freely recognised the truth of the Church's claims and beliefs cannot go back on them without separating himself from Christ and the Church. "The brethren born and baptised outside the Catholic Church are to be carefully distinguished from those who, though baptised in the Catholic Church, have knowingly and publicly abjured her faith" (*Ecumenical Directory*, Part I). A Lutheran and a lapsed Catholic could hold identical beliefs, but while the former (through his baptism and good faith) would be "in Christ", the later (because of his infidelity) would not.

This difference was first explicitly acknowledged in the early 19th century when, at the request of the English convert Fr. Ignatius Spencer (a collateral of Winston Churchill), the Holy See ceased to refer to Protestants in its official documents as *heretici* and substituted the word *a-catholici*. In doing so, it was recognising the difference between those who knowingly start a heresy and those who, as it were, inherit it. Those whom the Church is forced at the start of a heresy or schism to regard as "wolves" (her own apostate children), with the passage of time produce spiritual descendants who are innocent sheep. That is why the Church can today say of separated Christians, "The separated Christians who already belong in some way to God's Church ought to have full incorporation in it." As long as they fail to recognise the truth of the Catholic Church's claims, they enjoy some kind of associate membership of a kind not yet clearly determined.

But what about the status of the separated Christians as independent churches and communities? From the outset, the ecumenical movement has been concerned almost by definition with bringing together groups and collectivities rather than individuals. Here the Council was more guarded. This was partly perhaps to avoid hurting feelings. In the Catholic Church's eyes, a separated church or community with validly ordained bishops and priests and valid sacraments can more truly be considered a detached "piece" of the Church than can communities lacking them. "Although these churches and communities are defective, they are not without significance in the mystery of salvation . . . some, even very many, of the most significant elements and endowments which together go to build up and give life to the Church itself, can exist outside the boundaries of the Catholic Church." The elements mentioned are Scripture, the gifts and graces of the Holy Spirit and certain "visible elements". This is Fr. Congar's doctrine of *vestigiae ecclesiae* or elements of "churchness" existing outside the Catholic Church's boundaries. But disagreements about doctrine and discipline provide "impediments" and "serious obstacles" in the way of full membership of the Church.

Perhaps the best way to understand the import of the Council's teaching is to picture the Church as a sun surrounded at different distances by planets and clouds of star dust detached from it in the past by a succession of historical and spiritual calamities, but still drawing what light and strength they have from the sun, and being held within its orbit by the same gravitational pull. Somehow they have to be drawn back to form with the sun one single heavenly body. The attractive power of the sun is the holiness of Christ and his Church radiating from the centre. The factors weakening its gravitational pull are the lack of holiness in many of the atoms forming the sun's outer layers (us), and the centrifugal force imparted to the separated churches and communities by those who originally pulled them away from the sun.

However, by the end of the Council, large numbers of Catholic ecumenists had apparently adopted modernist-Protestant ideas about unity.

They had apparently decided that disagreements about doctrine and discipline should not be considered serious obstacles to unity, or even obstacles at all. Christians are already united in all that matters; baptism and belief in Christ as "Lord and Saviour". Catholics and other Christians should therefore be allowed to receive communion in each other's Churches instantly.

Differences of belief can be ironed out later – or tolerated as expressions of legitimate pluralism within an already existing one Christian Church.

Reunion with the Orthodox, on the other hand, should be put on the back burner, since an influx of Eastern Christians into the Catholic Church would reinforce the very beliefs and viewpoints which the theological revolutionaries were anxious to expel.

Notes to Chapter Twelve

[1] For "circles of dialogue", see: *Lumen Gentium*, arts. 15, 16; *Ecclesiam Suam*, arts. 96, 97.

[2] Fr. Congar was not an enthusiast for the encyclical. "I naturally situate what is called the *magisterium* in its due place. I can't be accused of having neglected that, but it expresses itself in history: O bull *Unam Sanctam*! O *Syllabus*! O encyclical *Mystici corporis*! . . ." (Address to a conference celebrating the anniversary of founding of *Concilium*, Cambridge 1981. Text in possession of the author). Fr. Congar did not want the boundaries of full or "real" membership of the Church so clearly drawn. In a conversation with him after the conference, he told me that he had been responsible for the use of the word "subsists" in the decree on ecumenism in the passage which states that "the unity . . . which Christ bestowed on his Church from the beginning . . . subsists in the Catholic Church as something she can never lose". (Art. 4)   The term "subsists in" has a certain indefiniteness. It could mean that the one Church of Christ subsists elsewhere as well. He also said that the Anglicans would have to be allowed into the Church without being required to accept the doctrines of the Immaculate Conception and Assumption. "Why?" I asked. "Because", he replied, "they had no part in defining them, they would therefore never accept them." "But of course they won't accept them as long as they remain Anglicans," I said, "I didn't. They haven't yet received the fullness of the gift of faith". "Ah," he said, "our experiences have been different." In his last years, disenchanted with developments within Protestantism, he pinned most of his hopes on reunion with the Orthodox. In his ideal Church there would be patriarchs over each region under a papacy much diminished in authority. General Councils in which the Orthodox had had no part (that is since Constantinople IV, 869–870) he regarded as regional councils of the Latin Church. As a theologian he did undoubted services to the Church and shortly before his death John Paul II made him a cardinal. But for many years his attitude towards Rome had been that of a grumpy old family servant, who, even in front of guests, doesn't bother to hide his dissatisfaction and discontent with the way the house is being run. I think it fair to say that this attitude after the Council did great harm.

[3] Whether in particular cases an individual has received such a grace and failed to respond to it, only God knows. The Church simply says, "they could not be saved who, knowing the Catholic Church was founded as necessary by God through Christ, would refuse either to enter it, or to remain in it". (*Decree on the Church*, art. 14; *Decree on the Missions*, art. 7).

Chapter Thirteen

THE CHURCH AND OTHER RELIGIONS

There are two ways of looking at other religions. They can on the one hand be viewed as systems of belief claiming men's total allegiance. In this respect they appear as rivals to Christianity and obstacles to its acceptance. Or they can be seen as part of a general effort by the non-Christian world to make sense of life and the universe without the help of divine revelation, unless with some dim relics of the primitive revelation given to Adam, each attempt containing elements of truth embedded in a greater or lesser number of errors. From this standpoint, the elements of truth can be regarded as a "preparation for the Gospel". (The exception of course is the religion of Israel, Christianity being its fulfilment).

Both the above ways of looking at the non-Christian religions say something true about them. But with the Second Vatican Council, the magisterium was persuaded to give pride of place to the second more sympathetic approach.

Pressure for the change came partly from missionaries. They pointed to the lack of success of the traditional approach with regard to Muslims, Hindus, Buddhists, Confucianists. Why had centuries of missionary effort not produced more conversions? The wise missionary, it was argued, does not immediately confront his hearers with the total wrongness of their beliefs. Like St. Paul on the Areopagus (the Athenian law court mentioned in *Acts*), he looks for points of agreement – in St. Paul's case, the Athenians' acknowledgement of the existence of an "unknown God". This had also been the approach of the 17th-century Jesuits, Frs. Matteo Ricci and Roberto de Nobili, towards the Chinese and Indians.

The new theologians, on the other hand, favoured the more sympathetic approach for theological reasons. It fitted their "universalism". God is interested in all men, not just Christians.

In his little book *The Salvation of the Nations* (Sheed & Ward, London 1949), the Jesuit Fr. Jean Daniélou describes the four stages through which thinking about non-Christian religions passed in the decades before the Council.[1]

Stage One

Non-Christian religions are inadequate rather than false, therefore a bridge rather than a barrier to the faith. This seems to have been the view of Fr. Pierre

Charles writing around 1929. When speaking of the moral and religious truths to be found in non-Christian religions, the second-century apologist and martyr St. Justin had used the phrase "seeds of the Word". These "seeds of the Word" he attributed in some way to God the Son, the Eternal Word, not just to human reason. Did that mean they were a kind of proto-revelation?

Stage Two

Should we not think of a revelation in three stages? First, God speaks through creation. Of this preliminary revelation the non-Christian religions are the main recipients and beneficiaries (even if they have got some of the facts wrong). Then comes the revelation to the Jews, and finally its completion in Christ. The non-Christian religions therefore represent the first step in a three-fold "mission of the Word". God could not call Abraham until the efforts of the non-Christian religions had raised mankind's "religious consciousness" to a sufficiently high level to receive it.[2]

Stage Three

The non-Christian religions and their cultures contain hidden spiritual riches which are necessary to the future development and completion of Christianity. "There may well be aspects of Christianity that we have not yet discovered and that we will not discover until Christianity has been refracted through every facet of the prism of human civilisation". So far "it has been refracted only through the Greek and Roman worlds, but it will have to be refracted through the Chinese facet and the Indian facet in order to attain its fulfilment" (op. cit., p. 36). Rather, therefore, than seeking to convert individuals, the missionary should concentrate on bringing about "an evolution within the culture itself" (ibid., p. 46). This, it seems, would be achieved through high-level discussions between experts in which the Catholics try to persuade the other side that their religion, good as it is, is now ripe for an evolutionary mutation. Without ceasing to be a distinct "religious experience", it must now open itself to receive a fully Christian content.

Stage Four

Non-Christian religions are valid paths to salvation in and by themselves. Trying to persuade non-Christians to change their religions is therefore wrong. The different "traditions" should live and let live, concentrating on joint efforts to make the world a better place.

The conclusion of stage two and stages three and four have not, needless to say, been endorsed by the Church, nor, as far as I am aware, were they by Fr. Daniélou, however much they have been touted as legitimate interpretations of the Council's teaching or in keeping with its spirit.

The Council confined itself to mentioning St. Justin's "seeds of the Word", echoing Eusebius of Caesarea, who described the "seeds of the Word" as a "preparation for the Gospel" (*Lumen Gentium* 16), and recommending that the faithful be taught to view the non-Christian religions with more sympathy and understanding.

Although the Church's first task – says *Nostra Aetate*, the Council's document on non-Christian religions – is to preach the Gospel, it also has "a duty to foster unity and charity among individuals and even among nations". "Let Christians, while witnessing to their own faith and way of life, acknowledge, preserve and encourage the spiritual and moral truths found among non-Christians, also their social life and culture." (*Nostra Aetate* 2). To which Pope Paul would add that the Church "esteems these non-Christian religions because they are the living expression of the soul of vast groups of people".[3]

The more sympathetic approach to non-Christian religions has been the justification for extensive liturgical "inculturation". The main problem here is that a religion is more than a collection of unrelated teachings and practices. It is an organised whole with an ethos that permeates the parts. Therefore an individual idea or practice, however seemingly true or innocent, when carried over into Christianity, can bring with it more than its own self, as, for instance, many Catholics fear has been happening with some of the Indian hierarchy's attempts to "Hinduise" the liturgy of the Mass.

The Church and the non-Christian's Salvation

Allied to the status of the non-Christian religions was the question of the non-Christian's salvation. About this there were four subjects of debate in theologically "advanced" circles before the Council:

(a) the non-Christian's salvation;

(b) the non-believer's salvation;

(c) universal salvation – everyone is saved;

(d) integral salvation – everyone and everything is saved, souls, bodies, animals, plants, stars, in other words the final transfiguration of the whole cosmos.

In this chapter I will consider points (a), (b), and (c). "Integral salvation" belongs to the next chapter.

(a) *The non-Christian's salvation* was not a subject on which much speculation was expended, as far as one can see, for the first 1500 years of the Church's existence. To the extent it was thought about, the consensus seems to have been that the chances were pretty slim. It was the missionary expansion accompanying the Spanish and Portuguese conquests in the Americas and the Far East which forced the subject on the Church's attention. Knowledge of these new realms impressed more deeply on men's minds the vast numbers of people who never had been and were never likely to become Christians. There was no debate about whether all men *can* be saved. The New Testament makes that clear. Only the 17th- and 18th-century Jansenists doubted it. God wills everyone's salvation. Christ died for all, even if all do not take advantage of his sacrifice. He is "the true Light" who "enlightens every soul born into the world". The subject of debate was how non-Christians are saved, given the Scriptural definition of the Church as the "one ark of salvation", the biblical and patristic insistence on the need for faith and baptism, and the age-old teaching, first explicitly formulated in the third century by Origen and St. Cyprian, *extra ecclesiam nulla salus* (no salvation outside the Church).

St. Peter speaks in a similar vein. "There is no other name (apart from that of Jesus) by which men can be saved". So does St. Paul: "neither is there salvation in any other". Texts could be multiplied to the point of weariness culminating in Christ's clear command "Preach the Gospel to all nations. He who believes and is baptised will be saved; he who refuses to believe will be condemned". To hear the Gospel preached, the Church has always insisted and continues to insist, is the greatest of opportunities, and the way men respond to it is of the utmost consequence. The Council reaffirmed the traditional teaching. "Basing itself on Scripture and tradition, it (the Church) teaches that the Church is necessary for salvation" (*Lumen Gentium* 14).

How then are the two sets of texts to be reconciled?

The Council, after saying that "the Church knows she is joined in many ways to the baptised who . . . do not profess the Catholic faith", speaks tentatively of "those who have not yet received the Gospel" being "related to the people of God in various ways" (*Lumen Gentium* 15). That it has their salvation in mind is clear from the context. The implication seems to be that if they are in the right dispositions they will receive the grace to persevere in them through the Church and will eventually enter heaven as members of the Church through having received what is called "baptism of desire". It is assumed that if they had truly heard and understood the Gospel message, they would have accepted it and asked to be baptised.

The right disposition presupposes, as a minimum, faith in a God who rewards and punishes, sorrow for sin and the desire to please Him. In every nation, says St. Peter, any one who fears God "and does what is right is acceptable to Him". And St. Paul, at the outset of his apostolate to the Corinthians, is told by God that, contrary to appearances, there are in Corinth already "many people on my side". Corinth was, on a small scale, a mixture of Los Angeles and Las Vegas.

But when exactly it is that the non-Christian who is sincerely seeking to serve God, however confusedly, receives this kind of baptism, no one knows. One thing, however, is certain. He will not owe his salvation to Buddha, Confucius, Mohammed, Vishnu, or anyone else real or imaginary. Only Christ was able to make satisfaction for the sins of the human race and win men eternal life. Only as members of his Mystical Body can men enjoy the vision of God.

It was to do justice to this wider vision that the new theologians started looking for an alternative to the definition of the Church as the "one ark of salvation", a definition that would still present her as the unique instrument of salvation, without seeming to imply that salvation was impossible without visible membership of the Church. The formula the Council adopted was "universal sign and sacrament of salvation".[4]

(b) *The unbeliever's salvation:* The main subject of concern here was the "good atheist", anxious to improve the living and working conditions of his fellow men. In the France of the 1930s, '40s and '50s, this mostly meant dedicated socialists and communists. Since they showed no signs of fulfilling any of the conditions necessary for baptism of desire, it was much harder to explain theologically how they could get into the kingdom of heaven – short of a death-bed enlightenment.

The simplest of the proposed solutions was that service of our fellow men is equivalent to belief in God. "In so much as you did it unto one of these, you did it unto me". Others built their theories on Fr. Rahner's or Fr. de Lubac's theologies of nature and grace. All that needs to be said at this point is that they seem to imply that every man has a germ of or disposition towards the supernatural in him by nature. He has an innate desire for the supernatural even when denying its existence, which led Fr. Rahner to postulate the existence of millions of "anonymous Christians".

Neither the Council nor the magisterium since has accepted either of these solutions. The Council merely says that divine providence will not "deny the assistance necessary for salvation to those who, without any fault of theirs, have not yet arrived at an explicit knowledge of God, and who, not without grace, strive to lead a good life." (*Lumen Gentium* 16)

(c) *Universal salvation:* By the 1940s there was a growing body of "advanced" theologians anxious for the Church to abandon, or at least take the sting out of the doctrine of eternal punishment. Some, like de Lubac and von Balthasar, favoured the idea that although hell exists, and is a real possibility for every individual, we cannot be certain that any particular person is in hell, and we must "dare to hope" that all men be saved. Others were for reviving in a modified form the ancient theory, repudiated by the Church but held by Origen, St. Gregory of Nyssa, and St. Jerome for a time, known as *apokatastasis*. Although some people go to hell, even a lot, in the end everyone or nearly everyone is let out, devils included. Hell is simply a more painful kind of purgatory. These ideas did not get through the mesh of the conciliar sieve either.

Nevertheless, it has to be said that the shift of emphasis from the defects to the virtues of the non-Christian religions and to the greater possibilities of salvation outside the visible boundaries of the Church, has been, of all the new orientations, the most difficult to control.

The collapse of missionary effort accompanied by priests and nuns preaching various forms of religious syncretism (Christianity being just one among many religions, all destined one day to be absorbed into a higher "world faith") have been only among the more sensational consequences.[5]

In theory, there was no reason why it should have had this result. When faith is strong, the Christian wants to obey Christ's command and to share what he regards as a priceless treasure with as many people as possible. How God deals with those the message fails to reach, he leaves to God. But when faith is not so strong, preaching the Gospel inevitably comes to seem a matter of less urgency.

Already before the Council, it was being suggested by certain French missionaries, discouraged by their failure to convert the north African Muslims, that rather than preaching the faith, they should be a "silent presence", preaching only by good example and good works.[6]

This inspired Frs. de Lubac and Daniélou to propose an alternative motive for missionary zeal. Even if salvation is possible outside the visible boundaries of the Church, Christians, they argued, should be anxious for the final coming of God's kingdom as soon as possible. But that will not happen until the Gospel has been preached to every nation.

Their alternative, however, was not able to counteract the weakening sense of Christianity's uniqueness and importance generated by the theories we have been examining. These were to have far more weight than any conciliar texts.[7]

Notes to Chapter Thirteen

[1] For Daniélou's views about the religious status of non-Christians, see also his *Holy Pagans of the Old Testament* (French original 1956, Eng. trans., Longmans, 1957). Daniélou, later made a cardinal by Paul VI, was a close associate of Fr. de Lubac. Soon after the war they started the publication of early Church writings under the title *Sources chrétiennes*, which now runs to over 320 volumes.

[2] The idea of an evolving "religious consciousness", compatible though it may be with Fr. Teilhard de Chardin's evolutionism, is hard to reconcile with the historical and anthropological facts. Are we to suppose that we today have a more developed religious consciousness than Abraham? And how do we explain the fact that South American Indians and Africans have accepted the faith without much difficulty, while the "superior" religious cultures of India and China have been more resistant? The work of Buddha and Confucius may, in God's providence, have been intended as some kind of preparation for the Gospel. But that is not how things have worked out. In practice they seem to have been an obstacle to Asia's reception of the Gospel. The subject is clearly not susceptible to easy solutions.

[3] The Apostolic Constitution *Evangelii Nuntiandi* 53, summarising the work of the 1974 Synod on Evangelisation. Elsewhere in the document the Pope found it necessary to say that appreciating the good points in other religions does not absolve missionaries from the obligation to preach the Gospel.

[4] The Council documents in fact express the idea in several forms. That revelation contains apparently conflicting affirmations should no more surprise us than the fact that in modern physics matter presents itself under conflicting aspects sometimes appearing as particles, sometimes as energy waves. Our inability to reconcile them demonstrates nothing but the fact that we are not omniscient.

[5] See the English catechetical programme "Weaving the Web", which introduces young Catholics to the rites and beliefs of Hinduism and Islam along with those of the Church, as though the former were viable variants.

[6] The idea of being "present" to other people without trying to have them share your beliefs seems to have its origin in the "personalism" of the German Jewish philosopher Martin Buber. The holy French priest Charles de Foucauld seems to have been touched by this idea prior to the First World War.

[7] By 2000, the situation had deteriorated sufficiently far for the Holy See to issue a document *Dominus Jesus*, insisting that Christ is the one and only Saviour, and the Catholic Church the one and only Church founded by him. In response, modernism stirred up an international clamour charging Rome, as usual, with being uncharitable – a charge which, according to its view of things, could just as easily be brought against Christ.

Chapter Fourteen

THE CHURCH AND OUR WORK
IN THIS WORLD

We have been considering salvation in the next world. What about our work in this one?

Most Catholics understood well enough that to win eternal life, strictly religious activities – prayer, fasting, alms-giving, the pursuit of virtue – are not enough. We have to earn our livings, bring up families, use our talents. A doctor who spent time on his knees which he ought to be giving to his patients, would not be pleasing to God. At this point, being on his knees would, as is now said, be "counter-productive". Nor was it difficult to understand why. The world, time and history exist in the first place for the creation, training and testing of future citizens of heaven. Life is essentially a school with a great final exam. Meanwhile the potential citizens of heaven have to be fed, clothed, provided with shelter and trained so as to rear future citizens of heaven in their turn. Beyond this, the use of our talents gives glory to God the way a work of art is a credit to the artist.

But does the use of our talents and the resources of nature have some further place in God's plan? Are all the things that make up what we call culture – Plato's dialogues, Shakespeare's plays, Greek sculpture, Florentine painting, Palladian architecture, Beethoven's sonatas, Balzac's novels, Newtonian physics, steam engines, airplanes, electric light, telephones, fireworks, farming – are they just accidental goods destined to sweeten life here during our time of testing, or do they have some lasting significance? In other words, if peopling heaven was God's primary purpose in creating the universe (did not an English poet call the world a factory for making gods?), was it his only purpose?

Most of the faithful, had the question been put to them, would, I think, have replied that the products of science and culture are accidental goods destined to vanish forever in the great final bonfire. After all, men can save their souls with or without the blessings of culture and material progress. As for the references in Holy Scripture to a "new earth" as well as a "new heaven" after the Last Day, the idea that they could mean the re-creation and transfiguration of the present world (as they indeed do) would have seemed to the majority like adding a belief in Cinderella to the articles of the creed. They tended to think of their eternal reward as a purely spiritual one. The reasons for the resurrection of the body – why a material body should have a permanent place in an immaterial heaven – remained obscure. There was no apparent reason. It seemed to be a divine whim, as perhaps did not a little else in their understanding of the faith.

The reasons the Church had hitherto said so little on the subject are plain enough. To get the majority of men and women to give more than a passing attention to God and the next world has never been easy. Tell them they ought to have a deeper appreciation of this world's goods, and it would be harder still. There was also the danger of giving the impression that the next world was going to be like a Muslim paradise. So in her day-to-day teaching the Church had limited herself to commanding and encouraging whatever in her eyes contributed to civilisation, culture and men's earthly welfare, leaving their place in God's final scheme of things to look after itself.

However by the mid-twentieth century that was no longer possible. With alien thinkers by the score flooding the world with their theories about the meaning of progress, civilisation and culture, it had become imperative for the Church to develop a teaching of her own.

The Human Endeavour

How does she view the "human endeavour", the term the new theologians will now start using for cultural and social progress? Is the age-old attempt of men to master the powers of nature, develop their talents, organise social life as best they can, and generally make the world a more agreeable place to live in, without theological significance? Do the history of civilisation and the history of salvation move through time on parallel tracks without point of contact, and with only the latter finding fulfilment elsewhere? Or are they in some way connected? How far, too, can the world be improved, and in what ways and to what extent should Catholics be allowed to take part in the efforts of their contemporaries to transform it into an earthly paradise?

In formulating their answers to these questions, the reformers were hyper-sensitive to atheist criticism of the Church.

These could be summarised as follows. "Why, O Catholic Church, hav-ing been in the world for nearly two thousand years, have you failed to produce the perfect world we are shortly going to create? Your doctrine of heavenly salvation is to blame. By teaching men to think of saving their souls in another world, you turn them into selfish individualists uninterested in improving this one. You are the enemies of men's earthly welfare." [1]

Hardline or Promethean atheists went a stage further: "Your teaching is not only useless. It is positively harmful. Belief in the Deity's existence means the extinction of man's rights, dignity, freedom and well-being. Whether as a fact or an idea, God is man's natural enemy, reducing this otherwise god-like being to slave-hood. As God's supposed representative you, O Church, are the ultimate obstacle to the full flowering of man's personality, creativity, genius and self-fulfilment. *Ecrasez l'infâme!*" ("Crush the brute") [2]

The extent to which the conciliar decrees, above all the decree on *The Church in the Modern World* (*Gaudium et Spes*), are intended to answer these accusations, and to remove anything real or apparent in the way faith and morals were presented that might seem to give grounds for them, can scarcely be exaggerated. Without some knowledge of what they were (which most of the faithful lack), the tone, style and even some of the substance of the conciliar teaching can hardly fail to be misunderstood. Passage after passage is devoted to rebutting the charge that the Church is indifferent or an obstacle to men's earthly well-being.

However, the reformers' immediate aims were practical. To rebut the main charge, Catholics must be encouraged to collaborate as much as possible with men of any religion or none in the "human endeavour". Collaboration between Catholics and "all men of good will" must become the basic principle of Catholic action. But for the collaboration to work smoothly, two misunderstandings must be cleared up.

One was the attitude Christians should have towards "the world". Was it true, as the Church's critics said, that she taught her children to despise, hate or fear the world? Did she see the world mainly as a source of temptations?

The Church's answer was "No", but some of the faithful had the impression that the answer was "Yes". This, according to the new theologians, was the fault of certain spiritual writers influenced by philosophical dualism (matter is bad, only spirit is good). These wrong ideas must be corrected. The faithful must be taught to love and appreciate the world.

What, then, about all the warnings, not only in spiritual writers, but in Holy Scripture itself against the dangers of becoming too attached to the things of this world, or Christ's telling his disciples that the world would hate them?

They had been stressed one-sidedly. To correct the balance, the faithful should be reminded more often that "God hates nothing he has made" and "loved the world so much that he gave his only Son to die for it".

The problem, of course, was the double meaning of the word "world"; either created things in general, or a disordered love of them. Everyone agreed that they are to be hated (kept spiritually at a distance) in so far as they turn our hearts away from God. The dispute was about how likely that is. After the Council it was won by those holding the view that, short perhaps of what goes on in down-town Las Vegas, the world has little in it to deflect us from the narrow path and the strait gate.

The other point to be clarified was what the Council would call "the legitimate autonomy of secular realities".

This means that, while all things are subject to and dependent on God, their physical and biological make-up and operations are not for the most part to be learned from divine revelation. Consequently, although the Church has the right to judge the morality of human acts and speak about the deepest meaning of things, it is not the business of the clergy as clergy, to tell scientists how to conduct experiments, painters how to paint, statesmen how to govern, or businessmen how to run their businesses.

Anxious to allay the ghost of the Galileo controversy, the reformers were sending a message to their opposite numbers in the secular intelligentsia. "No more interference by churchmen in matters scientific. No more ignorant old-fashioned bishops loosing off about Picasso and Corbusier, or influencing politics in a conservative direction". Catholic laymen and "men of good will" could work together at the human endeavour with the minimum of ecclesiastical intervention.

Now that many of the Western clergy want to take the lead in improving this world rather than concentrating on getting their flocks safely into the right department of the next one, we hear less about "the autonomy of the secular realities" or "secular realities" being the province of the laity rather than the clergy.

Creating a Christian Humanism

Attempts to answer the theoretical question "Does the history of civilisation, culture and progress have any theological significance?" resulted in the Council's "Christian humanism", of which *Gaudium et Spes* was the first official expression, and which has since been more fully developed by Popes Paul VI and John Paul II.

Many Catholics are allergic to the word "humanism" because, ever since it first came into use around 1815, it has been associated with unbelief and a quasi-idolatrous cult of man. But if we define humanism as the philosophy of civilisation and progress, or the development of man's natural talents and nature's potentialities, it becomes a neutral term, and in speaking about Christian humanism we are talking about what has been a fact and a reality since the

Church's beginnings. The Church has been the greatest of civilisers and one of the greatest promoters of culture.[3]

Compared to the way the faith was previously presented, the conciliar and post-conciliar "Christian humanism" involves a double shift of emphasis; from the importance of achieving salvation in the next world to our duties in this one; and from the sovereignty of God to the dignity and rights of man. The second shift is usually referred to as the "anthropological turn" or "shift to the human subject" in philosophy and theology. The object was to find common ground for dialogue with atheists, since modern atheism in its various forms is now the dominant "religion" of the West, and the West is culturally the most powerful influence worldwide.

"What kind of a being is man?" was judged to be a better starting point for discussion with atheists than the question "Does God exist?" About God's existence there is open conflict. About man's dignity and rights and the way he ought and ought not to act, the Church and modern atheism are in agreement on some points. It was hoped that by analysing the most fundamental human experiences, those common to all men, it would be possible to show that man is of necessity a being oriented towards God, and that if this is not so, theories about his dignity, rights or ultimate perfection and happiness go up in smoke.

In the words of Pope Paul, belief in man's dignity and rights without a God who confers them are like roses which can only live for a short time once cut from the bush (Christianity) on which they grew.

This has been the main thrust of the Church's case in its argument with atheism since the Council, a case based on the "personalist" philosophies of Jacques Maritain, Emmanuel Mounier, Martin Buber, Gabriel Marcel and Max Scheler. Maritain's and Mounier's "personalism" is more socially and politically oriented than Buber's and Marcel's. They wanted it made clear that the "human endeavour" is part of God's "one plan of creation and salvation", as *Lumen Gentium* puts it. (See Maritain's *Humanisme Intégral*, 1936). Buber and Marcel concentrate more on man's inner life than his external activities. Man is an "I" who only finds fulfilment in entering into communication with a "thou", and in responsibility and self-giving.

The other major thinkers influencing the "anthropological turn" or "shift to the human subject" were Martin Heidegger, the founder of existentialism and philosophical mentor of Fr. Karl Rahner, and Heidegger's French counterpart, Jean-Paul Sartre.

All these men – Buber, Marcel, Scheler, Heidegger and Sartre – could be called philosophers of the human spirit, and although Buber was Jewish, Marcel a Catholic, Scheler a spiritual vagrant who wandered in and out of the Church at different times, and Heidegger and Sartre were atheists, all drew heavily on the 19th-century Danish writer Søren Kierkegaard (1813–1855), arguably the most influential religious thinker since his works were first translated into the major European languages at the beginning of the last century.

The "anthropological turn", which has had the backing of John Paul II, has inevitably meant the introduction of a more subjective approach in Catholic philosophy than was hitherto allowed. In general one can say that the orthodox have mainly made use of Buber, Marcel and Scheler, with the heterodox favouring Heidegger and Sartre.

★　　　★　　　★

The main Scriptural foundations for the conciliar Christian humanism are the first chapter of *Genesis;* the doctrine of the Incarnation; and what could be called the "cosmological texts" in the epistles of St. Paul. Fr. de Lubac was their chief and earliest exponent. (See his *Catholicisme, les aspects sociaux du dogme,* 1939 [English edition: *Catholicism: Christ and the Common Destiny of Man,* Ignatius Press, San Francisco, 1988]).

In *Genesis* 1, God declares creation to be good, makes man "in his own image", and commands him to "fill and subdue the earth".

The Incarnation (God taking a human body as well as soul), exploded once and for all the notion, promoted by a number of oriental religions and philosophies, that matter could be evil or an illusion. Human nature was raised to unimaginable heights, and, most amazing of all, through "divine adoption", man's "deification" (a term familiar to Eastern theology) became a possibility.

In this teaching about man's "deification", the new theologians saw a way of stealing some of atheist humanism's thunder. What was its cult of man compared with what the Church has to offer? This explains Pope Paul's oft-quoted remark in his speech at the end of the Council: "The Church too has its cult of man."

It was perhaps not a very wise remark. As so often, the Pope had his eyes on cultivated unbelievers more than on the ordinary faithful, many of whom were not a little scandalised. Were statues of Beethoven and Einstein about to be set up as objects of worship? But his words were not without good theological foundation. Man is not an object of worship, but in each man the image of God and reflection of Christ, however defaced, should be venerated and the promotion of his bodily and spiritual welfare seen as a religious as well as a moral obligation.

What I have called St. Paul's cosmic texts are those in which the apostle of the Gentiles gives us a glimpse of the way the fate of the universe is bound up with man's. Nature has been mysteriously "condemned to frustration"; it "groans" as it waits for the "adoption of the sons of God".[4] But all things will be "reconciled in God", when Christ, having first "subjected them" to Himself, "hands them over to his Father."

Some of the Greek Fathers had likewise speculated about the dependence of nature's fate on man's, and the form of its final transformation, trying in the process to reconcile the Pauline texts with neo-Platonic philosophy. For this reason, they too were dear to the new theologians.

The Signs of the Times

The architects of the new humanism also made much of Our Lord's injunction about "Reading the signs of the times". If his hearers had read the signs of the times correctly, they would have recognised him for who he was. From the signs of the times we can sometimes learn how God wants us to act. But recent theology had been giving the expression a wider meaning. The signs of the times can give us an insight into the future. They can show us the way God's plans are unfolding and their theological significance. For the neo-Protestant theologian Karl Barth, the wise theologian carries a Bible in one hand, a daily newspaper in the other. From this it could be a short step – the step taken by modernists – to the notion of on-going revelation. Through current events, God is revealing new truths. The Council makes occasional if not clearly defined references to reading the signs of the times, but not in the last sense.

Which signs of the times, or features of contemporary history, did the new theologians regard as most charged with theological significance, and most influenced the development of their Christian humanism?

There were seemingly three: modern democratic political movements, in which they saw a belated fruit of the Incarnation; the growing unification of the world through rapid travel and communications; and the rain of riches, in the form of scientific knowledge, technology and cash, which has been pouring down on the once Christian industrialised countries of the West for the last 150 years, and since the second World War has become an inundation.

Democratic political movements: All that needs to be said here is that the more politically conscious reformers, like Maritain, Emmanuel Mounier and Fr. Marie-Dominique Chenu, wanted the Church to recognise the social and political movements of the last two hundred years, carried on in the name of liberty, equality, fraternity and democracy, as in some degree inspired by God. They also wanted the faithful launched into the quest for the perfectly just social and political system *en masse*.

To these two demands the Council, with due reservations, gave its assent. The faithful are urged to take their social and political obligations seriously. "Justice and peace" commissions (parish, diocesan and regional committees to implement the Church's social teaching) have multiplied.[5]

But how much justice is possible? Is perfect justice attainable, and how is the goal to be reached? Should it be by increasing or diminishing the powers of the state?

Here the Council refused to commit itself. It kept to general principles about social and political conduct. "The concrete forms, structure and organisation of public authority adopted in any political community may vary according to the character of the various peoples and their historical development" (*Gaudium et Spes* 74). However, the thinking of most of those responsible for drafting the text, reflected in its ethos, tended to be utopian and democratic.

One World: The unification of mankind as the climax of history is an idea which has been haunting the Western mind for at least two centuries, and under the influence of the evolutionary ideas of Fr. Teilhard de Chardin, had come to dominate the thinking of the new theologians too. History is moving ineluctably towards this consummation.

However, men are not united simply by being brought into closer physical contact or gathered together under one government. True unity presupposes some measure of agreement about the purpose of life and how to achieve it. Round what set of ideas, then, are men to be fully and finally united?

The Church's answer can only be: around belief in Christ. That is why the Council, after calling the Church "the universal sacrament of salvation", gives a further definition: "the sign and instrument of communion with God and unity among all men". Whatever some of the new theologians may have intended, the Council was rejecting the claims of Marxism, secular humanism, freemasonry, and every other "-ism" and "-ology", to be the instrument of mankind's final unification. A sign or sacrament does not have to achieve what it signifies. People are free to use or not to use it. But if full and final unity is to come about in this world, it can only be under the God-Man, the human race's Head and Redeemer. A unity based on mutual tolerance of diverse views would not be final unity.[6]

Western Prosperity: About the right way of using the inundation of knowledge and riches, the answers were again at hand in the Church's social teaching. All goods must be come by honestly. Those on whom God has showered them beyond measure must be generous and share them. Sharing includes helping the less well-endowed to help themselves.

These principles had long been recognised as applying to the internal life of nations. But the reformers, backed by the missionary orders, wanted it made plainer that they apply as much to relations between nation and nation, and region and region. This, in a nutshell, is the teaching of *Gaudium et Spes* on the subject.

But what is the deeper meaning of the inundation? Could it too, like the movement for civil and political rights, so the thinking of the reformers ran, be a continuation of the liberating work of the Incarnation? To begin with, men had had to be set free from false beliefs, false fears and evil desires. That had been the principal achievement of the first 1500 years of the Church's history – spiritual liberation. But beginning with the decline of slavery and accelerating as we approach modern times, can we not see flowing from that interior liberation an external liberation of man taking place; what will one day be a liberation for everybody from hunger, pain, disease and the drudgery of work as the forces of nature are increasingly harnessed to man's service?[7] In other words, God wants more than the salvation of souls. He wants *integral salvation:* the "salvation" of men's bodies as well, and, through men, of nature in its entirety.[8]

But if this is what the "reconciliation of all things in Christ" means, is it largely a work of men completed before the last day, or largely a work of God brought about after the last day? In other words, is the building of the kingdom of God, or is it not, to be identified with the building of an earthly Utopia?

To this question, which lies at the heart of the Church's struggle with modernism and about which the new theologians were divided, the Council gave a definite No; there is to be no such identification – though not, it seems, often and loud enough to silence those who wanted the answer to be Yes.[9]

"We know neither the moment of the consummation of the earth and of man, nor the way the universe will be transformed. The form of this world distorted by sin is passing away, and we are told that God is preparing a new dwelling and a new earth in which righteousness dwells" (*Gaudium et Spes* 39). Pope Paul and Pope John Paul II have also both repeatedly insisted that the "human endeavour" and the building of the kingdom of God are not to be identified. Building the Kingdom of God is not dependent on the success of the human endeavour. The Kingdom is built up principally by adding to the number of the saved.[10]

However the Council endorsed the idea that improving this world is a proper activity for Christians as Christians.

"The Church was founded to spread the kingdom of Christ all over the earth ... in order to make all men partakers of redemption and salvation, and through them to establish the right relationship of the entire world to Christ." (*Decree on the Laity*, art. 2). Or as *Gaudium et Spes* puts it, the spiritual and temporal orders "although distinct, are so connected in the one plan of God that he Himself intends in Christ to appropriate the whole universe into a new creation, initially here on earth, fully after the last day."

In other words, the Church, like marriage, has a primary and a secondary end, which in so far as possible should go hand in hand. Making men Christians not only sets them on the path to salvation, it contributes to making the world better; and making the world better (the human endeavour) is to be seen as an extension of the primal act of creation.

Building a better world is the Church's answer to modern atheism's notion of building a perfect world, and to get the accent in the right place, Paul VI launched the idea of building a "civilisation of love". Without love, no amount of prosperity will make the world better. It will be worse.

But if all the products of art and culture are eventually going to go up in smoke, as the first Pope has told us (II Peter 3:7), "what", asked the Council Fathers, "is the final meaning of man's activity in the universe?" (*Gaudium et Spes* 11). How will it have contributed to the "new earth", to which they refer?

On this point the Church has not said anything explicit, though there are hints in *Gaudium et Spes* and towards the end of John Paul II's encyclical on work, *Laborem Exercens*, that in some sense the products of our brains and hands in this life, will, if found worthy, have a place in transfigured form in the "new creation". Neither document goes so far as to say we shall hear Chopin or enjoy impressionist paintings. But the direction of the thought seems to indicate it as a possibility.

We have now covered, if not all, at least the main new orientations. Our next task is to see why the new theology, which was largely responsible for them, had become impregnated with error, as well as yielding valuable insights. For that we must go back to the early 19th century and the beginnings of the movement for coming to terms with "modern thought", which we can roughly define as the sum of 19th- and 20th-century knowledge and opinion, ideas and ideologies, clustered around the doctrines of the 18th-century Enlightenment.

Notes to Chapter Fourteen

[1] "Why is it so often said that Christianity does not work? 'You have been on the job for nearly two thousand years in this world: what is there to show for it?' – so runs the familiar accusation." Jean Daniélou, *The Lord of History*, Longmans, London, 1958, p. 87. For Teilhard de Chardin "the great objection against Christianity in our time . . . is . . . that our religion makes its followers *inhuman*" (*Le Milieu Divin*, Collins 1960, p. 41). In regard to the history of the Church as a whole, the accusations could hardly be more preposterous. The Church is not in the business of producing Utopias. In spite of this it is Christians who have filled the non-Christian world with hospitals, schools, orphanages and refuges for the poor, not apostolic disciples of Voltaire and Marx. Since the collapse of communism in eastern Europe, we can also point to the devastation these accusers have worked all over the world in a mere seventy years. Unfortunately the reformers did not have the benefit of this hindsight. It might have made them less sensitive to the accusations.

[2] Prometheus: the legendary Greek figure who was punished for stealing fire from the gods to benefit mankind.

[3] The renaissance had used the word "humanist", not the word "humanism", but the idea was already there, i.e. that scholarship, learning and the development of human talent and welfare do not have to be of a strictly religious kind to be pleasing to God. St. Thomas More, St. John Fisher and Erasmus are well known examples of Christian humanists. Many more instances can be found in *Vite di uomini illustri del Secolo XV* by the Florentine bookseller Vespasiano da Bisticci, first published from a manuscript in the Vatican library in 1839 (English trans., under title *The Vespasiano Memoirs*, Routledge, London, 1926, reprinted Harper & Row, New York, 1963). Humanism as an idea only begins to become toxic when it is assumed that the pursuit of man's earthly welfare and development can be conducted without reference to his supernatural end.

[4] The older translations of *Romans* 8:22 speak of nature or creation "groaning in travail" or "groaning and travailing together", to which the English translators of the Jerusalem Bible add the phrase "in one great act of giving birth". But these last words, seeming to imply some kind of Teilhardian evolutionary climax to history, are not found in the Greek text.

[5] In many cases, unfortunately, only to become unwitting channels for left-wing propaganda.

[6] Fr. de Lubac saw in mankind's final unification another motive for renewed missionary zeal. Before Christ comes again, the unification ought at least to be under Christian inspiration.

[7] See de Lubac, *The Drama of Atheist Humanism*, p. 5. Whether the scientific and technical marvels of recent times are or are not part of the liberating work of the Incarnation, one can easily think of some other purposes they might have: (a) They facilitate the preaching of the Gospel to all nations. (b) By putting much greater power for good and evil in our hands, they subject us to more demanding tests – we are being transferred to a higher classroom in God's high-school, not to a permanent apartment in a cosmic Ritz hotel. (c) Before the world ends, human nature is to display all its potentialities

before the watching, wondering, crowds of angels to whom St. Paul refers. For Maritain, "the manifestation of all the potentialities of human nature" is one of the world's "natural ends" (*The Peasant of the Garonne*, Chapman, London, 1968, p. 41).

[8] The concept of "integral salvation" was initially intended as a corrective to the misunderstanding I mentioned at the beginning of this chapter – the idea that God is not much interested in our bodies or the material creation; they are incidental to his overall plan. Unfortunately the concept rapidly received heterodox interpretations. Obviously, for the Church, the body is only "saved" in a metaphorical sense. Its "salvation" depends entirely on the soul. If the soul is lost, the most physically perfect body will be lost with it. Conversely, if the soul is saved the body will share in its glory. The body can do nothing towards its salvation apart from the soul. Modernism, on the other hand, rapidly gave the "salvation of the body" a largely this-worldly significance. Bodily salvation begins here below with advances in medicine and health care and keeping physically fit. The well-being of people's bodies should therefore be as much a concern of the clergy as the well-being of their souls. To think otherwise is to be guilty of "Platonic dualism". All this helps explain why in many places the traditional spirituality of self-denial has been replaced by a spirituality of self-fulfilment, and we have "centres of human development" as well as retreat houses.

[9] It should be remembered that much of the "advanced" thinking on this subject in the pre-conciliar decades was heavily influenced by the evolutionary optimism of Fr. Teilhard de Chardin, in whose scheme of things it is difficult to distinguish "the human endeavour" from the building of the kingdom of God. Men first "transform the world", and when the work is complete, Christ returns to take it over.

[10] "We likewise confess that the Kingdom of God, which had its beginning here on earth in the Church of Christ, is not of this world, whose form is passing, and that its authentic development cannot be measured by the progress of civilisation, of science and of technology." (Paul VI, *Credo of the People of God*, "The Solicitude of the Church"). And here is John Paul II, whom no one can accuse of disinterest in "transforming the world" in so far as that is possible. Addressing the Brazilian bishops on the then forthcoming celebrations for the new millennium, he observed that "it is not a matter of indulging in a new millenarianism (*Tertio Millennio Adveniente* 23) with the temptation to predict substantial changes in it regarding the life of communities and of each individual. Human life will continue, people will continue to experience success and failure, moments of glory and stages of decline, and Christ Our Lord will always be the one source of salvation until the end of time" (*Osservatore Romano*, 7th Feb. 1996).

PART IV

AGGIORNAMENTO AND
THE RISE OF MODERNISM

Chapter Fifteen

BEGINNINGS

In Chapter One, I said that the purpose of an intellectual or cultural *aggiorna-mento*, was to sift the wheat from the chaff in contemporary thought and life in order to keep the faithful from opposing what is naturally good, and to put the good at the Church's service. The chief hazard or occupational disease to which those taking part can succumb is trying to force the Church to eat chaff as well as wheat. We are about to see both things happening.

The Holy See's major changes of attitude and policy towards the under-taking fall conveniently for our purposes into four periods: from 1815 to the death of Pius IX in 1878; from the accession of Leo XIII in 1878 to his death in 1903; from St. Pius X's accession in 1903 to his death in 1914; and from the accession of Benedict XV in 1914 to the death of Pius XII and Pope John XXIII's election in 1958.

Up to 1958, these changes of policy were never total reversals of policy. They were a more or less vigorous putting on or letting off of the brakes, the strength of the pressure being dictated, on the one hand, by the necessity for adaptations of some kind, and, on the other, by the need to protect the beliefs of the bulk of the faithful.

Pope John XXIII initiated a fifth period – the one we are still in – by letting off the brakes with unprecedented suddenness. It was a complete reversal of policy, and Pope Paul who succeeded him touched the breaks so lightly, when he touched them at all, that the results were scarcely noticeable.

Returning to our starting point, by the mid-summer of 1815, the up-heavals of the revolutionary and Napoleonic era being over and Europe at peace once more, the effects of what could be called the "new realities" – the changes in men's ways of living and thinking and the factors responsible for them that mark off pre-revolutionary from post-revolutionary Europe – be-gan to make themselves felt. The revolution did not cause these changes. They had been in preparation for a long time. But by overthrowing the ancient but now decrepit political institutions which had been holding them in check, the French revolution and Napoleonic invasions let them out of the bag like the winds of Aeolus to blow about the world at gale force.

The most significant of the "new realities" for the Church was her loss of intellectual and cultural leadership. A high percentage of the most gifted thinkers, writers, artists, and scientists abandoned her. So too did large numbers of the actively enterprising middle classes. The departure marked the beginnings of the Church's long struggle with different forms of organised unbelief (liberal, masonic, socialist, communist) already referred to. It was the beginning of the end of Christendom as history had hitherto known it.

The other major new realities were: the spread of democratic or republican political ideas; the industrial revolution and the accompanying exodus of the farming populations from the countryside to the towns with their devastating social effects; the consequent growth of movements to win or defend the rights of workers, spear-headed by various forms of revolutionary socialism; as the century advanced, mass education; the spate of new scientific discoveries and inventions; and finally the torrent of scholarly and philosophical theories which in different ways seemed to undermine the foundations of belief.

How much of this immense collection of notions, speculation and reputed facts was true and to which could the Church therefore give her blessing?

Like nearly all important new initiatives, the beginnings of the movement for coming to terms with them were small. It was less a concerted undertaking than a tentative tackling of this or that topic by isolated individuals which at first seemed to be part of the general religious revival sweeping across Catholic and Protestant Europe. Nevertheless, though the same men were often active in both ventures, the objectives were different.

The religious revival was concerned with reawakening spiritual fervour (dulled by the tepid deism of the previous century); with restoring or preserving what is perennial in the Church's life; and, under the stimulus of the romantic movement, with rediscovering the treasures of the Church's past – not only what had been swept away by war and revolution, but things which had fallen into disuse through the attrition of time.

The *aggiornamento*, on the other hand, was concerned with ideas and practices originating outside the Church. For reasons which lie in their different histories it took a rather different form in the two countries, France and Germany, where the demand for it has always been strongest.

In France, for the greater part of the 19th century, political activity of some kind was possible, but the Church was excluded from the universities. In France, therefore, the movement's leaders were mostly writers, orators, or public figures of some kind, not university men; and what they sought was a measure of accommodation with 19th-century liberal theory and practice. Hence the name "liberal Catholicism" for this branch of the movement. The most representative figures were the abbé de Lammenais, the Dominican Fr.

Lacordaire, the Vicomte de Montalembert, and the Archbishop of Orleans, Msgr. Dupanloup. Although they differed about which items of liberalism's stock in trade were most valuable, they were at one in wanting the Church to approve political constitutions, government by elected representatives, equality before the law, the right of free association and so on. (There was in principle no objection to any of them). They also wanted the Church to speak well of individual liberty, particularly liberty of speech and opinion, and to accept religious freedom and the separation of Church and State as absolute goods, always and everywhere. These were a different matter. The agenda as a whole has been called "baptising the principles of 1789".

In Germany the opposite state of affairs prevailed. The royal and princely governments gave little scope for political activity. Interest in liberal theory and practice was in consequence relatively weak. Catholic writers of the period, like Görres, were more interested in the corporate freedoms of Germany's medieval cities. On the other hand, the Church still had a foothold in some of the universities. So it was mainly in the universities that the movement developed, the leaders were mostly professors, and what they chiefly wanted from the Church was her blessing on elements of German idealist philosophy and the use of the historical and literary critical method.

German Idealism

There are two main branches of this immensely influential school of thought. The first stems from Immanuel Kant's "Copernican revolution in philosophy" or "critical idealism", as he called it; the second from Hegel's "absolute" or "objective" idealism.

Building on the ideas of Descartes, Locke and Hume, Kant (1724–1804) decreed that we cannot know things as they really are, only as they appear, these appearances being the creation of our minds. Our minds impose on the incoming stream of impressions we receive through our senses a pattern of their own making. The world looks the way it does, not because that is how it is, but because that is how our minds make it look. Between the world of things as they appear (the world of *phenomena*) and the world of things as they truly are (the world of *noumena* or "things in themselves") a great gulf is fixed. The "noumenal" world remains forever unknowable.

It is not necessary for our present purposes to explain Kant's reasons for advancing these surprising ideas. We need only mention two of the more important consequences of his "Copernican revolution".

In the first place, it destroyed the foundations of natural theology. If the apparent order and design in nature are creations of our minds, they cannot be used as arguments for the existence of God. Nor can we have any knowledge of the kind of being that God is by reflecting on his works. The shape and form of things are dictated by us. The voice of conscience is the only evidence we have for the Deity's existence.

Although a Lutheran, Kant was in fact contradicting what St. Paul had plainly told the people of Lystra (not to mention a great deal that is said elsewhere in the Bible): namely that God, his purposes and the kind of being he is, can be known from his works. Kant is, in this respect, the father of modern religious agnosticism.

Kant's idealism is called "critical" because it calls into question the common-sense conviction that the appearance of things, for the most part, reveals rather than conceals what they essentially are.

Kant's theories about the relationship of the mind to reality were also responsible for the strongly subjective approach to religion and the great questions leading to religion with which we are all now familiar. "The way I feel about things is the way they are".

Hegel, on the other hand, rather than shutting men up in their minds, made us minuscule particles of God's mind. We and everything else in the universe are aspects or thoughts of a great universal Mind as it endeavours to reach a fuller understanding of Itself. The consequences in this case were to cast much of modern European philosophy into a strongly evolutionary pantheistic mould.

The Historical and Literary Critical Methods

This, the second of the two disciplines it was hoped the Church would bless, is the system of rules for testing the documents on which our knowledge of the past is based in order to determine their authorship and value as evidence, and to arrive at a more accurate understanding of the author's meaning. Already used in classical times, they were revived at the renaissance by humanists like Valla. Their development and application reached its apogee in the 19th-century under the name of "the higher criticism".

These rules are not unlike the rules of evidence in courts of law. The object is to determine whether the reputed authors really wrote the documents under examination, how truthful they were, and if they can be shown not to have been the authors, just how and when the documents were composed. Conclusions are reached partly by studying the documents' language, style and contents for inconsistencies and anachronisms (internal evidence), partly by bringing external information to bear. Does the language and style seem to be all from one hand or not? Does it fit the document's supposed date? Are the facts recorded consistent with each other? Do they agree or conflict with other historical evidence?

The critic, it is presumed, will not only have a good knowledge of the necessary languages, but also a good understanding of the conditions under which the texts were written, and, in so far as possible, of the ideas prevailing at the time. All this helps him to throw light on the meaning of obscure passages as well as the date of the texts. The method was also used for determining the date and authorship of literary works like the *Iliad* and the *Odyssey*.

Initially, the "higher criticism" had a stimulating effect on Catholic historians. The higher critics' industry, exacting standards and command of their materials, represented a challenge. Of the several Catholic historians matching them in erudition and industry, probably the most distinguished was the historian of Church Councils, Fr. Karl Joseph von Hefele (1800–1893).

These different focuses of interest – on liberal theory and practice west of the Rhine, on philosophy and critical scholarship to the east – were still to be found among the experts at the Second Vatican Council.

Outside France and Germany, curiosity was less compartmentalised. In Italy, Frs. Rosmini and Gioberti tried in different ways and with different degrees of success to come to terms with both liberalism and German philosophy, while in England Lord Acton was an apostle of liberalism and the higher criticism.

The Catholic social movement – the Catholic response to the evils of urbanisation, rapid industrial expansion and unchecked economic liberalism – developed separately. In France, most of the early social reformers were not political liberals (Armand de Melun, Albert de Munn, René de la Tour du Pin); nor was Cardinal Manning in England, or Bishop Ketteler of Mainz, the movement's chief protagonist in Germany. Ketteler was also distrustful of the rising pretensions, as he saw them, of the German Catholic scholarly world.

Unfortunately, the social movement and the liberal Catholic attempt to baptise the principles of 1789 introduced into French Catholic life, and later throughout the Catholic world, an internal struggle which eventually became as heated and bitter as the external conflict between Catholics and organised unbelief.

In this internal struggle, as in the external one, class, economic and political interests and prejudices again helped to confuse the issues. Nor were the faults all on the side of the liberal or "social" Catholics. If the liberals tended to see the principles of 1789 through rose-tinted glasses, and later generations of "social Catholics" came to idealise socialism, their opponents often tried to give monarchical government the appearance of an article of faith, or represented any attempt to correct social evils as support for revolution. Liberal and social Catholics were frequently at loggerheads too. Liberals like Montalembert and Dupanloup inclined to see the championship of workers' rights either as a violation of liberal principles, or as socially and politically dangerous.

Ultimately, however, the conflict came to be about more than straight-forward questions like "Should France be a monarchy or a republic?" or "Do workers have rights *vis-à-vis* employers?" Gradually a deeper question came to the surface. Should the laws and customs of nations express the mind and will of God, or the outlook of the majority of the inhabitants? In the long run, of course, a country's laws and customs always reflect the majority outlook (they also help to form it), whether or not they reflect the law of God as well. The question was only a burning one because the nations of Europe and the Americas were in a state of transition from being publicly more or less Christian, to being (what they mostly now are), publicly nothing, or atheist. The debate will eventually therefore be about whether to oppose the anti-Christian tendencies and save as much of Christian public law as can be saved, or whether to bow to what is regarded as a *fait accompli*, and, out of respect for majority opinion, surrender the field of public law to the anti-Christian tendencies without a fight.

The dispute is now of course at its height in regard to abortion and euthanasia, with modernism favouring co-operation in the work of demolition or surrender.

Such were the beginnings of the attempt to come to terms with the "new realities" – the first steps on the path leading to the Second Vatican Council's "new orientations".

Chapter Sixteen

FIRST SIGNS OF TROUBLE

That trouble lay ahead could have been foreseen in the way some of the scholars we have mentioned spoke about the work in hand – Gioberti, for example. The Church, it was said, must be reconciled with "modern times" or the "spirit of the age" as though the two things could receive a blanket blessing.

If the age is thought of as being run by a variety of spirits, a chaotic parliament of them so to speak, the problem is less intractable. Catholics can then make friends with the good ones and shun or shut the door on the bad – the guiding principle of all true *aggiornamento*.

There was also much talk about "bringing together faith and reason" or "faith and science". One knows what was meant. A naturally established fact, if it really is a fact, remains a fact. Our religion does not require us to deny it. But it may be a long time before the import of a particular fact is understood, while the mysteries revealed by God often seem to contradict what we take to be natural facts or appearances – as do certain scientifically established facts like the earth's movement round the sun. Things are not always as they seem at first sight. When we talk about reconciling reason and faith, is our object really to make the mysteries revealed by God appear what is considered reasonable by the average man, scientifically trained or otherwise?

There is another difficulty. Since faith is widely regarded as a matter of vague intuitions or feelings, while "science" has the reputation for dealing only with facts and being infallible, this kind of talk instantly gives the advantage to "reason" and "science" – whether thought of as representing the claims of natural knowledge or the unbelieving point of view – before discussion of the problems of trying to harmonise faith and reason has so much as started. The issue might have been easier to handle if, instead of talking about faith and reason or faith and science, Catholics had talked about supernatural and natural knowledge – two sources of information, the first being the more precious because it teaches man about his final end.

The first and most famous casualty in this opening period was Félicité de Lamennais (1782–1854). A convert, a priest and a brilliant polemicist, he started by championing the papacy against the surviving Gallicanism of the restored French monarchy and hierarchy. But gradually, captivated by the notions of popular sovereignty and progress, he started trying to refashion the Church as a Rousseauistic compact between Pope and people at the expense of the bishops, then transforming her mission into promoting temporal welfare of the faithful. The Church was to be their liberator from oppressive rulers, employers and foreign governments.

"Catholicism delivers man from the yoke of man", he was to write after his break with the Church, and "the day is approaching when (the Church) will mould all nations into one great society", appearing "between heaven and earth as a consoling sign".[1] But first she must regenerate herself by stripping herself of worldly goods and entanglements. For the first time we hear the accents of today's liberation theologians. It is an age-old dream.

Later still he was to make "the people" the source of religious truth. Christianity is true because what is essential to it agrees with what the generality of men has always believed about life's meaning and origins.

While Lamennais was still championing the papacy, Pope Leo XII is said to have thought of making him a cardinal. If the Pope really had such an intention, Providence must have intervened to make him change his mind. His successor, Gregory XVI, had to condemn Lamennais' principal theses in the encyclical *Mirari vos*, and in 1834 he was excommunicated. Excommunicating a cardinal would have been a considerable embarrassment.

The brushes with authority of other Catholic thinkers and scholars were less dramatic. At different times both Montalembert and Lord Acton were rebuked for pressing liberal ideas beyond the point of acceptability. Most of Gioberti's books were put on the Index of forbidden books, for philosophical or political reasons. His religion having become entangled with his passionate Italian nationalism, he wanted the Pope to see himself as a divinely appointed instrument for Italian liberation and unification. However, Rosmini's fidelity and holiness were never seriously in doubt, in spite of the censured propositions in his philosophical writings.

Scholarly pride seems to have been the undoing of the German historian Döllinger, who refused to accept the definition of papal infallibility in 1870. How could an ignorant Italian bishop be right about papal authority and a master of the higher criticism wrong? (Even Hefele, by this time Bishop of Rottenburg, had hesitated for a year before subscribing to the definition). Earlier, at a congress which he had organised in Munich, Döllinger had demanded total freedom from ecclesiastical control for Catholic scholars.

In retrospect, however, perhaps the most significant figures who got into deep waters before 1878 were the two philosopher-theologians Fr. Georg Hermes (1775–1831), a seminary professor in Bonn, and Fr. Anton Günther, a priest of independent means living in Vienna.[2]

Hermes, whose faith had been shaken as a student while reading Kant, and Kant's disciple Fichte, wanted to make belief easier for the highly educated. To this end he divided the faithful into philosophers and non-philosophers, justifying the step by adopting Kant's distinction between theoretical and practical reason. Philosophers, or the well-educated, only have to accept the truths of revelation in so far as they satisfy the demands of theoretical reason. In contrast, the uneducated, or anyone incapable of understanding the objections which theoretical reason raises against belief, are bound to accept the Church's teachings without question once they have a sufficiently strong practical inner conviction that there has been a revelation. He seems to have ignored the role of grace in believing. He also taught that theology should start with methodical doubt.

Günther thought that with a judicious mixture of Kant and Hegel, mysteries like the Trinity and the Incarnation could be demonstrated by reason alone. Revelation was not absolutely necessary. Furthermore, with the progress of science and philosophy, such mysteries would become ever clearer and more easily demonstrable. The Church's doctrinal definitions were therefore always subject to revision and improvement.

For a time, "Hermesianism" had a following in the Rhineland important enough to cause serious anxiety in Rome, while Günther's ideas had repercussions throughout Catholic Germany. Both died in the Church, but their efforts to put Kant's and Hegel's idealism at the Church's service were condemned in 1835 and 1857. Several of Günther's disciples left the Church after the First Vatican Council, some joining the Old Catholics.[3]

What was the attitude of the magisterium to these first attempts at making German philosophy, critical scholarship and the "principles of 1789" into handmaids of divine revelation?

If, to most of the Popes and bishops of the time, there did not seem to be much in what then passed for modern thought that could be reconciled with the faith, it is hardly surprising. The struggle to preserve the Catholic character of Catholic Europe was at its height; they were having to fight off attacks on the Church and the faith from half a dozen different directions. Many of the new ideas, moreover, seemed to be bound up with atheism, materialism, naturalism, or some other equally undesirable philosophical position. In these circumstances, attempting to make fine distinctions about the merits and demerits of the enemy positions seemed likely to confuse the faithful about essentials. It seemed better to stick to the condemnation of manifest errors and wrongs.

The high point of this policy was Pius IX's *Syllabus of Errors* (1864), with its famous final condemnation of the proposition that the Pope should be reconciled with "liberalism, progress and modern civilisation". Pius IX meant civilisation and progress as continental liberalism understood them: no divine revelation, no religious influence on government or in education, legalisation of divorce, expulsion of religious orders, conscription of seminarians in order to destroy vocations, confiscation of Church property.

★   ★   ★

With the death of Pius IX came the first policy change. In Leo XIII, Pius's successor, the Church received a Pope sympathetic to some kind of coming to terms with contemporary ideas for the first time since Pius VII had tentatively acknowledged the possibility of baptising the principles of 1789 shortly after his election in 1803, and Pius IX had trifled with liberal theory and practice during the first two years of his pontificate (1846–8). The burned fingers which the latter pontiff received in the course of his experiments explain his determination not to repeat them.

Among the more conspicuous signs of Leo XIII's change of policy were his decision to open the Vatican archives to the world's scholars, and his call to French Catholics to accept the Third Republic as a legitimate government. The call was not well received by many of the children of the Church's eldest daughter.

In 1879, at the request of the Duke of Norfolk, Leo made Newman a cardinal, an indirect way of removing doubts about his theology, which would have included his theories about the development of doctrine and the role of the laity.

The first encyclical of Leo's reign, *Aeterni Patris* (1879), was devoted to "the restoration of Christian philosophy". By Christian philosophy he meant the philosophical realism of the high middle ages, of which St. Thomas Aquinas is regarded as the greatest exponent. For Pope Leo, a lover of philosophy as well as a skilled diplomat, sound philosophy was the necessary starting point for any successful grappling with contemporary ideas and ideologies. To this end he encouraged the foundation of the higher institute of philosophy at the Catholic university of Louvain in Belgium, under the direction of Msgr. (later Cardinal) Mercier. A restoration was necessary because the scholastic and Thomist traditions were considered to have been distorted by the introduction of alien philosophical ideas during the 16th and 17th centuries. The editing and publication of accurate texts of St. Thomas was part of the restoration.

Louvain, swept away during the revolution and re-founded in 1834, was by now the chief centre of Catholic scholarship in Europe outside the German universities. Although the institute of philosophy subsequently interpreted the philosophy of St. Thomas in a way with which it is hard to think Leo XIII would have sympathised, the Pope's support for the "restoration of Christian philosophy according to the mind of St. Thomas", the sub-title of *Aeterni Patris*, can be seen as providential. Catholic scholars who have tried to come to terms with contemporary philosophy without their feet firmly planted in Christian philosophical realism, have nearly all been swept away in the powerful currents of German subjectivism.

Later came the encyclical *Rerum Novarum* (1891), on the rights and duties of capital and labour, the first of the modern papal "social encyclicals". Written at the urging of leaders of the social movement, like Bishop Ketteler and Cardinal Manning, its doctrine of co-operation, "capital needs labour, and labour needs capital", was the Church's answer to Marx's doctrine of social progress through class warfare. It laid the foundations for the social teaching of the popes of the 20th century.

However, Leo XIII's change of policy was no naïve "opening to the world" of the kind favoured by modernism. He was no less aware than his predecessors of the problems raised by the new learning and of the need to mark out the danger zones. Nor, despite his diplomatic tact, was his pontificate without political troubles. The campaigns against the Church, launched by the recently founded German imperial government under Bismarck, and the statesmen running the new united Italy during the early 1870s, persisted; and in 1877, when deputies of liberal-masonic affiliation won control of the French Republic, that government too embarked on an aggressively anti-Catholic policy.[4]

Meanwhile, the movement for intellectual and cultural *aggiornamento* was growing in strength and becoming more consolidated.

In the late 1870s the Church realised that she was not going to recover control of the universities in the foreseeable future, but that to reply effectively to the intellectual attacks on her beliefs she must train scholars capable of meeting the masters of the new historical scholarship and philosophy on their own ground. A group of French bishops set about founding five Catholic institutes of higher studies or free universities (the Instituts Catholiques) at Paris, Toulouse, Lille, Angers and Lyons.

Other centres of Catholic scholarship in France and the Low countries at this time were the Jesuit houses of studies in Paris and at Fourvière outside

Lyons, and the Jesuit College of St. Michael in Brussels. The latter, whose members are known as the Bollandists after one of the college's founders, had been established in the 17th century to collect and edit the sources for the lives of the saints. Dispersed, when the Jesuits were suppressed in 1773, and coming together again for the same purpose after the restoration of the Society of Jesus in 1814, the Bollandists had been applying the historical-critical method to their work with increasing rigour.[5]

A series of international congresses for Catholic scholars organised by Msgr. d'Hulst, rector of the Paris Institute between 1888 and 1900 also helped to consolidate the movement. There were six congresses in all: at Paris in 1888, 1891 and 1892, at Brussels in 1894, at Fribourg in 1897, and at Munich in 1900. They enabled scholars who had hitherto only known each other through their books or by letter to meet and talk informally. Their object was, to use their own words, "the reform or renewal of Catholic studies". By this they meant a greater use of the critical method in Bible study and Church history, acceptance of a greater or lesser number of the higher critics' conclusions, and admission of "modern philosophy" into the curriculum of Catholic universities and seminaries in place of, or alongside, the reigning scholasticism.

These were the circumstances in which modernism made its first appearance in the Catholic Church. The *aggiornamento* was about to give birth to its illegitimate child. But, as a system of ideas, modernism was not a Catholic invention. Its foundations had been laid a good sixty years earlier in Germany when Lutheran scholars started applying the critical method to the Bible. Why were the results to be so devastating? To answer this question, we must first say something about Bible study in general.

Notes to Chapter Sixteen

[1]   Rops, *The Church in an Age of Revolution*, Dent, London, 1965, p. 202.

[2]   Msgr. Eugene Kevane has suggested that the cases of Hermes and Günther should be seen as a kind of curtain-raiser to Catholic modernism. See his *Creed and Catechetics*, Westminster, Maryland, p. 279.

[3]   Old Catholics, a fusion of two schismatic groups: the Jansenists of the "Church of Utrecht" who broke with Rome in 1724, and the groups of Catholics who left the Church after the definition of papal infallibility in 1870.

[4]   Bismarck's campaign, known as the *Kulturkampf*, aimed at the complete subjection of Church to state. The need to ensure the unity of the new German empire was the supposed justification. Catholic resistance led Bismarck to reach an agreement with

Leo XIII, by which the laws were modified. The campaign in France reached its climax between 1901–4 with the suppression of religious orders, the closing of Catholic schools, and the wholesale confiscation of Church property.

[5]   The Society was suppressed by Clement XIV under pressure from the the kings of France, Spain, Portugal, and Naples, and their Voltairean ministers. The Empress Maria Theresa, hitherto pro-Jesuit, but influenced by her chancellor Kaunitz, remained neutral.

Chapter Seventeen

ENTER MODERNISM

The Bible, the Word of God in human speech, is not like a manual of instructions – though it has often been treated like that. While most of it is straightforward enough, there are also many passages whose meaning is far from immediately self-evident. This is why Bible study has a history going back to Old Testament times.

The obscurities are basically of three kinds.

The first are due to mistakes by copyists. In the transmission of the manuscripts down the ages, the attention of the copyists sometimes wandered, or they added comments in the margin which later became incorporated in the text. As a result, the surviving manuscripts contain numbers of variant readings. The kind of scholarship that tries to determine which of these different readings comes nearest to the original is called textual criticism. It is largely a matter of comparing manuscripts to determine which seems most reliable.[1]

It is not difficult, I think, to see why God, in his providence, allowed the texts to become corrupted in this way. Had he prevented it, had he ensured that the thousands of copyists working over two to three millennia had never made a mistake, the Bible would so obviously be a work of divine origin that faith would no longer be a free act. The variant readings are never sufficient to make the main substance of the biblical books uncertain. They only affect particular sentences or phrases.

Obscurities of the second kind flow from the human limitations and character traits of the inspired human authors. While ensuring that they wrote what he wanted, God did so through the medium of their particular personalities and styles of writing and the kinds of literary composition characteristic of their age. Since they were writing a long time ago, they, not surprisingly, used modes of expression or referred to events and things sometimes beyond the comprehension of later readers.

Difficulties arising from this second class of causes are resolved, in so far as they can be, by the study of ancient languages, history, archaeology, and literary forms or *genres* (not to be confused with "form criticism"). Are some words to be taken literally or metaphorically? Is a certain book or passage intended to be history in the strict sense, or an allegory or parable, or is it some combination of the two? The search is for what the human author intended to say and how. This is called "the literal sense".

These first two forms of Bible study simply prepare the ground for what in the Church's eyes has always been the most important branch; the study of the religious significance or theological meaning of the texts.

Obscurities in this field are due to the mysterious nature of the subject matter, or, according to St. Augustine, are deliberately put there by the divine author himself. "The Sacred Books inspired by God were purposely interspersed by him with difficulties both to stimulate us to study and examine them with close attention, and also to give us a salutary experience of the limitations of our minds and thus exercise us in proper humility".[2] God does not disclose the full meaning of what he is saying to mere cleverness or sharp wits.

Most of the problems connected with these three branches of Bible study were familiar to the scholars of the ancient world, with the school of Antioch concentrating on the literal meaning and those of Alexandria on possible symbolic or "spiritual" meanings. The critical approach was not unknown either. Origen and St. Jerome, for instance, on the basis of internal evidence, doubted whether the Epistle to the Hebrews was really by St. Paul.[3] But whatever the problems, down to 200 years ago the end in view was always the same: to strengthen belief, deepen understanding and increase love of God.

Since around 1800, on the other hand, "advanced" biblical scholarship has followed a markedly different course with the precisely opposite results. The critical method has been given pride of place over every other approach; attention has focused on technical rather than spiritual questions (when and in what circumstances were the books written), with a high percentage of those trying to answer the questions losing most of their beliefs in the process. This is a plain historical fact which receives surprisingly little attention. Does it mean that the Bible cannot stand up to close examination? No. We have to distinguish between the method and the spirit in which it is used, or between the critical method and the critical movement.

That the critical method, once formulated, would be applied to the Bible was more or less bound to happen, but it was clearly a much more sensitive business than applying it to other historical documents, seeing that implicit in its use was the assumption that the origin of at least some of the books would turn out not to be what had hitherto been thought.

The method also carries with it a number of temptations. Experts like to exercise their skills. But if a text is the work of a single author, without additions or interpolations and written when it was thought to have been, there is nothing for the critic to do. The method, of its nature, therefore carries within it a kind of bias against single authorship. There will be a tendency to see any ancient text as necessarily a patchwork of literary fragments put together by groups of editors at some considerable time after the events described, which is different from recognising, as has always been done, that the biblical authors, like other writers about past events, when not writing about events they had themselves taken part in, depended on external sources. We can see the tendency at work in 19th-century Homeric studies, where it came to be more or less taken for granted that any work before the fifth or sixth century A.D. must be of composite authorship. Homer's very existence was doubted, and the authorship of the Iliad and Odyssey assigned to a mob of Greek poets spanning several centuries. Since then Homeric studies have changed course. A real Homer is credited with the bulk of the epics.[4] But there has been no such change of course in advanced biblical scholarship.

Another temptation will be to try to ape the exact sciences by assigning a certainty to conclusions, which, because of the nature of the subject matter, can only be conjectural.[5] Nevertheless, as we have already said, there is nothing objectionable about the method itself. The Church has approved it, and its use by biblical scholars with faith and a sense of proportion has thrown light on numbers of incidental scriptural obscurities.

The critical movement is another matter. Although forerunners like the 17th-century French Oratorian priest Richard Simon and the 18th-century French physician Jean Astruc were Catholics, we can take as the movement's starting point the publication of *The Wolffenbuttel Fragments* (1774–1778) by the German Lutheran dramatist and writer Lessing. The "fragments" were actually extracts from an unpublished manuscript by the rationalist scholar Reimarus, which Lessing pretended he had found in the royal Hanoverian library at Wolffenbuttel. A few years later, Gottfried Eichorn, the Lutheran professor of oriental languages at Jena (and subsequently Göttingen) published his *Introductions* to the Old and New Testaments (1780–1783 and 1804–1812), and from then on the movement was dominated by scholars whose conclusions about the time and the way the biblical books were written were influenced as much by philosophical assumptions and cultural prejudices as by concrete evidence.

Their principal assumption was that supernatural phenomena like miracles and prophecy are impossible, and therefore a large part of the Bible must be folklore. They also tended to see people in the past as necessarily inferior, uninterested in objective truth and incapable of transmitting facts accurately, while regarding priests as by nature deceitful and only interested in the maintenance of their collective authority. Evidence that the art of writing was practised by the Hebrews at least by the time of the Exodus, and of the capacity of non-literate peoples to orally transmit religious traditions faithfully over long periods of time was either downplayed or ignored.[6] These assumptions had in most cases already been made before they set to work.

The Pentateuch and Gospels were the main objects of attention. The crucial question about the composition of the Pentateuch is not "When were the books written or put together in the form we now have them?" but "Was the information they contain, whether recorded by Moses or others, transmitted accurately down the centuries?"

The crucial question about the composition of the Gospels is "Were they, or were they not, written by eye-witnesses, or by men with more or less direct access to eye-witnesses?"

To both questions the critics' conclusions tended towards a negative answer.

If Moses existed, it was maintained, little could be known about him except that he was neither the Pentateuch's author nor Israel's lawgiver. The Pentateuch was put together after the Exile out of four collections of documents and oral traditions, the earliest written four or five hundred years after Moses' death, with the books of the Law coming last. *Deuteronomy* had been composed at the time of King Josiah's religious reform (640–609). The clergy responsible pretended they had found the book in a part of the temple undergoing reconstruction. Before that the Jews had no fixed laws. They lived by a shifting mass of customary rules and regulations. Most of *Leviticus*, also the work of priests, was written during and after the Exile. But in order to convince the Jewish people that these two codes of laws were not the innovations they must have appeared to be, the post-exilic clergy combined them with two sets of oral and written traditions ("Yahwistic" and "Elohistic") about the supposed early history of the world and the Jewish people, now found in *Genesis, Exodus, Numbers* and *Joshua*.

Most of these ideas are associated with Julius Wellhausen (1844–1918). But long before he was born, Eichorn had been suggesting that *Leviticus*, for which he invented the name "priestly code", had a different origin from the other four books of the Pentateuch, while between 1802 and 1805, J. S. Vater had introduced the "fragment theory" of the suspended Scottish Catholic priest, Alexander Geddes. According to Geddes, the Pentateuch had been put together at the time of the Exile from 39 separate sources. In 1833, E. Reuss was teaching that no traces of the law can be found in the early prophetical and historical writings, consequently the law could not have existed in the early period of Jewish history. In a book published at Gotha in 1850, Eduard Riehm attributed *Deuteronomy* to the reign of King Manasses.

It was less easy to dismiss the New Testament miracles as myths and the Gospels as patchworks of folklore. Between the death of Christ and the writing of the Gospels there were no long centuries during which myths could form and orally transmitted information become garbled. The best the critics could do was date the Gospels as long after the death of the last eye-witnesses as possible.[7] This in a sense is what a great part of New Testament scholarship outside the Catholic Church has ever since been about.

For Reimarus the New Testament miracles were due to conscious deception. In the case of the Resurrection, the apostles simply stole the body, then lied about it. (Reimarus also seems to have been the first modern scholar to present Christ as a political agitator.) Less crude were the theories of critics like Semler (d. 1791) and Paulus (d. 1803). They attributed the miracles to natural causes misunderstood by the witnesses. The apostles thought they saw Christ walking on the water when he was actually walking on the lake-shore. But if this was the way Christianity began (lies or poor eyesight), how do we explain its phenomenal expansion and later triumph? Efforts to answer this question took a more sophisticated philosophical form.

The leader of this new school of thought, Ferdinand Christian Baur, founder of the Tübingen school, side-stepped the question as to what prompted the apostles to invent the myths, or give them the form they did. He concentrated on the way the myths developed. The rise of Christianity was explained in terms of Hegel's theory that progress takes place through the clash of contradictory ideas.

According to Baur, a conservative Jewish party under St. Peter and St. James (thesis) came into conflict with the Gentile-oriented party under St. Paul (antithesis). The eventual result was a compromise (synthesis) from which sprang the Catholic Church. St. Matthew's and St. Mark's gospels represent the conservative view, St. Luke's gospel and St. Paul's epistles that of the innovators, and the "Johannine writings" (not from the pen of St. John) the standpoint of the party of compromise. Baur attributed the bulk of the New Testament to the late second century. He was also one of the first critics to regard the Gospels as primarily a record of the early Christians' collective thinking rather than a record of events and facts. However, he was at least honest enough to admit that if the Gospels were written by eye-witnesses or the friends of eye-witnesses, his theories fell to the ground.

But how, asked Bruno Bauer, another critic of the period, can a collective consciousness produce a connected narrative? A good question. However Bauer (with an "e") was even more radical than Baur (without an "e"). For Bruno Bauer, Christianity originated with the author of St. Mark's Gospel, an

Italian living in the Emperor Hadrian's time, who never intended his book to be anything but a work of fiction. Nevertheless, the idea got about that the hero was a real person, a sect of admirers formed, and the other New Testament books followed. Bauer eventually lost his teaching post.

Such, roughly, were the beginnings of the biblical critical movement. The Bible, it would seem, is like an atomic reactor. Anyone working on it without the protective coating of prayer and reverence rapidly has his faith burned to cinders.

This is not the place to consider to how many of the theories we have been describing contemporary scholarship still attaches weight. Here we are only concerned with the immediate results.

At first sight it may not seem to matter much when or by whom the biblical books were written, provided they are still believed to be inspired by God, in the sense intended by him. It is true, however, that most men and women will, rightly or wrongly, assume that the greater the span of time between the occurrence of an event and its being recorded in writing, the less likely the record is to be true.[8] It was therefore not long before the readers of Reimarus, Eichorn and their successors were believing the Bible to be largely a work of fiction too, the critics' immense erudition being the principal factor enabling them to carry the day. Their readership included growing numbers of Lutheran pastors, who were simultaneously being exposed to Kant's idea that God's existence could no longer be proved from his works.

Seeing that, as Lutherans, they believed neither in an infallible Church nor a tradition complementary to Scripture, there seemed no longer to be any reliable basis for belief. Religion appeared to be at its last gasp, and for many it was in fact so. Most of the fathers of modern German atheism, like Feuerbach, the forerunner of Karl Marx, began life as Lutheran theological students.

However, men can rightly want to go on believing in God even when they are unable to answer the formal objections to belief, and so it often was in this case. The situation was saved for the poor victims of Reimarus' scepticism, Eichorn's doubts, and Kant's agnosticism – or they thought it had been – by the Lutheran theologian Friedrich Schleiermacher.

★   ★   ★

Schleiermacher (1768–1834), a leading figure in the German romantic movement, had likewise had his belief in the reliability of Scripture and the value of natural theology undermined by Eichorn and Kant, but he thought he had discovered a way out of his impasse.

His message was roughly this: "Take heart. All is not lost. Religion does not need outside evidence to justify its existence. Religion is not knowledge, whether in the form of creeds, doctrines or the content of sacred books. It does not need philosophical reflection either. The essence of religion is piety, and piety is feeling. If you have a feeling of dependence on God you have all that is necessary to make you a member of the worldwide 'communion of saints' or company of the truly religious. The separate beliefs and practices of the various religions scattered through time and space are simply different ways, all more or less valid, of cultivating and expressing this fundamental instinct or attitude, which by itself is sufficient".[9]

Such was the tenor of the book which first made Schleiermacher famous: *On Religion – Addresses to its Cultured Despisers* (1799).

Equating religion and feeling had of course long been a feature of certain kinds of Protestantism, not least with the Moravian brethren, one of whose schools Schleiermacher had attended as a boy. But no professor of theology had hitherto denied the Bible and creeds any objective value, or made feeling – even if it was a feeling of absolute dependence on God – the sole substance of Christianity.

In 1811, Schleiermacher, who had been teaching at Halle, was offered the chair of theology at the recently founded university of Berlin, a post he held until 1830, and in 1821 and 1822 he published in two parts the other book on which his fame chiefly rests, *The Christian Faith*.

In *The Christian Faith*, in spite of its title, Schleiermacher does not retreat from his previous position. Christianity remains only one of many expressions of the feeling of dependence or "God-consciousness". But he tries to show why it is the best expression so far: Christ was the man in whom God-consciousness reached the highest intensity. Christ was not God. He did not found a Church. But the followers who naturally gathered round so remarkable a man received the impress of his personality, his special way of feeling dependence on God, and later, by forming themselves into a permanent community were able to transmit his special way of feeling or personhood down the ages. We do not know how many, if any, of the words attributed to Christ by the Gospels actually come from him. But each Christian receives the impress of Christ's way of feeling, by living and experiencing the sense of absolute dependence within the Christian community.

What differentiates the Christian religious consciousness from other forms of religious consciousness, and makes it superior to them, is the sense of having been redeemed from sin by Christ. This does not mean that Christ paid the debt for mankind's sins by his death on Calvary. Such a notion borders on magic. Redemption means that by receiving the impress of Christ's personhood, the Christian is better able to overcome sin (or whatever is an obstacle to the feeling of absolute dependence) and reach the highest level of God-consciousness of which he is capable.

One is inclined to agree with Karl Barth a century later that a characteristic note of Schleiermacher is an astonishing self-assurance. Schleiermacher is the real founding father of modernism. With Schleiermacher, everything essential to modernism has arrived. Radical biblical scholarship destroys belief. There follows a desperate attempt to construct a gimcrack religious shelter out of the ruins with the help of some form of modern philosophical subjectivism. This in turn leads to the positing of the two fundamental modernist theses. First, since there is no reliable external source of religious knowledge, it can only be found in personal experience (early modernists inclined to stress individual experience, today's modernists communal experience). Secondly, doctrines – those at least which are found "difficult", or, as would be said today, "lacking in credibility" – should not be regarded as statements of fact, but symbolic expressions of personal experience. Supernatural happenings, like the parting of waters at the Red Sea or the Resurrection, take place in people's minds or imaginations, never in the real world.

Personal experience is therefore the judge before which every objective statement of belief, whether in the Bible, the creeds, or any other source, will have to justify itself. If a teaching finds an echo in personal experience it can be accepted, if not, it should be left on one side or rejected. That is why, in *The Christian Faith*, Schleiermacher relegates the Trinity to an appendix: "What is not directly given in Christian consciousness", as a contemporary admirer of Schleiermacher puts it, "is of no primary concern to faith". We can have a feeling of sinfulness (concupiscence), or of having had our sins forgiven (redemption). These ideas are therefore "meaningful", but we no more feel that there are three persons in the One God, than that there are four, five or six.

Schleiermacher stands at the turning point in the history of Protestantism where the fierce certainties of Luther, Calvin and the other reformation patriarchs start to crumble, and doctrine or any clear statement of belief comes to be seen as something repulsive, something that, instead of giving light to the mind, weighs on it like a sack of cement which the mind wants to throw off.

As the 19th century proceeds, this turning away from doctrine will become first a flight, then a stampede, and finally a Gadarene rush, until in the mid–20th century it hits the rocks at the bottom of the cliff in the patronising agnosticism of Bultmann and the barely disguised unbelief of Tillich. Catholics swept into the stampede usually express their dislike of religious certainty with the lament "Oh, no! Not another infallible doctrine".

The one interesting feature of Schleiermacher's theology, from the Catholic standpoint, is his shift of attention away from the Bible to the "Christian community". What Schleiermacher meant by that term is not what Catholics mean. Nevertheless he reintroduced into Protestantism as a whole an awareness of the Church as a factor in Christianity of at least equal importance with the Bible. The Bible might be untrustworthy. But the Christian community with its personal experiences was an indisputable past and present fact.

Notes to Chapter Seventeen

¹ The term "higher criticism" was reserved for analysing texts, whether biblical or profane, in order to elucidate their authorship, date and meaning. The higher critics regarded textual criticism as a lower branch of scholarship.

² Quoted by Pius XII, *Divino Afflante Spiritu*, 47.

³ For Origen's doubts, see Eusebius, *Hist. Eccles.*, 6.25, 11–13. For St. Jerome's: *Eph.* 129. C.S.E.L. 55169.

⁴ See *Geschichte der Griechischen Literatur*, Franke Verlag, Bern, 1963 (English translation 1966) by Albin Lesky, professor of Greek, University of Vienna.

⁵ Some examples will help to illustrate the difficulty of assessing the significance of stylistic differences. (a) Dr Johnson's two accounts of his journey to the Western Isles – one in letters written on the spot, the other in book form published after his return – are so unalike in style that, in Macaulay's opinion, if we did not know otherwise, we should find it hard to credit that they were written by the same man. (b) The 17th-century mystic St. Margaret Mary Alacoque was ordered by her superiors to write her memoirs. The result was found too unpolished for the intended readership, so they were rewritten in a style suited to the Grand Siècle. Should we infer from this that St. Margaret Mary had nothing to do with them? (c) There are versions of Chaucer in contemporary English. If these alone were to survive, what conclusions would be drawn about their authorship? The style of a text can belong to a period later than that of the author, with the content remaining essentially his product.

⁶ See Ricciotti, *History of Israel*, Vol. 1, Milwaukee 1955, who cites a succession of cases where texts of enormous length have been handed down orally, with apparently little if any alteration, for centuries. See also William Dalrymple, *City of Djinns*, HarperCollins, 1996. According to this author, in India today there are still "bards" who can recite from memory the whole of the *Mahabharata*, an epic longer than the Bible.

[7] In taking this line, the critics were making, even by their own standards, an illegitimate inference; namely that the books of the New Testament were necessarily formed in the same way as those of the Old Testament as though literary composition and culture had remained unchanged between the period of Sennacherib or Cyrus and the age of the early Caesars. In fact, after two centuries of debate, there seems to be no compelling reason not to accept the already ancient tradition enshrined in the *History* of Eusebius of Caesarea (264–340), that the Gospels were written by the four Evangelists at roughly the time and in the way always believed. Justin Martyr (100–165) calls them the "Memoirs of the Apostles". Vatican II affirms both their "apostolic origin" and "historicity". (*Dei Verbum* 18 & 19). How could St. John have recalled lengthy speeches like Our Lord's at the Last Supper? We have only to recall similar feats of memory on the part of Macaulay and Mozart to realise it is entirely possible even without special divine assistance.

[8] It is now common, in Catholic Bible study groups and popular commentaries, to hear the *Exodus* miracles described as merely literary devices used by the author to convey the idea of God's power. See, for example, *A Catholic Guide to the Bible*, Oscar Lukefahr C.M., Liguori Publications, Liguori, MO.

[9] Livingston, *Modern Christian Thought*, Macmillan, New York, 1971, pp. 96–113.

Chapter Eighteen

DRAMATIS PERSONAE

In the Catholic Church, the first modernist outbreak ran from about 1875 to 1910, and, unlike the eruption after Vatican II, was confined to the well-educated. France, Italy and England were the countries mainly affected. What came about was one of those intellectual brotherhoods of like-minded men which seem to arise spontaneously; men who are reading the same books, thinking the same thoughts, swimming in the same sea of ideas.

England's part in the drama is surprising, considering how few Catholics she had. It can perhaps be explained by the prestige she enjoyed as head of a world empire, and the fact that modernism already had a hold on that empire's established church. The relatively modest part played by Germany is even more puzzling, given the dependence of modernism on German scholarly and philosophical ideas.

The most active figure was Baron Friedrich von Hügel, a naturalised British subject, Austrian by birth, who lived most of his later life in England.

Highly cultivated, widely read, a prolific writer of books on mysticism and the spiritual life, a devotee of Schleiermacher, von Hügel devoted himself to putting priests and laymen with doubtful or extreme ideas in touch with each other, encouraging them to persist in their work when they showed signs of flagging, and generally trying to keep them together as a group. No doubt he sincerely wanted to bring about a spiritual and intellectual revival, but too much according to his own ideas.

As a writer, he has always enjoyed a considerable reputation among cultivated English Catholics and Anglicans, some minimising his modernism, others being unaware of it. Misunderstandings are largely due, I think, to his strange and bland (one is tempted to say, intellectually slippery) personality. In addition to writing, he devoted a considerable amount of time to acting as a spiritual guide to troubled souls.

Exactly what he believed at different moments between 1880 and 1910 is not easy to determine. But that he can be classified as a modernist, at least during this period, is beyond dispute. Fr. George Tyrrell, after listening to him talking one evening about religion, summarised his viewpoint thus: "Nothing is true, but the sum total of nothings is sublime".[1] Although Tyrrell was obviously exaggerating, the testimony of other contemporaries is not dissimilar.

According to one of his closest friends, Professor Clement Webb, von Hügel did not subscribe to the doctrine of a "kernel" or "hard nucleus" of revealed truth, which for believers must be beyond criticism, and "was to the end wholly impenitent in his adherence to modern critical views of the sacred books".

Maude Petre, herself deeply involved in the movement, was of the same opinion. Without the Baron, she wrote to Alec Vidler, "Fr. Tyrrell would have been a spiritual and moral *pioneer* (sic), but not strictly a Modernist". In spite of all this, von Hügel was rather conspicuously pious, to the surprise of his more logical French friends.[2]

Although he cannot be called the movement's leader, his knowledge of languages, social position, and financial independence did enable him to act as its impresario in a way that would have been impossible for any of the other members. Vidler calls him the movement's "chief engineer", while von Hügel's contemporary, the French liberal protestant Paul Sabatier, referred to him as its "lay bishop". In particular he helped to keep the French, Italians and English in touch with what was going on in German historical and biblical scholarship. He thus gave the movement a cohesion it might not otherwise have had, and without which the measures taken by St. Pius X to put an end to it might have been unnecessary.

Msgr. d'Hulst's congresses also unwittingly helped to consolidate the movement. Participants with modernist inclinations discovered there were more people inclining to their way of thinking than they had realised.

Von Hügel was never publicly reproved, but the censure and excommunication of some of his friends came as a shock, suggesting that he perhaps only half understood what he was involved in. Before his death in 1925, he seems to have returned to more Catholic views. Perhaps his piety – his daily saying of the rosary and visits to the Blessed Sacrament – was responsible.

Of the other key figures, the scripture scholar, Alfred Loisy, (1857–1949) is probably the best known. An exceptionally bright seminary student, and, like von Hügel, pious to match, he was sent by his bishop, the Bishop of Chalons, to complete his studies at the Institut Catholique in Paris. After a brief spell as a parish priest, he returned in 1881 to become lecturer in Hebrew and then professor of biblical exegesis. Many years later (1930), when he came to write his memoirs, he admitted that, in spite of his repeated claims to the contrary, he had begun to lose his faith around 1880. About the time he took up his lectureship at the Paris *Institut*, he had started attending Renan's lectures at the Collège de France.

Fr. Laberthonnière, an Oratorian, and Edouard Leroy, a layman, were

philosophers. Fr. Hébert was head of the Ecole Fénelon, a well-known Paris-
ian boys' school; his interests included philosophy, scripture and history. Fr.
Houtin, a teacher of history in the diocesan school at Angers, became a self-
appointed and perhaps not very reliable historian of the movement, and the
Protestant Paul Sabatier just referred to, author of a highly successful life of
St. Francis of Assisi, gave support from without.

The chief Italian modernists were Frs. Minnocchi, Bonaiuti and Semaria,
and the novelist Antonio Fogazzaro. Minnocchi and Bonaiuti edited reviews.
Semaria, a member of the Barnabite order, was a scripture scholar. As a successful writer, Fogazzaro was able to introduce the general public to the
modernist religious outlook. The hero of his novel, *Il Santo*, did for modernism what the Vicaire Savoyard of Rousseau's novel *Émile* had done for the
18th-century Enlightenment – provide the movement with an ideal holy man.

In England, Fr. Tyrrell, northern Irish and protestant by birth and upbringing, had entered the Society of Jesus in 1880 about a year after becoming
a Catholic at the age of eighteen. Ordained in 1891, he worked a few years in
a parish before being put to teaching philosophy at Stonyhurst, the Jesuit
college and boys' school. The turning point in his life was his meeting with
von Hügel in the mid-90s. Von Hügel introduced him to the writings of
Schleiermacher, Loisy, Bergson and Blondel. Before their meeting he had
been an enthusiastic Thomist, but, with characteristic abruptness, became
henceforward an equally ardent devotee of religious and philosophical subjectivism and Loisy's scepticism about the Bible. Among his friends he had a
reputation as a mystical thinker and reformer of the philosophy of religion.[3]

In both Loisy and Tyrrell there was a strong dash of the *enfant terrible* – the
gifted child with an uncontrolled urge to shock, attract attention and annoy
the grown-ups.

These were the men who made a noise; who were prepared to say openly
what others were only thinking, or to take to their limits and beyond, ideas
which these others were only beginning to touch.

More worldly-wise men, like the English liturgical scholar, layman and
convert, Edmund Bishop, only expressed their views in letters to friends but
otherwise lay low. The abbé Brémond, historian of 17th-century French
spirituality, another religious *enfant terrible*, darted in and out of the game,
but mostly ran up and down the touchline keeping out of serious trouble.
Meanwhile the French Church historian, Msgr. Louis Duchesne (1843–
1922), could be said to have sat in the grandstand, watching the sport without
getting sunburnt or wet, at one moment egging a man on, at others crying
a warning.

This famous, enigmatic figure, who in 1877 became professor of Chur... history at the Paris *Institut,* was the first important French Catholic scholar to apply the principles of the higher criticism to ecclesiastical history in a thoroughgoing way. A whole generation of young Catholic scholars and teachers were trained by him. Loisy, his most gifted pupil, seems to have acquired from him his uncritical belief in the infallibility of the critical method.

For a time Duchesne's views led to his being suspended from his professorship. However, he recognised early on that the Church was not going to meet any of the modernists' demands and quickly shed any appearance of leadership. In 1897 he was made director of the Ecole Française in Rome (a government appointment), where he remained till his death. His apartment became a centre where dissatisfied visitors to the Eternal City could express their resentments against the Holy See or make it the butt of their wit. His reputation rests chiefly on his edition of the *Liber Pontificalis,* and his three-volume *History of the Early Church.*

Unquestionably learned, his attitude to the reigning authorities seems to have been mostly sardonic contempt. Hébert said that Duchesne helped him to see the "reasons" for not believing in the Resurrection. Duchesne later denied this. On his instructions, his papers were burned after his death. Loisy always stressed Duchesne's scepticism, but rather than a sceptic, the surviving letters suggest a man moving uneasily in a kind of no-man's-land between scepticism and faith. Here is part of a letter to Hébert, dated 18th January 1900, urging him not to give up the headship of the Ecole Fénelon:

> "Religious authority counts on its traditions and the most de-
> voted members of its personnel, who are also the least intelligent.
> What can be done? Endeavour to reform it? The only outcome
> of such attempts would be to get oneself thrown out of the
> window ... Let us then teach what the Church teaches ... We
> need not deny that in all this there is a large part of symbolism
> that calls for explanation. But leave the explanation to make its
> own way privately. It may be that despite all appearances the old
> ecclesiastical edifice is going one day to tumble down ... Should
> this happen, no one will blame us for having supported the old
> building for as long as possible." [4]

On the other hand, after Hébert's resignation, Duchesne urged him to take a country parish which he said would revive his faith, as he found that his own invariably was by his annual visits to Brittany. And in 1903 he was to write to Loisy: "On the whole, I do not think that Catholicism is irreconcilable with the kind of criticism you practise ... but I cannot see cardinals and theologians presiding over the feast you will serve up to them ... In fifty years' time, so I am told, everyone will find these ideas natural. Possibly – but will this 'everyone' still be Christian?" [5]

Finally in Msgr. Mignot, the Archbishop of Albi, the modernists had a cautious episcopal patron.

The philosopher Maurice Blondel (1861–1949) acted as an intermediary, trying to bring the wilder spirits back within bounds, while explaining to authority what the more moderate ones who were unjustly suspected of modernism were actually saying. Without subscribing to modernist principles himself, like others pressing for a "reform of Catholic studies", he sympathised with some of the modernists' practical aims, such as their demand for an end to the privileged position of scholastic philosophy.

According to Blondel, traditional metaphysics (classical Christian realism) "is impotent when it is a question of bringing modern spirits to Christianity ... If there is one conclusion to which modern philosophy attaches itself as a certainty, it is the idea, basically justifiable, that nothing can enter into a man which does not come from him".[6] Because of this, all future philosophy should start with some aspect of man's inner life. In other words, he was the first prominent Catholic to ask for what has come to be called a "shift to the human subject".

His own philosophy, which he, perhaps rather misleadingly, called a "philosophy of action", focused on our acts of choosing and willing. If we analyse what happens when we will something, he claimed, we inevitably arrive at the supernatural. The most minimal act of will is made with a view to some good, but no good achieved in this world exhausts the will's capacity for willing something more – a supreme good only found elsewhere. The natural order therefore presupposes the supernatural order, towards which the will has a natural tendency, as its necessary fulfilment.

Blondel named his method the "method of immanence". His aim was to undercut the materialism and atheism prevailing in the majority of French university philosophy departments. It was probably the term "method of immanence" and the assertion that for modern times this was the only effective philosophical method, which initially drew on him the suspicion of modernism. To his philosophical opponents it smelled of Kantian subjectivism. The idea that the natural order in some way requires the supernatural order for its completion or fulfilment was another philosophical and theological hot potato. In spite of this, at different periods of his life he was commended for his work and fidelity by Leo XIII, St. Pius X and Pius XII, and after his death acquired a positive admirer in John Paul II.

Blondel's theories about the relationship between the natural and super-natural orders ("the natural presupposes the supernatural"), taken up in the 1930s by Fr. de Lubac, were to become central to the new theology. In this respect, he is a key figure. His relationship to modernism anticipated that of the orthodox new theologians to neo-modernism; the relationship we have already seen of "This, yes, but not that; thus far, but no further".

Notes to Chapter Eighteen

[1] Alec Vidler, *A Variety of Catholic Modernists*, Cambridge University Press, 1970, p. 117. The author, an Anglican, who has written extensively on "Catholic" modernism, is far from unsympathetic to von Hügel. For the other figures mentioned in this chapter, see also, Jean Rivière, *Le modernisme dans l'église*, Paris 1929, the first in-depth study of the movement, and Michele Ranchetti, *The Catholic Modernists*, Oxford University Press, 1969.

[2] For Prof. Webb and Maude Petre, see Vidler, *op. cit.*, p. 111.

[3] Philosophy of religion: what used to be called natural theology.

[4] Vidler, *op. cit.*, p. 71. It is possible that by the "old building", Duchesne meant the Church as it was *then* run, not the Church as such.

[5] Ranchetti, *op. cit.*, p. 33.

[6] *Les premiers écrits de Maurice Blondel*, Paris 1956, quoted John K. Ryan, *Twentieth-Century Thinkers*, New York, 1967. However, a few decades later, Maritain's conversion was to falsify the dictum.

Chapter Nineteen

BELIEFS AND DISBELIEFS

How did Catholic modernism differ from the modernism of Schleiermacher and his followers?

Fundamentally they were the same. Radical biblical scholarship shook or destroyed belief, and some kind of philosophical subjectivism was then called in to shore up the ruins, with dogmas as symbolic expressions of personal experience. However, in the fifty years since Schleiermacher's death in 1834, there had been developments both in the critical movement and in philosophy, and some new arrivals of a different kind had made their appearance. Their impact gave "Catholic modernism" its somewhat different colouring or flavour. Of these new arrivals, "evolution" was by far the most potent.

Darwin and Evolution

By giving an apparently different account of the creation of species from the Bible, and a manifestly different account of the origin of men, Darwin's *The Origin of Species* (1859) and *The Descent of Man* (1871) seemed directly to challenge the Bible's truth and reliability. And since, by the same act, a number of fundamental doctrines constantly taught by the Church like original sin appeared to be called into question, belief in the Church as a trustworthy teacher also began to be shaken. If Adam and Eve, the Garden, and the Fall were myths and had to go, where did the process stop? A thread had been cut and the whole fabric of revelation seemed about to come apart.

As for the idea that living things came into existence through the interplay of accident (natural selection), it seemed to reduce God, when not extinguishing belief in him altogether, to a cold and remote First Cause and implicitly to repudiate his providence. What room was left for him to care about sparrows?

Finally, if the philosopher Herbert Spenser was to be believed, evolution was a universal law governing everything: life evolves, history evolves, civilisation evolves, religion evolves. Religion is perhaps after all just another natural phenomenon like music and dancing, a way in which man expresses himself.[1]

Although, in the destruction of belief, the part played by radical biblical scholarship was in the end to be greater, it took longer for the consequences to be felt. The effect of Darwin's books was instantaneous. For many of von Hügel's generation, of whom the young Teilhard de Chardin will be typical, those theories seemed to be empirically proven facts in terms of which the whole Catholic faith must be reinterpreted.

New Testament Studies

In this field the most momentous event since Schleiermacher's death had been the publication in 1835 of the *Leben Jesu* (Life of Jesus) by David Friedrich Strauss (1808–1874), a pupil of the critic Ferdinand Baur, who taught theology and philosophy at Tübingen before being compelled to retire to private life. *Leben Jesu* carried the critics' theories beyond the scholarly and clerical worlds to the general reading public. The novelist George Eliot translated it into English, and the Prince Consort Albert, Queen Victoria's husband, was an enthusiastic admirer. Strauss did for the Anglo-Saxon educated classes much what Voltaire had done in the previous century for educated Europeans of French culture.

For Strauss, the origin of the New Testament myths was no problem. The essence of religion is clothing universal spiritual truths or ideas in concrete imagery. In all religions, myth and fact are interwoven from the beginning, Christianity being no exception. Clothing ideas in myths was as natural to the early Christians as distinguishing myth from fact is natural to men today. Moreover, in the apostles' case, the work was already half done for them. They simply took over the myths about the Messiah current among the Jews at their time.

In this way Strauss presumably justified to himself his otherwise disingenuous claim that his assaults on the Gospels' historical value did not endanger Christian belief. "The supernatural birth of Christ, his miracles, his resurrection and ascension remain eternal truths, whatever doubts may be cast on their reality as historical facts." [2] In his last book, *The Old and the New Faith* (1872), he declared Christianity to be dead and called for a new religion built on art and science.

Just under thirty years after Strauss's *Leben Jesu*, Renan's *Vie de Jésus* (1863) brought the critical movement's doubts and denials to the French-speaking Catholic public.

What, I think, those doubts and denials chiefly show is that the path to unbelief has not been a linear one, starting with tentative inquiries, followed by serious suspicions, leading in turn to absolute conviction. Nothing said by

Bultmann or Tillich in the twentieth century would have shocked or startled the earliest members of the movement. The most extreme positions were taken from the start.

However, around 1850, a reaction set in. The more moderate critics may have been as little willing to believe in miracles as Reimarus, Eichorn, Baur or Strauss. But they were not prepared to see Christ vanish altogether in a mist of scholarly doubt. In their view, when the myths and miracles were stripped away, enough historical material remained in the gospels to construct a reasonably accurate picture of the kind of man Christ was and what he taught, or, as will from now on be said, to distinguish the "Jesus of history" from the "Christ of faith" (the product of early Christian imagination). The search for the historical Jesus had begun.

What the searchers with all their learning and labour eventually discovered was an ethical teacher like Confucius or Buddha preaching a simple religion of the heavenly Father's love and a kingdom of interior righteousness freed from dogmas and what were claimed to be Hellenistic philosophical accretions. Their view of Christ and Christianity, which was dubbed the "liberal" view, is now the "orthodoxy" of the 20th century's occasionally church-going Protestant. In the scholarly world it held the field from about the mid-1860s to the end of the century. The pillars of the liberal position were Albrecht Ritschl (1822–1889) and the famous Berlin court theologian and scholar Adolf von Harnack (1851–1930).

But by the 1890s the tide of opinion in the critical movement was turning again. A pamphlet (1892) by Johannes Weiss heralded the change. According to Weiss, who was teaching at Göttingen, the liberals' Jesus was an historical anachronism, the product of wishful thinking, not historical evidence. The liberals' Christ was an enlightened 19th-century Lutheran pastor dressed in first-century clothing. The totality of "reliable" gospel texts give us a quite different figure – a typical rabbi of the Jewish apocalyptic tradition, who believed in the rapid arrival of the end of the world and the inauguration of a supernatural new creation which his death would hasten. His world-view had passed away for good and all.

Albert Schweitzer (1875–1965) was to give these views their classic expression in his *Quest for the Historical Jesus* (1906), whose basic message was that the quest was over: as historical documents, the gospels were almost worthless. The critical movement had come full circle back to where it started.[3]

It was into these currents that von Hügel, Loisy and their associates were being swept in the 1890s.

Philosophy

Between 1890 and 1914 the fashionable philosophies in France were the *creative evolution* of Henri Bergson (1859–1941) and the *pragmatism* of the American William James (1842–1910) – neither of them directly in the German idealist tradition. The two philosophies complemented each other, the philosophers themselves becoming friends. Their success was partly due to their charm as speakers and writers, but still more to the fact that they were challenging the determinism and materialism of which the more refined elements of the European cultured classes were momentarily wearying. Both philosophers spoke well of religion, recognised some kind of "higher power", and insisted on the spirituality of the soul and the reality of free will. Believers of all varieties therefore welcomed them enthusiastically.

Bergson, who had first made his name in 1889 with his *Essai sur les données immédiates de la conscience*, became almost the object of a cult after the publication of his *l'Evolution créatrice* (1900). Had he not reconciled evolution and religion by giving evolution a mind (the *élan vital*)? Unfortunately, in the excitement of the moment many Catholics tended to overlook some of his ideas' more serious deficiencies.

Bergson's notions of creator, creation and creature were in fact deeply ambiguous. Nothing is ever completely made, but always on the way to being made, or if already made, made differently. This applies to the *élan vital* or vital impulse, Bergson's pantheistic "creator", as much as to his creatures. Being incomplete, the *élan vital* has need of its creatures both as objects of love and co-operators in the work of creation. It also creates without foresight or plan since these would limit its freedom, and what limits freedom kills life. Perpetual process and change are the necessary consequences.[4]

If all this had not been sufficiently appreciated before, that – for Bergson – was because European philosophy had overvalued the intellect. By cutting up reality's indivisible continuity into separate categories and things, the intellect obscures its fundamental nature, which can only be discovered by empathy or intuition. To know reality as it truly is we must sink ourselves in the flow of consciousness and the experience of duration. It is these which reveal that the substance of reality is change.

Bergson also set up a dichotomy between "closed" and "open", or static and dynamic, religion and morality. Closed or static religions and moralities depend on fixed beliefs, principles and practices. These may have a certain social usefulness, but basically impede the creativity and upward ascent of the vital impulse. Open and dynamic religion and morality are the work of free religious spirits like Christ and Buddha. Such free spirits, and their disciples (was Bergson thinking of Tolstoy?) can dispense with fixed beliefs and practices because they are in tune with the evolutionary creativity of the vital impulse. (In fact, if beliefs are true and practices good, one of the first things they do is protect religion and morals from becoming the playthings of private whim and personal eccentricity.)

While Bergson was providing his contemporaries with an evolutionary metaphysics, William James was supplying them with an evolutionary ethics. An experimental psychologist turned philosopher with a special interest in the practical consequences of religious belief and its accompanying phenomena, his *Principles of Psychology* had appeared in 1890, to be followed in 1902 by his much more widely read *Varieties of Religious Experience*.

The burden of the latter work is that, while some of the phenomena described can be put down to emotional disturbance or mental illness, it is reasonable to suppose that at times the believer or mystic was in touch with another order of reality. For the sake of convenience, James was prepared to call this other something "God". But he preferred to think of God, or "otherness", as something finite and limited rather than infinite and sovereign, and of the universe as in a state of being experimentally put together, since an omnipotent God with a pre-existing plan would mean a "dead, static universe".

However, for our present purposes, the important thing is James's view of truth. In James's philosophy an idea is true *not* when it corresponds with reality, but if (a) it is alive, or (b) has what appear to be beneficial results. An idea is alive when a lot of people believe in it, and beneficial when it makes them better, or happier, or gives them spiritual satisfaction. Belief in Moloch was therefore presumably once alive and in this sense "true". For the Canaanites, as they flung their babies into the furnace, Moloch worship was, as people now say, "meaningful". When there were no more Moloch worshippers, people having turned to other forms of spiritual satisfaction, the idea was dead and no longer true. Christian beliefs are true in so far as they make people unselfish or act as psychological stabilisers. The worth of ideas is to be judged by their "cash value". Such is the heart of his pragmatism.

(People who use the word truth in this way are not really talking about truth but about utility or human convenience, though they will mostly claim that what they see as useful is also good and right.)

Bergson's view of truth had equally unfortunate implications. Since everything that happens is part of reality as it makes itself, more or less anything can seemingly be justified.

Needless to say, neither philosopher acted strictly in accordance with the logic of his ideas. Both were thoroughly upright men. Their influence on the Catholic modernists will appear shortly.[5]

The Higher Criticism and Church History

By the 1880s the critical method applied to the records of the Church's past was generating the same doubts about the divine origin of the Church as its use on the Bible had been generating about the Bible's inspiration and inerrancy. The causes in this case were largely psychological.

From the time of the renaissance a crowd of part-time scholars, doctors, lawyers, monks, parish priests, eccentric nobles and country squires – along with professional historians – had, as never before, been searching libraries and lovingly collecting manuscripts dispersed by wars and revolutions. By the mid-19th century their labours, which are one of the glories of European civilisation, had produced an avalanche of specialised studies and rediscovered facts.

However, in any subject, the sudden appearance of a mass of new information can bring about a temporary increase of darkness rather than light, and something like this happened to Catholic scholars as they applied themselves to sorting and assessing the deluge of new documents and monographs about the Church's past. Rather as Christ's divinity became less visible under the blows and bruises of the Passion, so the Church's supernatural character started to fade from view as she was looked at through a thicker and thicker screen of natural and human appearances. "Behold the man", Pilate had cried to the crowds. "Behold the purely human institution", seemed to be the message of the mountain of historical records. There was also a temptation to adopt a neo-Protestant view of Church history; the true nature of the Church has been lost, but it can be reconstructed from the surviving documents – though fewer and fewer were being judged trustworthy.

The temptation to lose sight of the Church's supernatural dimension was aggravated by a factor of a different kind – the spirit of the German higher critics, the leaders in the field, who for the most part, when not Protestant, were unbelieving. By the mid-19th century they had turned the higher criticism into something like a religion and themselves into a ruling class able to batter down all but the toughest opponents with their erudition and self-assurance.[6] Because of their prestige, Catholic scholars were tempted to treat the Church's historical records, oral traditions and devotional life in the same iconoclastic spirit.

We have noted the influence of this aspect of the higher criticism on Döllinger, Acton and Duchesne (though, being French, Duchesne affected an amused Voltairean manner rather than the imperial style of the university autocrat). It also influenced the Bollandists, and left its mark on the Thurston-Butler *Lives of the Saints.*[7] The intentions were praiseworthy: to show that the Church is not afraid of genuine facts. Moreover, the facts in this area were not on the same level as those in the Bible. Divine revelation was not involved. But too often the authors left their readers with the impression that "science" was the protector and preserver of truth, while the Church was the mother of forgeries.

I am not suggesting that Catholic scholarship should be served up under an artificial coating of piety. But there are aspects of learned debate – the acid footnote, the sardonic aside, the coldly clinical approach – which may be appropriate for disputes about Ptolemaic tax records but become seriously harmful when holy things are at stake. The damage to the faith and reverence of the scholars themselves was often bad enough. When this spirit reached the non-scholarly, the consequences could be ruinous. The rough handling by Catholic scholars of the traditions relating to the origins of many French dioceses was one of the factors contributing to the abbé Houtin's loss of faith.

Historicism, the History of Dogma, and Doctrinal Development

The great increase in historical knowledge, by focusing minds on the factor of change, intensified the evolutionary climate of the age which in turn prepared the way for historical relativism or "historicism", whose chief representative at this period was the German philosopher and historian Ernst Troeltsch.

Historicism is not the same as being sensitive to the fact that most things, whether ideas, practices or institutions, come to fulfilment over the course of time, being to some degree both influenced by the times they exist through, while at the same time helping to shape them.

By historicism, I mean the notion that our thoughts and acts are largely or entirely determined by the period we live in. Our minds are incapable of reaching a kind of knowledge unconditioned by their times. The ever-moving times make men, ideas, and institutions what they temporarily are, before the never-ceasing river of time and change turns them into something different. Only the historian, for unexplained reasons, is assumed to be capable of standing outside the flux and forming a judgement which is not conditioned by his times.[8]

At the turn of the century, the scholars perhaps most subject to the seductions of historicism were the historians of dogma.

For the Church, the history of doctrine and dogma is the history of her ever-deepening understanding of divine revelation. When God committed his revelation to the care of the apostles and their successors, it was not in a neat tidy form, as we have already remarked in relation to the Bible. It was a cornucopian torrent in an almost bewildering variety of forms – history, prophecy, poetry, parable, proverb, law, letters, meditations, religious instruction, sacred rites, along with what Christ had told the apostles to do and teach and all they had learned through simply observing and living with Him. All this, if one can say so without irreverence, God poured into the Church's lap in what one can only call a vast confused heap. The main features stood out clearly enough. The rest was unmapped virgin forest. It was left to the Church, who is herself part of the revelation, to organise this vast accumulation (the "deposit of faith" as it is called), interpret it, and draw out its implications with the help of the Holy Spirit.

The catalyst for the process was to be ordinary human curiosity. Since the divine communication was not only largely unorganised, but was mainly about supernatural mysteries, it was natural that as soon as the faithful started telling the world about it, their hearers started asking questions. So did the faithful themselves. Thus was born Christian theology. Christian theology is the attempt to give as rationally intelligible an explanation of the different aspects of revelation as is compatible with the mysterious nature of what is being explained.

From the start, however, not all explanations proved satisfactory. Some the Church rejected as heretical. Those she approved became part of her official teaching (doctrine). Dogmas are simply doctrines that have been proclaimed with a greater degree of solemnity – usually because they have been challenged in some way.

This is why there is doctrine and dogma, why they have a history and why they develop. However, not all points of belief develop simultaneously, nor continuously. Development is not an "open-ended" process. Dogma is the end point of development in regard to a particular point or area of belief. The fact, for instance, that in the One God, there are three persons, one in substance and equal in majesty, is in itself incapable of further development, even if further light can be shed on subordinate aspects of the mystery. Around 1900, the question at issue was whether the history of doctrine was to be regarded as a development (the moving towards a deeper, fuller, clearer understanding of the meaning of a belief and its implications) or an evolution (a constant change of meaning). It is also the question at the heart of today's crisis.

Von Harnack dominated the field. His seven-volume *History of Dogma* (1894–99) presented that history as an evolution. The work also had a practical purpose: to liberate Christianity from dogma altogether, by showing how far Christian doctrine had deviated from the original meaning. The French Sulpician, Fr. Tixeront replied with his three-volume history from the Catholic standpoint (1904), and the Jesuit Fr. Jules Lebreton with his *Histoire des origines du dogme de la Trinité* (1910, 6th ed. 1927), but not before a number of Catholics had been influenced by von Harnack's view.

Comparative Religion

From the time Columbus discovered the Americas, the merchants, colonists and missionaries of the Spanish, Portuguese, Dutch, British and French empires had been providing the West with a knowledge of other peoples and religions such as it had never possessed before. The input reached its climax in the mid-19th century. The comparative study of religions was the result. By the 1890s one of its best known products, Sir James Frazer's now largely discredited study of primitive religion and magic, *The Golden Bough*, was replacing the Bible on the bedside tables of cultivated Anglo-Saxons.

The object was not to discover whether one religion rather than another was specially sanctioned by God, or which contained most truth. The aim was to determine what the beliefs and practices of each religion meant to its members, and to find psychological and other natural explanations for them. If in the process faith went into decline, it would seem to have been partly because common sense was affected too.

To conclude that because all religions have certain features in common (the members pray, fast, give alms, or offer sacrifice to an unseen Being or beings), therefore one of them cannot be unique, is like thinking that, because all houses have certain common features such as windows and doors, there is nothing special about the White House or Buckingham Palace. The common features are simply traces of the natural religious truths (the seeds of the Word we met with earlier), knowable in principle by all men, even if frequently distorted or lost from sight.

Students of comparative religion are easily led into regarding the boiled-down residue of these common features as the essence of religion, ending as devotees of some kind of one-world ethical monotheism towards which, they consider, the religious consciousness of mankind is evolving. This idea too made an important contribution to the development of early modernism.

Notes to Chapter Nineteen

[1] It is well to remember that Spenser propounded his evolutionary philosophy before Darwin published *The Origin of Species*.

[2] *Life of Jesus*, London 1906, xxx, quoted in Livingston, *op. cit.*

[3] But why should the texts used by Weiss and Schweitzer be considered more historical than those preferred by Ritschl and von Harnack? Weiss and Schweitzer were in fact just as selective as their opponents.

[4] Later, in censuring "immanentism", the Church would no doubt have Bergson as well as Hegel in mind.

[5] From the Catholic standpoint there is something mysterious about the providential role of thinkers like Bergson and James, whose writings led some towards the faith, others away from it. In his will, Bergson declared his moral adherence to Catholicism. He did not ask for baptism only because, as a Jew, he did not want to seem to be deserting his people at the height of the Nazi persecutions. For useful summaries of Bergson and James, see J. Macquarrie, *Twentieth-Century Religious Thought*.

[6] For protests by distinguished contemporary historians against the higher critics' overweening self-confidence, see Hodgkin, *Italy and her Invaders*, seven volumes, London 1892, and Freeman, *History of Sicily*, London 1881.

[7] See Feb. 5th, St. Agatha, where the accounts of her martyrdom are stated flatly to be "of no historical value", while the 1911 *Catholic Encyclopaedia* says of them that their "details have no historical credibility". This could mean one of three things. That the information is all false; but how can anyone know? That where there is no corroborative evidence, recorded matter is not to be considered historical; in this case much accepted history has to be jettisoned. Or that the content of the account seems to the authors improbable. But what may have seemed improbable to scholars living in the relative security of the early 20th century may well not seem improbable to generations familiar with the history of the Nazi and communist regimes. Indeed, the behaviour of St. Agatha's torturers has a decidedly contemporary ring. See also the martyrdom of a newly baptised American Indian chief, witnessed by the Jesuit St. Isaac Jogues in 1638. Had that chief's incredible sufferings been recorded of an early martyr, they would have assuredly been dismissed as fantasy. (*Saint Among Savages: the Life of Isaac Jogues*, Francis Talbot S.J., Image Books 1961, pp. 136–7; republished in 2002 by Ignatius Press, San Francisco).

[8] In *What is Christianity*, von Harnack had tried to reach the "essence" of Christianity. Troeltsch's final conclusion was that there is no such essence. Christianity is a formless historical process. "The essence of Christianity can be understood only as productive power ... to create new interpretations and adaptations." Livingston, *op. cit.*, p. 305.

Chapter Twenty

THE CRISIS

How much of what we have been describing in the last two chapters could the Church agree to? In particular, how many, if any, of the biblical critics' theories about the origin and dating of the biblical books were allowable – at least as hypotheses?

By the late 1880s, a number of Catholic biblicists were pressing the Church to abandon the Mosaic authorship of the Pentateuch; to allow that the flood was not of universal dimensions; recognise the second half of Isaiah as the work of a prophet living after the exile and therefore after the events it appeared to foretell; admit the dependence of the authors of the synoptic gospels on a vanished source document of unknown authorship, designated "Q"; permit the idea that St. John was not the author of the fourth Gospel, and that that Gospel was more "theology" than history.

In 1893 Leo XIII issued his encyclical on Bible study, *Providentissimus Deus*. It was the Church's first official response to the critical movement. In it the Pope called on Catholic scholars to answer the critics on their own grounds and with their own weapons. Nine years later, in 1902, he established the Pontifical Biblical Commission to give authoritative answers to questions about the Bible. In 1909 the Biblical Institute was established as a department of the Gregorian University in Rome for training teachers conversant with the new methods and problems. Meanwhile the French Dominicans under Fr. Marie-Joseph Lagrange had founded the Ecole biblique in Jerusalem (1890), and in 1892 started the *Revue biblique*.

But in von Hügel's circle there were deeper doubts.

In 1881, about the time he had taken up his lectureship at the Paris Institute, Loisy had started attending Renan's lectures at the Collège de France. "I instructed myself at his school," he later wrote, "in the hope of proving to him that all that was true in his science was compatible with Catholicism sanely understood".[1]

What a "sane understanding" meant for Loisy began to show in 1890. In that year he completed a thesis on the canon of the Old Testament (which books came to be held as divinely inspired, and why) that proposed a view of divine inspiration incompatible with that of the Church. This was followed by a history of the canon of the New Testament (1891) and a work on the early chapters of *Genesis* (1892) raising questions about their historicity. As a result, the students of St. Sulpice, the major seminary for the archdiocese of Paris, were forbidden to attend his lectures. To protect his professor, reassure those in authority, and defend a controlled use of the critical method, Msgr. d'Hulst, the rector of the Institut catholique, published an article entitled *La question biblique.* But it only attracted more attention to Loisy, and d'Hulst was forced to dismiss him.[2] The encyclical *Providentissimus Deus* appeared shortly afterwards. In 1900 Cardinal Richard of Paris condemned a series of articles by Loisy on the religion of Israel, whereupon the government, ever happy to embarrass the Church, offered him a post at the Ecole des hautes études (School of higher studies) at the Sorbonne.

Loisy was by this time a figure of major importance. Having been appointed chaplain to a convent of nuns at Neuilly just outside Paris, he had time to develop his ideas which were moving more and more in the direction of Weiss's and Schweitzer's. In 1902 he published *L'Evangile et l'église* (The Gospel and the Church). Purporting to be a critique of Ritschl's and von Harnack's scriptural "liberalism", he used it to expound his own much more radical views.

Loisy now saw Christ as an apocalyptic visionary, fallible in his knowledge and judgements, who had had no intention of founding a Church or teaching lasting truths. Since Christ clearly expected the instant end of the world, founding a Church would have been pointless. Christianity as we know it was the invention of the early Christians. Christ's achievement was launching a new religious ideal or spirit, which the Church incarnates and perpetuates. That is the value of the Church. But to survive, she must continually change the teaching in which that spirit finds expression in each generation as the world and men's experiences change. "Reason never ceases to put questions to faith, and traditional formulations are submitted to a constant work of interpretation".[3]

"The incessant evolution of doctrine", Loisy wrote towards the end of the book, "is made by the work of individuals . . . and these individuals are they who think for the Church while thinking with her".[4] But that Loisy was thinking with the Church was just what the Church would deny. And it was clear that in thinking so, Loisy was not a lone figure. Von Hügel and the English Catholic writer Wilfred Ward, among others, found *The Gospel and the Church* a valuable apologetic for Catholicism.

Fr. Tyrrell's views started coming to light in a series of signed and anonymous or pseudonymous books and articles over a period of roughly ten years starting in 1899 with *A Perverted Devotion*, which called for agnosticism about the punishment of the damned.

For Tyrrell, what mattered in the Church was not doctrine or hierarchy, but the "collective subconscious of the *populus Dei*, through which the Christian religious idea "unfolds itself and comes into clearer consciousness in an infinity of directions and degrees." But "from the nature of the case, its presentiment of the transcendent order ... can never be more than symbolic ... the transcendental can never be expressed properly".[5]

Nevertheless, as long as the Church's doctrines or "symbols" continue to promote the spiritual life of the soul, the Church has a duty to protect them, even if demonstrably false. What the Church says "is often absolutely wrong, but the truth (or spiritual idea) in whose defence she says it is revealed ... That a lie should be sometimes protective of truth is a consequence of the view of truth as relative to the mentality of a person or people".[6] Only when a doctrine or symbol ceases to be beneficial, when it starts to suffocate spiritual life (as Tyrrell now believed to be the case with most of the Church's dogmas) should they be jettisoned.

What is the essential Christian idea always seeking new forms of expression? "Otherworldliness". Christ and the Church both see this world as "but a preparation and a purgatory". The other world is the one that really matters. But in Jesus the idea was in a primitive stage of development. Jesus thought the purgatorial period was soon to end. Now we know better.

To this one could reply that, even if it were right to protect truth with lies, we would still be left wondering why the Church needed to erect such a bastion of myth and falsehood to protect such a very simple idea.

In the development of "Catholic" modernism, Loisy and Tyrrell played much the same part as Eichorn and Schleiermacher had played in the development of Lutheran modernism. Loisy's radical biblical scholarship, like Eichorn's, destroyed belief. Tyrrell, like Schleiermacher, tried to rebuild belief of some kind on subjective experience.

In Fr. Laberthonnière we chiefly see the influence of Bergson and James. Philosophy, in his view, "gets worked out in living ... it is not a set of abstract propositions ... derived from certain axioms or fundamental principles. Its truth is to be viable."

In support of this opinion he contrasted Greek "idealism" (meaning presumably Platonic metaphysics) with Christian "realism" to the disparagement of the former. His Christian realism ultimately led him to see the fall of Adam, not as a past event, but as the symbolic expression of something we are aware of in ourselves, and Christ himself as a reality the believer experiences in his daily life more than as an historical person living at a particular date.[7]

Le Roy's "philosophy of action" was a synthesis of Bergson's evolutionary view of reality and James's opportunistic view of truth. Here is an example of the way he applies his philosophical principles to the interpretation of Catholic dogmas. Dogmas, he argued in *Dogme et critique*, do not give information; they are not truths to be believed but guides to action. The doctrine of the Trinity, for instance, does not tell us anything about God, but is a way of teaching us to value personal relations.

In another passage, after saying "I believe without restriction or reserve that the resurrection of Jesus is an objectively real fact", he starts whittling down this bold profession of faith by declaring that no Council has defined what a real fact *is*. The Resurrection, we are told, has nothing to do with the "vulgar notion" of the "reanimation of a corpse". How then can he say it is a *real* fact? – By reinterpreting the word "real". Things are real (he is actually talking about ideas not things at this point) if they can be put to use without breaking down, and if they are "fertile for life". The belief that Christ rose from the dead has inspired generations of men to lead self-sacrificing lives. In this sense it is real and a fact. Macquarrie calls Le Roy "the most radical pragmatist among the modernists".[8]

All these equivocations show us, I think, how old most of the "novelties" of today's modernism are beneath their wigs, rouge, and eye-shadow.

In 1905, in a famous article *Qu'est-ce qu'un dogme?* (What is a Dogma?), Le Roy publicly demanded that the Church commit herself to regarding her doctrines as merely symbolic expressions of ineffable intuitions. Shortly before, Hébert had made the same demand.

Taking modernism as a whole, in so far as it tended to reduce the faith to a refined and watery theism under a Christian veneer, we can see it as part of the *fin de siècle* decadence of cultured European society. In the twenty-five years leading up to World War I it was both rationalistic and anti-rational, sceptical and superstitious at the same time, uniting "scientific unbelief" with an interest in mysticism and psychic phenomena, while craving for spiritual experiences of more or less any kind, religious or non-religious. The German poet Rilke and his patroness Princess von Thurn und Taxis typified these tendencies, which are also well portrayed in Thomas Mann's *Magic Mountain*.

Why, given their doubts and denials, did the modernists not leave the Church? For the same reason as others who have set themselves to reform Christianity according to their own ways of thinking. They saw themselves as an elite destined to save the Church from herself. The ordinary rabble of Catholics, including St. Pius X (often snobbishly referred to as the "peasant pope") and most of the episcopate, might not understand their high purposes.

But for the good of the Church and the world they must be made to do so. Accepting the modernist thesis that Catholic doctrines are only blundering attempts of the religious sense to express the inexpressible did not mean the Church would have to go into retirement. Myths, like parables, can have a spiritually uplifting effect. While leaving the hard business of objective facts and practicalities to science, she could still be the "moral educator of mankind".

If she accepted this view of her role – as the wife of science and modern thought, though you may think a rather abjectly submissive one, and the midwife of man's "religious sense" – she still had a great future ahead of her. But if she ignored modernist warnings and insisted that her teachings be taken literally, then she and the modern world would meet in a head-on crash and she was doomed to succumb.

For highly educated men, yesterday's modernists like today's had a strangely naïve attitude to science – both what it is and what it can achieve. They were in some ways like bright schoolboys who have discovered science with a big "S" for the first time.

On the other hand, they were totally unlike the sceptical abbés of the century before, who were contented with their unbelief while living comfortably off the Church's revenues. For the sceptical 18th-century abbé, religion was superstition and that was that. Why make a fuss? The modernists, many of whom had their psychological roots in happy pious childhoods, were fascinated by religion. As a universal phenomenon it was of all-absorbing interest to them. Whether a particular religion was true or false mattered less and in some cases not at all. This partly explains their hostility to Rome. Rome not only blocked their efforts to bring modern man to their new re-interpreted Christian faith which he would at last find acceptable. Its opposition seemed to challenge their claim to be spiritual men. Rome was harsh, brutal, ignorant. The rest of the faithful were silly, superstitious or purblind. They themselves, in the words of Msgr. Mignot, were *âmes sincères et intelligentes*. From their lofty view of their role the more perceptive developed the practical principle we have seen Duchesne recommending. Stay put. Transform belief from within.

By 1900, they seemed to be succeeding. Their ideas were spreading to the cultivated clergy and penetrating the seminaries. Priests started having crises of faith. (Von Hügel's daughter had had a crisis of faith in 1899 when her father disclosed his spiritual doubts to her and his hopes for a change in the meaning of certain doctrines. Fr. Tyrrell was called in to settle her mind).

To contain the damage, the authorities started issuing warnings, books were put on the Index, reviews prohibited. In 1902, Cardinal Richard of Paris condemned Loisy's *L'Evangile et l'église*. Loisy made a qualified submission, but without changing course. The following year he published *Autour d'un petit livre*, a defence of *L'Evangile et l'église*, which treated the beloved disciple's memories of his master as a theological fantasy. Rome responded by putting five of Loisy's books on the Index of forbidden books. Tyrrell, who had been retired from active work, likewise continued to pour out books and articles. In 1906 his Jesuit superiors dismissed him from the Society. He was also suspended from acting as a priest.

Then in July 1907, the Holy Office issued the decree *Lamentabili* listing and condemning sixty-five modernist errors. Von Hügel hurried to Italy where he met Fogazzaro, Bonaiuti and others in order to decide their terms of submission. *Lamentabili* was followed by the Pope's encyclical *Pascendi*, which analysed and synthesised modernists' teachings, showing how they hung together as a system.

Tyrrell attacked the encyclical in two letters to the London *Times*, and was excommunicated shortly afterwards. He died two years later.[9] Loisy's response was an abusive little book about the authorities in Rome, which led to his excommunication in 1908. After 1910 priests were required to take a special anti-modernist oath, and bishops were instructed to make sure that none of their seminary teachers held modernist views. They were also asked to set up diocesan vigilance committees.

St. Pius X is often bitterly criticised for these measures. But the Church has to think of the ordinary faithful as well as of her scholars and theologians. Who can blame a Pope for condemning theories which led to the denial of Christ's divinity, the rejection of the Church's authority to teach and rule in his place, or the reduction of her doctrines and dogmas to being merely symbolic? One does not have to be a scholar to imagine what St. Peter and St. Paul would have said.

The Pope in fact showed great forbearance. Six years passed in the case of Loisy, five in the case of Tyrrell between the appearance of the books in which their disbelief became manifest and their condemnations. Semaria was allowed to take the anti-modernist oath with reservations.[10] And when Fr. Romolo Murri, whom we shall meet in the next chapter, later fell on hard times, St. Pius secretly provided him with an annuity.

The clergy and laity leading the opposition to modernism have also been severely criticised. Much is made of the *Sodalitium Pianum*, an international network of committees for informing authority about clandestine cases of modernism or supposed modernism, founded and directed from Italy by a Msgr. Benigni, whose activities resulted in suspicion being unjustly cast on a number of scholars and clerics. Writers sympathetic, if not to modernism, at least to some of the modernists' aims, speak of a "white terror". But the fact is that, however regrettable or deplorable, in any really serious conflict, whether about ideas or material things, a proportion of people, even with right on their side, are going to act badly, and in the heat of the contest give blows below the belt. In this case, given what was at stake, when all the incidents have been accounted for where individuals flung accusations at the wrong target, took advantage of the crisis to work off grudges or advance their interests, or in other ways acted badly or over-hastily, the strength of the anti-modernist reaction should cause no surprise. In the third century, the Alexandrian faithful responded in a similar way to certain of Origen's ideas. Although those ideas were not condemned by the Church until long after his death, he had to leave Alexandria. The faithful, says Newman, writing about the Arian crisis in the fourth century, when they truly are faithful, experience heresy as something utterly repulsive.

However, when reaction to heresy is too violent, there can be a danger that portions of the faithful will start setting themselves up as the arbiters of orthodoxy and unorthodoxy in place of the magisterium, and be carried out of the Church in the opposite direction.[11]

Something like this started to happen in France, where the reaction to modernism was strongest and gave birth to the movement or tendency which both its opponents and exponents called "integral Catholicism" or "integralism". Integralists saw themselves as defenders of the faith as it had been traditionally expounded. They viewed with suspicion any concessions, real or apparent, to contemporary scholarship or philosophy. The only question was whether everything they regarded as traditional was traditional in the sense of being unchangeable.

The movement also had a socio-political side. For integralists, "full or complete Catholicism" meant the conjunction of the Catholic faith with a fully Catholic society or state, preferably monarchist. Attempts to baptise the principles of 1789 would, they believed, not only undermine belief but end by destroying the Christian character of French life and culture.

It was from this reservoir that the political movement L'Action Française, founded in 1908, drew much of its support. Charles Maurras, its leader and moving spirit, was an unbeliever with a talent for rhetoric and polemics, who valued monarchy and Catholicism as inseparable parts of the national way of life and, after the fashion of Napoleon, as indispensable forms of social cement. In 1929 Pius XI forbade Catholics to belong to the movement under pain of excommunication. His chief reasons were its aggressive nationalism, subordination of religion and morals to the state, and harmful influence on Catholic youth. Not a few French monarchists and integralists ignored the ban. Any enemy of the Republic, it seemed, was to be regarded as a fitting ally. They were often as severely punished for their disobedience as the modernists for their heresies. Many leading French Catholics publicly dissociated themselves from the movement, and a reconciliation began in 1937 when Maurras wrote the Pope a letter of apology. Pius XII lifted the ban at the outset of the second World War.[12]

On the socio-political plane, integralism can be seen as the counterpart of Maritain's integral humanism.

The rift between these two viewpoints, their disputes about which was right, were a continuation on a more theoretical plane of the quarrel we have noticed disturbing the inner life of the French Church during the previous century. Eventually the conflict will engulf the whole Church, with modernism as the *tertius gaudens* or chief beneficiary.

Notes to Chapter Twenty

[1] *Mémoires I*, 1930, p. 118, quoted Livingston, *op. cit.*, p. 277.

[2] Msgr. d'Hulst, although keen on the scholarly *aggiornamento*, was politically a monarchist, another example of how unsatisfactory the categories "progressive" and "conservative" can be.

[3] *L'Evangile et l'église*, English translation, 1908, p. 211 (Livingston *op. cit.*, p. 281).

[4] *Ibid.*, p. 224 (Livingston p. 282).

[5] *Christianity at the Crossroads*, reprint, London, 1963, p. 25 (Livingston p. 286). In 1963 the Council is only in its second year. A reprint suggests a revival of interest in Tyrrell already under way.

[6] *Ibid.*, p. 59 (Livingston, p. 286).

[7] *Oeuvres*, Vol. I, pp. 1–2 (Macquarrie, p. 183).

[8] *Dogme et critique*, p. 25 (Macquarrie, pp. 184–5). Le Roy, as we shall see shortly, was to transmit his viewpoint to the young Teilhard de Chardin.

[9] Of Bright's disease. Its onset may partly account for his intellectual and psychological instability.

[10] According to Ranchetti, *op. cit.*, p. 31, only Semaria was granted this privilege.

[11] For a case in point, see the schism in northern Italy after the second Council of Constantinople, brought to an end some 50 years later by St. Gregory the Great.

[12] Daniel Rops, *A Fight for God*, Dent, London 1965, pp. 296–303. In Jan. 1914, a condemnation of seven of Maurras' books and his newspaper was drawn up on instruction from St. Pius X. But he delayed publication so as not to divide French Catholics still further in view of the approaching war.

Chapter Twenty-One

THREE RELATED MOVEMENTS

Before leaving early modernism, we must glance at three related movements. They too provide examples of *aggiornamento* going off the rails, foreshadowing things that were to happen in the late 20th century.

France and Italy

The first was the attempt by French and Italian Catholics interested in the rights and conditions of workers to move from social action to political action through the creation of Catholic political parties acting independently of the hierarchy.

By the 1930s they had come to believe that social action by itself – the founding of trades unions, co-operatives, night schools, loan banks, educating the public in their social obligations – could not work the desired changes. State intervention was necessary, and that, in states with parliamentary governments, meant winning elections.

At the same time, on the theoretical plane, they began searching for an ideal political system, which, while securing everyone's rights, would perfectly incarnate liberty, equality, and fraternity. This meant coming to terms with the meaning of democracy, and its realisation in practice. In part, it was a taking up again of the work Lamennais had attempted and so conspicuously failed at sixty years earlier. In it we see the liberal Catholicism of Montalembert and the "social Catholicism" of de Munn and Ketteler flowing together, and the birth-pangs of 20th-century "Christian democracy".

Matters came to a head in France with the Sillonists and the *abbés démocrates*, and in Italy with the *Opera dei Congressi*.

Le Sillon was a Catholic lay association founded around 1894 by a group of university students in Paris in order to re-evangelise young working men by showing that as Catholics and Christians they were sympathetic to their needs and claims and anxious to help satisfy them in a Christian way. Their leader, Marc Sangnier, had an apostolic soul, a gift for organisation and oratory, exceptional charm, and a large private fortune. The name, Le Sillon (The Furrow), came from a small periodical which the association took over.[1]

Once launched, the movement spread rapidly and soon reached the provinces. Reading rooms, study circles, people's institutes were set up. By 1904 there were 50 study circles in the Paris area alone. *L'Eveil démocratique*, a popular paper, reached a circulation of 60,000 within a year of its founding in 1905. There were frequent public debates and lectures and a yearly national congress. Annual retreats fostered the members' spiritual lives. The obvious good the movement was doing won the approval of numerous bishops. Leo XIII gave Sangnier the Order of St. Gregory the Great, and in 1903 St. Pius X received a Sillonist pilgrimage in Rome.

Trouble only began as Sillonist publications and public utterances increasingly showed signs of the influence of unacceptable secular political ideas, and Sangnier himself took the first steps towards founding a political party. To give himself more freedom of manoeuvre, he announced that Le Sillon was "not properly speaking and directly a Catholic work". In his encyclical *Graves de communi* of 1901, Leo XIII had forbidden Catholics to form or join a Christian democratic party.[2]

Close in aims and outlook to the Sillonists, and eventually succumbing to the same influences, the *abbés démocrates* were a loosely linked group of priests anxious to spread the social teachings of Leo XIII. They were not an organised body. They aired their views as journalists, public speakers, editors of periodicals, and in a few cases as members of parliament.

The Italian association, the *Opera dei Congressi*, was an early example of what later came to be called Catholic Action – organised lay action under the guidance of a bishop or bishops. Growing out of a series of public meetings in the early 1870s, and officially approved in 1874, the association was formed to enable Italian Catholics to defend and promote their rights as citizens and members of the Church against the anti-Christian policies of the new government in Rome, dominated by extreme liberals and freemasons. This they could not do by ordinary means. Since participation in politics would look like tacit recognition of the new Italian state and its right to Rome and the old papal territories, the Church had forbidden Italian Catholics to stand for parliament or to vote in elections.

But in the 1890s the association fell under the control of Don Romolo Murri, a priest with a gift for fiery political oratory. An enthusiast for Leo XIII's *Rerum Novarum*, like Sangnier and the *abbés démocrates*, Murri started an agitation for the Holy See to lift the *non expedit*, the ban on taking part in politics, and made the defence of workers' rights *vis-à-vis* their employers, rather than the rights of Catholics and the Church *vis-à-vis* the government, the association's main concern. The shift of focus split the association. Murri's opponents appealed for the intervention of the Holy See.

We can call the members of these three groups – the Sillonists, the *abbés démocrates*, and the Italian *Congressisti* – "Catholic democrats". Not all the democrats' aims and ideas were unacceptable to the Church. With the passage of time, and changed circumstances, she has allowed or endorsed many of them. Those she immediately objected to were the ambiguous or ill-defined use of the word democracy; treating it (however defined) as the only legitimate form of government; teaching that the authority of governments comes from the people rather than God; suggesting that the government of the Church should in some way be made democratic; rejecting the guidance of the Church in social and political matters, questioning the right to private property and identifying democracy with socialism.

The Sillonists were also censured for encouraging the discussion of conflicting moral and religious opinions at their meetings (in keeping with the ideal of freedom of expression) and for encouraging their working-class members to join unions affiliated to the anarchist Confédération Générale du Travail, rather than Catholic trades unions, on the grounds that the former better represented working-class interests.

Leo XIII had tried to control the situation by de-politicising the notion of Christian democracy, which he had defined in *Graves de communi* as "benevolent Christian activity with regard to the people". But as time went by the rhetoric of the democrats grew ever wilder. The theories of Robespierre and Danton were described as "of the substance of the Gospel", and the "mystic-souled Russian anarchists" as "witnesses of Christ". No one, it was said, had "embodied the republican idea so perfectly as Jesus Christ". The Holy Trinity was proposed as the archetype of democratic equality, and the eucharist of democratic brotherhood.[3]

In 1904 Pius X decided there was no way of extracting the *Opera dei Congressi* from Murri's control. At the association's meeting in Bologna the year before, the majority of members had given him an ovation. The Pope therefore dissolved the organisation, replacing it with a new one, the Italian Catholic Movement, from which Murri was excluded. Murri thereupon founded his own National Democratic League. He was suspended from his priestly functions in 1907 and excommunicated in 1909. In 1908 the *abbés démocrates'* two leading journals were condemned. Le Sillon was suppressed in 1910. The reaction of Sangnier and the Sillonists was exemplary. There was no opposition or rebellion of the kind there had been among the scholars condemned by *Pascendi*. Most of the *abbés démocrates* submitted too. Only Murri held out. He was reconciled to the Church shortly before his death in 1944.

Can the Catholic democrats' attempts to make democracy, however understood, an absolute good or article of faith be described as "social and political modernism"? In the opinion of most writers, not in the strict sense. Von Hügel and his circle had no noticeable interest in social and political questions, while the democrats were for the most part uninterested in the theories of biblical critics or the relationship of religious experience to doctrine. Any ties of sympathy seem to have been due to both having attracted Rome's disapprobation.[4] As yet there was no true convergence of aims and ideas. The incorporation of social and political utopianism into the evolutionary experience-based Christianity of early modernism will only begin in the late 1930s, and not reach its climax until the appearance of liberation theology in the late 1960s. Murri seems to have been the only democrat with a real interest in theological modernism; he was the only democrat at the meeting called by von Hügel in August 1907 to work out terms of submission to *Pascendi*.

Germany

The second of the three related movements was the German phenomenon known as *Reformkatholizismus*. To distinguish it from modernism proper, Jean Rivière, author of the first major history of modernism, describes it as "university liberalism." Inspired by a professor of history at Freiburg, Franz Xaver Kraus, and a professor of apologetics at Wurzburg, Herman Schell, it seems to have been chiefly a manifestation of 19th-century German nationalism, fortified with a strong dash of the older 18th-century Gallican or Josephite spirit.

19th-century German nationalism owed much of its original force to a national inferiority complex about the long dominant cultures of Italy, Spain and France. An insistence on the *superiority* of German culture to inferior "Latin civilisation", especially to everything emanating from its centre, Rome, was one result. Protestant sentiment and Germany's scholarly, scientific and military triumphs during the course of the 19th century also helped to fuel these prejudices, which eventually affected Catholics too.[5]

The adherents of *Reformkatholizismus* declaimed against Roman centralisation, scholastic philosophy, the Jesuits, the Index, *ultramontanism*, the oppressive use of ecclesiastical authority, and Church involvement in politics, while calling for freedom of research, the "progress of religion and culture", "Germanism", and the acceptance of modern art. They also liked to describe themselves as "progressive Catholics", possibly the first use of the term.

All this sounds not unlike Fr. Hans Küng on the rampage. Enough of the movement's spirit seems to have survived the war and inter-war periods to fuel the developing German modernism of the 1950s when it began testing its engines, and, with Pope John's announcement of the Council, taxied towards the take-off. Of the movement's less preposterous demands, some will find a place on the new theologians' agenda.

The United States

Completing our trio of quasi-modernist movements was *Americanism*. Americanism, like *Reformkatholizismus*, was a form of religious nationalism. It could be described as the absorption by the American Catholic mind of the dye of the secular American spirit. At this stage, like integralism, it was more a tendency than a movement.

The quintessential element of the American spirit is, presumably, the belief that every man is as good as his neighbour, that there are no difficulties he cannot surmount by himself if he is the kind of man he ought to be, and that he needs no help from outside authority. It is the independent, practical, self-sufficient spirit of a pioneering people, which in the right place is admirable. But in the raw, it is not easily reconciled with Catholicism and the spirit of the Gospel.

The French translation of the life of Fr. Paul Haeker, founder of the American Paulist order, and still more that translation's introduction by the French abbé Felix Klein, first alerted the Holy See to the dangers. Leo XIII explained what he saw those dangers as being in his apostolic letter, *Testem Benevolentiae* (1899) to Cardinal Gibbons of Baltimore. They were: making good works the heart of religion, rather than obedience, humility and union with God; downplaying the role of grace; and the idea that certain aspects of faith and morals should be adapted to suit the culture of each people. He had previously warned the American hierarchy against taking the American constitution as the model for relations between Church and State always and everywhere (*Longinqua oceani*, 1895). Separation of Church and State was not to be considered the ideal. The best state of affairs was when a people was religiously largely of one mind, and as a politically organised body acknowledged and worshipped God according to the one true religion.[6]

Since few Catholics gave explicit voice to the ideas censured by the Pope, it was easy to deny that anyone held them. Americanism in consequence used to be laughingly called "the phantom heresy". The Holy See, it was said, did not understand how the American mind worked, or, in today's parlance, "the American experience". However, the last twenty-five years have made it clear that the phantom had more substance than was supposed. It also seems to have had holiday homes in a number of other countries.

Notes to Chapter Twenty-One

[1]   The founders had been pupils of Blondel at the Collège Stanislas, a Parisian Catholic high school.

[2]   The Church's reservations about specifically Catholic parties were due to the possibility of their seeming to commit her to ideas and policies which she could not endorse, and to the term "Christian democracy" because of the ambiguities surrounding the term.

[3]   Daniel-Rops, *A Fight for God*, Dent, London, 1965, pp. 194–5.

[4]   Although Vidler (*op. cit.*, p. 195) notes that Le Roy was associated with Le Sillon in its early days, and that Laberthonnière became a friend of Sangnier and a contributor to the movement's paper, he attaches no particular significance to the fact.

[5]   French nationalism and English nationalism had no less preposterous aspects. They were merely expressions of different prejudices and illusions. For *Reformkatholizismus* in general, see, in addition to Rivière (*op. cit.*), Fliche et Martin, *Histoire de l'église*, Vol. XXI.

[6]   In 1939, in the encyclical *Sertum Laetitiae*, commemorating the 150th anniversary of the establishment of the American Hierarchy, Pius XII, while praising the great achievements of the Church in the U.S.A., felt it necessary to draw attention once again to the aspects of U.S. culture incompatible with a truly Catholic outlook.

Chapter Twenty-Two

AGGIORNAMENTO 1918–1958

Although the spread of modernist ideas had made a partial reversal of Leo XIII's policies unavoidable, it was only a temporary reversal. In his first encyclical *Ad Beatissimi*, Benedict XV, who succeeded St. Pius X in 1914, began to relax the pressure on the brakes. Referring to modernism as a "manifest heresy" and speaking of its "monstrous errors", he nevertheless said that "in regard to questions on which the Holy See has as yet given no ruling . . . no one is forbidden to put forward and defend his opinion".

Even while the crisis was at its height, the *aggiornamento* had continued. Orthodox Catholic scholars had been applying the critical method to the Bible and Church history without losing either their faith or their sense of proportion. Among more notable examples were the Jesuits Frs. Jules Lebreton and Léonce de Grandmaison, the Dominican Fr. Marie-Joseph Lagrange, Frs. Battifol, Tixeront, and Labriolle, Ludwig von Pastor, and Horace Mann.

Fr. Henri Pesch was developing a social ethics based on the principle of "solidarity", an idea later made use of by Popes Pius XI and John Paul II. Pierre Duhem, the theoretical physicist and historian of science, was demonstrating that the foundations of modern physics were laid in the late middle ages not the renaissance as previously assumed, pulling the rug from under the idea that the advances of modern science were in some way connected with the growth of atheism.

The careers of Pesch and Duhem show that it is not always thinkers who make the most noise during their lifetimes who do the most valuable work. Only recently have they become names outside their own countries.

In the social field, Marius Gonin and Adiodat Boissard were founding the *semaines sociales* (1904), annual conferences for stimulating interest in Catholic social teaching.

The 1890s and 1900s also saw the beginnings of the 20th-century Catholic literary revival. Péguy was in full career, and Claudel's first books were appearing. Léon Bloy too was already exerting an influence. They would be followed a decade or two later by Mauriac and Bernanos. Nor is there any sign that the condemnation of modernism checked the flow of prominent literary converts to the Church.[1]

Then came the First World War, at the conclusion of which the Church, like everyone else, found herself in a new world.

The Russian, German and Austrian monarchies had been swept away, long established patterns of economic life broken up, old nations brought back to life, new ones created. In Russia, the Bolsheviks had established the first officially atheist state. Elsewhere, through the influence of the victors, parliamentary governments mainly hostile to Catholicism were in the ascendant. But their leaders seem to have lacked the moral fibre or political acumen for dealing with the economic stagnation and resulting social unrest of the post-war years. The inclusion in their number of a humiliated Germany and a discontented Italy, did not contribute to making them a force for international stability either.

The devastation to souls was greater still. Millions of men and women, who had grown up in villages where belief was taken for granted and protected by custom, had been suddenly uprooted and thrown pell-mell among men of other ways of thinking and into sufferings and moral evils for which the faith of the majority was no match. Europe was still Christianity's heartland, but there was now a hole in the heart more than half the size of the heart itself, and it was only a question of time before something else came to fill it.

This is why the twenty inter-war years were a time of uneasy peace and why the partisans of totalitarian ideologies posed the threat they did to the tottering democracies, with Italian fascism and German national socialism step by step gaining the lead over Soviet-led communism. More and more the West was looking to politics rather than religion for salvation.[2]

The success of the totalitarians was due as much to continental liberalism's philosophical bankruptcy, as to its economic and political inefficiency. To give meaning to life the liberals could only offer more irreligion (now like a drug on the market), increased material prosperity (which they were failing to provide), or promises of still greater individual freedom (useless to men and women on the breadline and, as a philosophical ideal, one of the root causes of social disintegration). Why should men live together in harmony if individual liberty and gratification are presented as the supreme goals? In other words, they could fill neither the hole in the heart, nor the hole in the stomach, while as a motive for social cohesion they could only offer a vague and ineffective doctrine of universal brotherliness.

The totalitarians, on the other hand, offered ideology and party discipline. Ideology (meaning, in this case, deification of the nation, race or working class) would temporarily fill the spiritual vacuum. By lifting the individual's sights above personal self-interest, it gave to life an at least quasi-transcendent meaning. Party discipline and total state control, it was thought, would solve the problems of material well-being.[3]

In these respects, the totalitarianisms, whether of left or right, had more in common with each other than with their victims, the enfeebled democracies. Their successes were also due to their novelty. The peoples of Europe were like invalids running desperately from one medical practitioner to another. The totalitarianisms had the advantage of not yet having had their incompetence tested.

The autocracies which won.control in Spain, Portugal and elsewhere where something *sui generis.* If ideology was present it was something peripheral.

To try to explain all this as a simple conflict between right and left, rich and poor, dictatorship and democracy, or good and evil, as is too often the custom in England and the USA, is like trying to get light out of a torch with the wrong kind of battery.

European Catholics found themselves confronted with three social, economic and political systems or philosophies – liberal, fascist and communist – all godless, all from the Catholic point of view in divergent ways and degrees deficient or undesirable. This is the key to understanding much of the papal teaching during the inter-war years and the Holy See's diplomatic activities. It explains too the shifting alignments of many Catholics, intellectuals included, before, during and after the second World War. It was a question of deciding which of three ugly sisters was the least repulsive.

Then came the six years of World War II, which, by throwing groups of Catholics and Protestants together in Germany against Hitler, and groups of Catholics and communists together in France against the Vichy regime and German occupying army, stimulated interest in Christian reunion, and sympathy towards Marxism. It was also responsible for much guilt and heart-searching. Why had not more Catholics been openly on the Allied side? The lunacy and wickedness of the Nazi regime, coupled with Allied propaganda in favour of Russia, helped to disguise the vileness of the Soviet Union's equally brutal but less demented and far more universal and long-lasting form of totalitarianism, as well as the ambiguous nature of a "triumph of freedom and democracy" which left Europe split down the middle with the eastern half subject to Stalin.

Western Europe, propped up by the power and wealth of the United States, was now committed to economic and political liberalism modified by semi-socialist welfare policies, with the United Nations replacing the League of Nations as, in theory, the cement holding the international community together. The resulting economic recovery, this time benefiting nearly all classes, eventually produced the mood of euphoria that was moving towards its climax just as Pope John announced his plans for calling a Council. Could it be that a world of plenty for everybody really was just round the corner?

The dismantling of the French, English, Portuguese and Dutch empires mainly affected missionaries. Anxious to identify themselves with their flocks, sensitive to the charge of having been agents for the colonial powers, many were inclining to see only virtues in the local culture, and only defects in European culture and the colonial past, including the way Church affairs were run.

These were the main factors influencing the *aggiornamento* from without, which, once it got going again after World War I, took three forms.

First there was the kind of adjusting to the times which Catholics of all periods make without waiting for papal encyclicals or episcopal pastorals. New ideas and events overtake them before the magisterium has had time to assess their significance and give guidance. It is therefore usually a hit and miss affair. Sometimes the faithful's Catholic sense points to the right solution. Sometimes weak faith or moral imperfection lead to the kind of worldly compromise or "social modernism" reproved by Pius XI. In the latter case, the magisterium's subsequent verdict is likely to be ill-received. In the dramatic social and political upheavals between 1920 and 1958, there must have been a great deal of this *ad hoc* adjusting to the times, preparing the ground in good and bad ways for what was to come.

Secondly there was a continuation of the kind of steady *aggiornamento*, stimulated or guided by the popes, that had begun with Leo XIII.

Over a period of 38 years, in a stream of encyclicals and addresses to pilgrims, Pius XI and Pius XII instructed the faithful in almost every aspect of modern life, from the obligations of governments to the duties of midwives, pointing out what was and was not compatible with Catholic belief and practice. They also began opening the door to some of the ideas and initiatives that would triumph at the Council. The teachings of Pius XII are among the most frequently cited authorities in the conciliar documents.

But Popes do not teach in isolation. Their teaching incorporated the work of scholars in many fields. This was the third form taken by the interwar *aggiornamento*.

In theology, men like the Belgian Jesuit Fr. Emile Mersch were preparing the ground for the more organic, spiritualised conception of the Church described in Chapter 9. It was officially approved by Pius XII in his encyclical *Mystici Corporis Christi* (1943).

In philosophy, the Thomist revival was probably this moderate *aggiornamento*'s most striking achievement. Outside the Church, St. Thomas and the scholastics had for centuries been treated as philosophical non-persons. But by the 1940s, sixty years after Leo XIII's call for the restoration of Christian philosophy, the situation had been completely reversed. Thinkers like Gilson and Maritain had forced even die-hard adherents of the "religion equals superstition" school, represented by Bertrand Russell, to admit that St. Thomas, even if wrong, was a figure of world stature.[4]

War and revolution having shaken belief in the inevitability of progress, the first half of the 20th century also saw the publication of a number of influential philosophies of history, with Spengler's *Decline of the West* and Toynbee's *Study of History* in the forefront. These sought to determine the laws governing the rise and fall of civilisations and whether, if decay had set in, there was any way of arresting the process. The 18th-century Neapolitan philosopher, Giovanni Battista Vico, with his cyclical vision of history, became fashionable. If, for Marxists, history was to end in the triumph of the proletariat, others, inspired by Vico, saw it as endlessly repeating itself. This was the background to the new theologians' interest in the meaning of secular history. The English Catholic social and cultural historian, Christopher Dawson, made one of the best contributions to this debate.

The dramatic social and political changes helped to stimulate the development of the Church's social teaching. Pius XI had stringent things to say about unbridled economic liberalism as well as about communism, fascism and national socialism. He proposed a "sane corporative system" as the best basis for a just and peaceful social order. By "corporative" he did not mean the Italian fascists' system of state-regulated industries. He meant taking into account the natural hierarchical order of men's talents, encouraging them to form self-governing professional associations at every level, and getting those associations to co-operate with each other instead of trying to do each other down.

During the inter-war period, the Italian priest Don Luigi Sturzo, founder of the Italian Popular Party suppressed by Mussolini in 1921 and revived as the Christian Democratic Party after 1945, made important contributions to the theory of "Christian democracy" or Catholic parliamentary republicanism.[5] So too, both before and after World War II, did Jacques Maritain, an even more influential figure in this field. In the 1950s, Pius XII recognised the legitimacy of nationalising a limited number of industries and services where the common good required it.

By this time, the number of governments that could be called remotely

Christian having dropped to near zero, and of governments actively hostile to Christianity mounted into the two-figure range, a shift in papal teaching began from the duties of states towards the Catholic religion to the right of Christians to worship God without state interference.

Meanwhile, the first steps had been taken towards Catholic participation in the movement for Christian unity. In 1924, Pius XI called on the Benedictines to work for reunion with the Orthodox. A centre for studying the questions responsible for the separation was set up at Amay-sur-Meuse in Belgium (later moved to Chevetogne) under Dom Lambert Beauduin. Shortly afterwards, the Dominican Fr. Christophe Dumont opened a similar house of studies, the Istina centre, in Paris. Later, both houses extended their work to include Catholic-Protestant relations.

Reunion with the Protestant churches was likewise the aim of the Möhler Institute and the Una Sancta fraternity begun in Germany by Fr. Josef Metzger, who was later executed by the Nazis. In 1935 the abbé Couturier started the "week of universal prayer for Christian unity". All Christians were to take part. Two years later, unofficial Catholic observers attended the Protestant ecumenical Faith and Order conference in Edinburgh. After World War II came the Holy Office's "Instruction on the Ecumenical Movement", laying down guidelines for Catholic participation, and the foundation of two more houses for ecumenical study and work: *Unité Chrétienne* in Lyons in memory of Couturier, and Fr. Charles Boyer's *Unitas* in Rome.

The 1950s likewise saw the first liturgical changes: the restoration of the Easter vigil service, "dialogue" Mass (with the faithful making a number of responses), evening Mass and relaxation of the fasting laws for receiving Holy Communion (to make weekday Mass attendance easier for city workers).

Other changes of practice or policy were: the settling of the dispute between the Holy See and the Italian government about the one-time papal states, and the establishment of the present Vatican City State (by the Lateran Treaty of 1929); the consecration of more and more native bishops in mission territories; and the conclusion of the centuries-long Chinese rights controversy (could Chinese converts continue to venerate their ancestors, i.e. was ancestor worship in the strict sense "worship"? Rome finally decided it was not).

The 1920s, '30s, '40s and '50s were notable too for the growth of international lay movements: Schoenstatt, the Legion of Mary, Opus Dei, Focolare, Communion and Liberation, Foyers de Charité. Less directly under the control of the local bishop, they were also less socio-political than the Catholic Action movements like the Young Christian Workers which had sprung up in the previous century in Italy and France.

Even without the Council, there is no reason to think this moderate updating would not have continued.

Meanwhile, the new theologians' plans for a more far-reaching *aggiornamento* were taking shape. Pius XII tried to keep it on track during the 1940s and 50s with three major encyclicals, *Divino Afflante Spiritu* (1943) on Bible study, *Mediator Dei* (1947) on divine worship and the liturgy, and *Humani Generis* (1950) on new theological and philosophical ideas, but with only partial success. Why, in addition to providing the Church with new insights, did the *aggiornamento* of the new theologians become the vehicle for a revived modernism?

Partly, it is now clear, because modernism as a way of thought or temper of mind did not, as was widely assumed, die under the blows of the encyclical *Pascendi.*[6] Scholarly young men, touched by modernism while having their minds formed in the seminaries around 1907, were, at the end of World War II, still only in their early sixties. Where faith survived, it was often with disgruntled feelings or a grudging attitude towards authority. Meanwhile, throughout the 1920s and 30s, leading modernists were pouring out books and apologies, thereby enlarging this pool of discontent.

Loisy, whose memoirs appeared in 1930–31, lived on until 1940. Laberthonnière, although forbidden to publish, continued to write, and these later works appeared after his death in 1932. Le Roy survived until 1954.

As a layman and professor at the Collège de France, Leroy was not prevented from publishing. His books were merely censored as they came out. Each time he submitted, but without changing course. The same ideas would be developed in the next book. Official formulas, he maintained, should receive only official submission and be interpreted to bear an acceptable meaning; he was not dealing with an infallible authority.

Other modernist or semi-modernist writings circulated in the scholarly world in mimeograph. One of the most influential contributors to this ecclesiastical samizdat was Fr. Teilhard de Chardin. Teilhard's speculations also got into circulation through his friendship with Le Roy. Le Roy confessed that he and Teilhard had discussed their ideas together so often that he could no longer say which were Teilhard's and which his own.

But it would be a mistake to attribute modernism's persistence solely or even mainly to a handful of survivors from the first phase. Modernism persisted because the causes which had originally brought it into existence persisted: the increasingly secularised culture in which the bulk of Western Catholics now lived, and the complexity of many of the questions raised by "modern thought".

How much neo-Protestant biblical scholarship, how much evolutionary theory, could be incorporated into a genuinely Catholic Christian world-view? Which aspects of modern philosophy, which democratic social and political ideas? How far can personal experience throw light on doctrine and dogma, or is it only in the light of divine revelation that personal experience becomes fully intelligible?

These questions and the theories giving rise to them are examined, discussed and explained more fully in a sequel to this book which it is hoped will appear shortly. Along with a study of the movement for liturgical reform, and the unique role played by Fr. Karl Rahner in the conciliar and post-conciliar dramas, it will include topics like existentialism and the human sciences, which, although they played little or no part in the early modernist crisis, had an impact later on Catholic thinking. The arrival of these new-comers is what justifies speaking of today's aberrations as "neo-modernism".

Notes to Chapter Twenty-Two

[1]   The Maritains came into the Church in 1906, drawn to a great extent by Bloy. Other well-known converts to the Church between 1900 and 1960, included Ernst Pischari (Renan's nephew), Jacques Rivière, Julien Green, Alexis Carel, Gertrud von Le Fort, Edith Stein, Sigrid Undset, Johannes Jorgensen, G. K. Chesterton, Christopher Dawson, Maurice Baring, Graham Greene, Evelyn Waugh, Edith Sitwell, Dorothy Day and Walker Percy.

[2]   Today the word "fascism" usually has one of three meanings: (a) the anti-communist political movements which sprang up in Italy, Germany and Spain after World War I in response to the economic and political crisis in those countries – the original and historically accurate meaning; (b) any authoritarian regime or nationalist reaction to the universalising tendencies of the political philosophies stemming from the Enlightenment; (c) a term of abuse in the vocabulary of the political left for anyone opposing or criticising their policies or practices.

[3]   Ideology: a political or social theory acting as a substitute for religion, while claiming to be capable of solving life's problems, down to the last detail.

[4]   For the French historian Octave Hamelin, Descartes was "in succession with the ancients, almost as if ... there had been (philosophically) nothing but a blank between". Quoted, *One Hundred Years of Thomism*, Houston 1981, p. 34.

[5]   See Luigi Sturzo, *Church and State*, 2 Volumes, Notre Dame, 1962, and Richard Webster, *Christian Democracy in Italy, 1860–1960*, Hollis and Carter, London, 1961.

[6]   Writing about half a century after the first modernist crisis, Fr. Creehan S.J. speaks of "this now half-forgotten heresy" (*Father Thurston*, Sheed and Ward 1952, p. 48); Daniel Rops (*op. cit.*, p. 238) citing fellow author J. Rouquette, calls it "a completely outmoded phenomenon"; while in his *A Short History of the Catholic Church*, (Burns & Oates, London, reprinted 7 times between 1939 and 1967), Msgr. Philip Hughes says of the modernists "within a very short time the Church was rid of them".

191

Chapter Twenty-Three

WHAT DOES IT ALL MEAN?
– AN INTERPRETATION

We have returned almost to the point where we began – the turmoil which broke out in the wake of Vatican II, which we compared to a sieve, separating the life-giving from the toxic elements in modern thought and in the reform party's agenda.

We could also compare it to a water filter. From the moment Pope John announced his plans for a Council, the faithful were deluged with a flood of ideas and opinions from theologians, scholars and writers of every description about what needed to be done, how the faith should be re-presented, or which elements of modern thought could safely be taken on board.

In so far as they were channelled through the conciliar decrees, or the Holy See's subsequent instructions about the way the decrees were to be understood, these ideas could be called "safe to drink" or swim in. But most of the flood-tide – whether conveyed in books, articles, lectures, sermons or workshops – swept around and over the filter plant, carrying the bulk of the Western faithful along with it into a vast uncharted ideological and theological lagoon, where the majority are still, spiritually, floundering or swimming. As a visible entity, they are held together by the boundaries of parish and diocese, but internally their beliefs can vary as widely as the species of the animal, insect, reptile and bird kingdoms. What they believe as individuals depends largely on which group of free-wheeling theologians or religious writers has most influenced them.

In examining the origins of this state of affairs, I hope I have managed to throw at least some light on how and why it all happened.

Symptoms of genuine renewal in the Western world, as I mentioned earlier, are chiefly to be seen in the "new movements". But Christ did not intend the Church to be a federation of movements. Movements and religious orders have always played an auxiliary role – by prayer, preaching, example and good works – to raise the spiritual level of the Church as a whole. Renewal only fully takes off when it begins to touch dioceses and parishes, and that presupposes a renewal of the episcopate of the kind brought about in the 16th and 17th centuries through the agency of great saints like St. Philip Neri, St. Charles Borromeo and his cousin Federico. A striking example of what can be achieved by a bishop truly faithful to his vocation are the reforms carried out by Pope John Paul II when he was Archbishop of Krakow. If the number of his imitators or equals in the West is not yet large, hope for the future lies in there being more and more of them.

The hurdles immediately confronting the Church are: the growing pressure for ordaining women and making homosexual practice morally allowable; an ecumenism oriented almost exclusively towards liberal Protestants, which prizes togetherness above truth; and a revival of the plans scotched by Paul VI to cut down papal authority and transfer the bulk of it to national episcopal conferences. Each conference, it is thought, will then be free to adapt the faith to meet local majority demands.[1]

A *Kulturkampf* ("culture war") waged by politically correct liberal governments seems another possibility in the not-too-distant future.[2] A recent newspaper article referred to a measure being considered by the Swedish parliament making it a punishable offence to say that homosexual practice is morally wrong. What does a truly Catholic bishop or teacher do then? However, this latter eventuality would not in itself be an obstacle to renewal. Indeed it could have the opposite effect.

There then remains the question, what does it all mean? Granted that God was not altogether satisfied with us as we were in the period before the Council, and that he required adjustments of some kind in our behaviour and thinking, why did he allow what he wanted to be said, to be written and presented to his people in a way that was almost certain to mislead large numbers of them? Why did he allow a flock of heterodox theologians to become to a great extent the most influential interpreters of the Council and its new orientations?

I suppose most of my readers have asked themselves this question at some time. As for myself, the only answer I can find is that, in the mystery of God's designs, the Council had a double purpose.

The main and long-term purpose, I suggest, was to lay down guidelines for an eventual renewal which would smooth the path for the newcomers of all nations and races who are going to come across the Church in the first centuries of the third millennium. These newcomers are going to be unlike any potential converts the Church has ever encountered before.

Let me explain. Through its formidable scientific, technical and scholarly achievements, the West is rapidly destroying all other cultures from the roots up. The attractions of Western know-how and the wealth that has so far accompanied its achievements, appear, for great masses of the world's populations, to be proving irresistible. But adopting a Western life-style, and still more a Western education, is next to impossible without imbibing a good measure of the philosophical ideas and mental attitudes on which the West's successes have to a great degree depended.

I believe that, once its members are exposed to Western industrial development and adopt a Western middle-class outlook, then every religion, Islam included, is going to have a modernist crisis – and it will be much tougher for them than for Christianity. Not only are the grounds for Christian belief more solid, but Christianity is much better equipped to cope with the Western spirit of rational inquiry, partly because it helped to give birth to it and has always been glad to use it.

This means that a high percentage of the 21st century's men and women of non-European origin are going to be children by adoption of the European Enlightenment, and to be a child of the Enlightenment means taking on board a whole lot of Christian ideas and attitudes uprooted from their Christian soil and replanted in secular or atheistic earth. The Enlightenment, having developed out of a centuries-old Christian civilisation, has, I believe, to be seen as a secularised Christian heresy. Because of this, they are not going to be like people meeting Christianity for the first time. They are going to be quasi ex-Christians without even knowing it. With their Western education they will have imbibed not only uprooted and distorted Christian ideas, but the typical Western secularist's incomprehension of Christianity, and many of his prejudices against it too.

That, I believe, is why it was necessary for the Church to embark on the wide-ranging *aggiornamento* initiated by Pope John and given its guidelines by the Second Vatican Council. It was necessary, if for no other reason, so that non-Westerners can understand how much of what they have absorbed from the West, and now take for granted, is compatible with the faith, how much conflicts with it, and how much is actually Christian in origin. It was necessary, too, for the sake of the majority of contemporary Westerners who are now ignorant about the origin of most of the ideas they live by and assume to be self-evident. As for the surviving Christians, they need this knowledge to equip them for their task as evangelists to these hosts of quasi ex-Christians.

This, I believe, was the Council's main or long-term purpose, which will not, I think, be fully understood until most of those who took part in it, and their immediate successors, have gone to their reward.

It would be unjust and ungenerous not to give the reformers credit for having seen that the work needed to be done, and for having prepared the ground for it. Nor can the fact that a proportion of them fell into heresy in the process be blamed fairly on the party as a whole or used as grounds for dismissing the work as unnecessary. But, like the generality of reformers, in their eagerness to make their ideas prevail, they tended to exaggerate the gravity of the defects they meant to correct, and as a result created new imbalances, which have proved to be far more dangerous.

Their chief weakness, it soon became obvious, was their too uncritical admiration of the beauties and virtues of modernity. But it was this very modernity about which, shortly after the Council was over, the modern world itself began to have serious doubts, many of its younger members abandoning political engagement for transcendental meditation, and Western efficiency for hippy impracticality.

The reformers' lack of balance in this respect is what so often made them, and even more their followers, such poor judges of what it was important to preserve from the Church's past life and culture, and also as regards matters of faith and morals. It is not that one would want them to have condemned modern life *in toto*, rather to have had a greater sense of proportion about it.

This, I would say, is why the People of God have had to suffer so painfully while on the operating table. The operation was necessary. But the Divine Surgeon had to use instruments which – with some distinguished exceptions – were neither fine nor sharp enough. They seem not to have seen that the "eternal man", who lives under the skin of every man and woman who has ever existed, or will ever exist, can never be satisfied with modernity as such, except in a superficial way.

It is the voice of eternal man that we hear whenever the psalms are sung or recited. If it were not so, there would be no point in wearying God's ears with them; we could not make the psalmist's words and sentiments our own. It is the crimes, follies and miseries of the eternal man which we read about every day when we pick up the tabloids. They are essentially the same as those of Joseph's eleven brothers and Potiphar's wife. Karl Barth used to talk about the "strange world of the Bible". But the Bible will only seem strange to people who think that, with modernity, a new kind of human being has come into existence. Nothing but a similar myopia on the part of the reformers can explain the eagerness of so many of them to try to force-feed poor modern man with more and more of the kind of stuff that, in the depths of his soul, he already half-loathed even while he was wallowing in it.

If the Church, which is chiefly concerned with the eternal man, has adjusted her tone of voice or mode of expression from time to time throughout history, it is only so that her message can more easily penetrate the carapace of modernity in which the eternal man is forever encased, and resonate in those depths of his being which never alter. This is the sole reason why "modernity" as such has to be taken into account. In itself, modernity is always a passing phenomenon, the greater part of it being a matter of fads and fashions, as we can see from the speed with which particular fashions become unfashionable. Increases in knowledge do not alter the eternal man either. They can usefully enlarge his understanding of particular aspects of the things he studies. But they can equally fill him with illusions about himself, which hide from him the needs of his deepest being.

As with "modern man", so it was too often with the reformers' assessment of the "modern world". The modern world meant of course the industrialised Western world and, for the reasons we have just explained, it was important to clarify the Church's role in relation to its aims and ambitions. Unfortunately, many of those engaged in the undertaking ended by giving the impression that the modern world's aims and ambitions were all but identical with those of the Church. As a result, St. Augustine's vision of history as, at the deepest level, a battle between the forces of good and evil, has all but vanished from the faithful's consciousness, to be replaced by the conviction that personal salvation is not a matter of any consequence, and that there are no serious obstacles to building a better world together with men who hold radically different views about what "better" means.[3]

It is imbalances like these which have so far delayed the full realisation of what I have suggested was the Council's long-term purpose.

But it was first to have an immediate or short-term purpose. Before the desired renewal could take place, God was going to subject his people to a test. By letting loose a flock of heterodox theologians and scholars who gave an alternative interpretation of the Council's teaching – an interpretation differing in major respects from that of the Church – the secrets of hearts were to be revealed. Which did his people want? God's version of the conciliar teaching, mediated in the final resort through his Vicar, or a modernist or semi-modernist version?

That has been the test for the majority of Catholics throughout the West. But, in one way or another, all of us, I believe, are being tested, regardless of rank, inclination or shade of opinion.

It is right to feel an abhorrence for heresy. It was the mark, as we saw Newman noting, of the faithful of the fourth century in their resistance to Arianism. The faith has to be defended. But there are better and worse ways of doing it, and if one is not careful, love of the Church and faith can become entangled with natural bellicosity or the spirit of domination. We can forget that our opponents need prayers more than maledictions. In our eagerness to stop an abuse or establish a truth, we can find ourselves unintentionally demanding or requiring more than the Church herself demands, or denigrating something which God wants promoted, even if it is not being done always or everywhere in the way that he wishes. The grace that we most need to pray for is the gift of discernment.

When will the test stop? No one can say. All we do know is that, after the outbreak of any major heresy in the Church, it is quite usual to find both Catholics and those who have adopted the new ideas living jumbled together in what appears to be the same fold for several generations, before things sort themselves out. It happened in the Roman empire in the fourth, fifth, sixth, seventh and eighth centuries, and in Europe for part of the 16th century; and in the 20th–21st century, a comparable state of affairs has been going on for nearly forty years. There will certainly be an end to the situation, because the Church could not survive if she allowed truth and falsehood to have equal rights in her pulpits and seats of learning forever. But exactly when and how unity of belief and stability will be restored is at present impossible to foresee. History and logic seem to allow for one of two possibilities.

There have been occasions when the bulk of those adhering to a new heresy have abandoned it and been absorbed back into the Church. Such was the case with the fourth-century Arians, with the seventh-century monothelites, and with the eighth-century iconoclasts. This is one possibility. But in the instances just mentioned, the state, having first promoted the heresy, after a change of ruler helped to bring it to an end. Today no state regards itself as having such a duty.

The alternative to re-absorption is separation. The dynamism with which all heresies are imbued – they would scarcely succeed without it – ends by carrying their members out of the Church. Once they find they cannot take it over, they set themselves up more or less permanently as a separate entity, as did the Nestorians and Monophysites in the fifth and sixth centuries, the Waldensians in the twelfth century, and the Protestants in the sixteenth. The Church will then break off communion. But long before that, the dissenting body will have shown it had no real desire for communion.

Today the situation is different. The Christian world is already divided into three great bodies (Catholic, Orthodox and Protestant), and in all of them modernism has established itself just as they were beginning to try to reconcile their differences. However, in other respects, the possibilities for the future remain more or less the same. Either the modernist leadership will have a change of heart and let itself be re-absorbed into the parent bodies, or it will continue its efforts to take them over. In the case of the Catholic Church, we believe this second alternative can never succeed and, for the time being, the Orthodox hierarchies and traditional Protestants seem even more resolute in their determination not to be "taken over".

The most likely future would therefore seem to be the emergence of modernism as an independent "fourth denomination", made up of liberal Protestants, ex-Catholics, and anyone else with a taste for a "Christianity" without substance. And this is what actually appears to be happening. Already the World Council of Churches acts as a kind of modernist international headquarters, while much that goes on under the name of ecumenism, in contrast to genuine ecumenism, looks like the coming together not of Christians to discuss their disagreements, but of modernists who already share the same beliefs – even if most of those beliefs consist of denials. Once publicly established as a separate institution and belief system, one can see this new fourth denomination having a longish career as a protégé of Western secular governments – a Western version of the Chinese patriotic church.

But we have not yet reached that point. Nor, I think, is it likely to come soon, if only because, for reasons already explained, the Catholic Church has committed herself to a policy of reconciliation through dialogue for as long as is humanly and supernaturally allowable.[4]

This being so, I suggest that anyone over forty will be wise to accept the fact that the present confused situation is the one in which they are going to have to practise their faith for the rest of their lives.

Should this be a cause for nostalgia and regrets? Not, I believe, if we understand our faith properly. The practice of Christianity has never been dependent on ideal political, social or even ecclesiastical conditions. Even in the most unpromising conditions, there is nothing to prevent Christians from doing more fervently the necessary things: loving, praising and thanking God at all times and in all places; deepening our spiritual lives; fulfilling the duties of our state more faithfully; trying to be apostles of our environment; seizing all the opportunities for small acts of charity, mercy, forgiveness and penance that the present circumstances provide in abundance. And if we are tempted to regard all this as not likely to achieve anything of world-shaking importance, we have the teaching and example of the latest saint to be made a doctor of the Church, St. Thérèse of the Child Jesus, to remind us that it is through trifles such as these – or what the world regards as trifles – that, if done with sufficient love, God works major miracles like the salvation of great sinners and the conversion of whole nations.

One of the only two things we know with certainty about the future is that, before Christ comes again, the Gospel must first be preached to *all* nations; and who can say that that has yet happened to most of the peoples of

Asia, except in a rudimentary form? They are the 'islands' referred to in Scripture that are still awaiting Christ's light and his law, and in the fashion I have just described we can contribute to bringing them that light and that law, even if we live in the Bronx or in Bermondsey. Then indeed shall 'many islands be glad'.

Notes to Chapter Twenty-Three

[1] See "Battle for the Keys", *Inside the Vatican*, June–July 2002. The "plans" have been outlined in a four-part series of articles in the Italian clergy magazine *Rocca* ("The Fortress"), by an influential Italian journalist, author and "Vatican expert", Giancarlo Zizola.

[2] Bismarck's *Kulturkampf* (1871–1878) included the expulsion of religious orders and the imprisonment of several priests and bishops.

[3] At the 1999 Synod for Europe, Cardinal Varela of Madrid made a direct connection between the crisis in the Church and interpreting the faith "in a secular way as a strategy for better organising the things of this world" (*Challenge*, Canada, December 1999).

[4] In the fourth century, no one can have cared more about the faith or suffered more at the hands of the Arians than St. Athanasius. But as Newman makes a point of showing in the last chapters of his *Arians of the Fourth Century*, the saint was conspicuous in his efforts to make it as easy as possible for his one-time opponents in the episcopate to return to the Church.

INDEX